BEING H

the companion a⌐
Staying Alive and

'I love *Staying Alive* and keep going back to it. *Being Alive* is just as vivid, strongly present and equally beautifully organised. But this new book feels even more alive – I think it has a heartbeat, or maybe that's my own thrum humming along with the music of these poets. Sitting alone in a room with these poems is to be assured that you are not alone, you are not crazy (or if you are, you're not the only one who thinks this way!) I run home to this book to argue with it, find solace in it, to locate myself in the world again' – MERYL STREEP

RESPONSES TO *STAYING ALIVE*:

'*Staying Alive* is a magnificent anthology. The last time I was so excited, engaged and enthralled by a collection of poems was when I first encountered *The Rattle Bag*. I can't think of any other anthology that casts its net so widely, or one that has introduced me to so many vivid and memorable poems' – PHILIP PULLMAN

'Usually if you say a book is "inspirational" that means it's New Agey and soft at the center. This astonishingly rich anthology, by contrast, shows that what is edgy, authentic and provocative can also awaken the spirit and make its readers quick with consciousness. In these pages I discovered many new writers, and I've decided I'm now in love with our trouble-some epoch if it can produce poems of such genius' – EDMUND WHITE

'A vibrant, brilliantly diverse anthology of poems to delight the mind, heart and soul. A book for people who know they love poetry, and for people who think they don't' – HELEN DUNMORE

'*Staying Alive* is a wonderful testament to Neil Astley's lifetime in poetry, and to the range and courage of his taste. It's also, of course, a testament to poetry itself: to its powers to engross and move us, to its ability to challenge and brace us, and to its exultation. Everyone who cares about poetry should own this book' – ANDREW MOTION

'This is a book to make you fall in love with poetry…Go out and buy it for everyone you love' – CHRISTINA PATTERSON, *Independent*

'I don't often read poetry, so *Staying Alive* was a revelation' – IAN RANKIN, *Sunday Telegraph (Books of the Year)*

RESPONSES TO *STAYING ALIVE*:

'When you choose your book for *Desert Island Discs*, this should be it. *Staying Alive* proves that poetry is the most sustaining and life-affirming of literary forms. A triumph' – HELENA KENNEDY, QC

'A revelation...An anthology like this should make poetry reviewers feel not just enthusiastic but evangelical. Buy it. Leave it around the house. Give it to friends. It could keep them alive' – JOHN CAREY, *Sunday Times*

'Anyone who has the faintest glimmer of interest in modern poetry must buy it. If I were master of the universe or held the lottery's purse strings, there would be a copy of it in every school, public library and hotel bedroom in the land. On page after page I found myself laughing, crying, wondering, rejoicing, reliving, wishing, envying. It is a book full of hope and high art which restores your faith in poetry' – ALAN TAYLOR, *Sunday Herald*

'The book is without equal as a handbook for students and readers' – SIAN HUGHES, *Times Educational Supplement*

'*Staying Alive* is a book which leaves those who have read or heard a poem from it feeling less alone and more alive. Its effect is deeply political – in a way that nobody ten years ago could have foreseen. Why? The 500 poems in it are not political as such. But they have become subversive because they contest the way the world is being (and has been) manipulated and spoken about. They refuse the lies, the arrogant complacencies, the weak-kneed evasions. They offer 500 examples of resistance' – JOHN BERGER

'The best anthology I've read or am likely to read...devastating' – MICHAEL COLGAN, *Irish Times* (Books of the Year)

'A book that travels everywhere with me...It is full of beautiful writing that can blow your mind' – BETH ORTON, *The Times*

NEIL ASTLEY founded Bloodaxe Books in 1978, and was given a D.Litt by Newcastle University for his pioneering work. As well as *Staying Alive*, *Being Alive* and *Being Human*, he has edited over 1000 poetry books, and has published several other anthologies, including *Passionfood, Do Not Go Gentle, Earth Shattering, Soul Food* [with Pamela Robertson-Pearce] and the DVD-book *In Person: 30 Poets* [filmed by Pamela Robertson-Pearce]; two poetry collections, *Darwin Survivor* and *Biting My Tongue*; and two novels, *The End of My Tether* (shortlisted for the Whitbread First Novel Award), and *The Sheep Who Changed the World*.

BEING HUMAN

the companion anthology to
Staying Alive and *Being Alive*

edited by
NEIL ASTLEY

BLOODAXE BOOKS

ISBN: 978 1 85224 809 3

First published 2011 by
Bloodaxe Books Ltd,
Highgreen,
Tarset,
Northumberland NE48 1RP.

www.bloodaxebooks.com
For further information about Bloodaxe titles
please visit our website or write to
the above address for a catalogue.

*In memory of Simon Powell (1952-2009),
passionate champion and lover of poetry,
courageous and extraordinary human being.*

Supported by
**ARTS COUNCIL
ENGLAND**

Cover design: Neil Astley & Pamela Robertson-Pearce.
Cover photograph courtesy of Lord Taylor of Warwick.

Printed in Great Britain by Bell & Bain Limited, Glasgow, Scotland.

CONTENTS

4 About time

8 Body and soul

9 More to love

EDITORIAL NOTE: An ellipsis in square brackets […] in this anthology denotes an editorial cut to the text. An ellipsis without square brackets is part of the original text. American spellings are retained in work by American authors, except for *-ize* suffixes, which are modernised to *-ise*. Punctuation follows Bloodaxe house style (single inverted commas for quotation, double for qualified expressions).

ABBREVIATIONS: SA: *Staying Alive* BA: *Being Alive* BH: *Being Human*

INTRODUCTION

Being Human is the third book in what has now become the *Staying Alive* poetry trilogy. *Staying Alive* and its sequel *Being Alive* have introduced many thousands of new readers to contemporary poetry. *Being Human* is the companion volume to those two books – a world poetry anthology offering poetry lovers an even broader, international selection of poems with emotional power, intellectual edge and playful wit. *Staying Alive* has the subtitle 'real poems from unreal times', and *Being Human* extends that territory with selections of poems that are not just relevant and timely but universal in addressing the human condition. The thematic thread linking the poems in all sections of *Being Human* is our relationship with time.

The range of poetry in *Being Human* complements that of the first two anthologies, presenting another 500 thoughtful and passionate poems about living in the modern world. It has more great poems from the 20th century as well as many more recent poems of rare imaginative power, with an even greater emphasis on world poetry, showing what it means to be human in different cultures. *Staying Alive* and *Being Alive* only cover modern and contemporary poets, but *Being Human* also includes new versions or translations made by contemporary English-language poets.

Many of the poems in *Staying Alive* (2002) and *Being Alive* (2004) were selected from books first published during the 1990s and over the turn of the millennium. *Being Human*'s coverage includes work from later collections published in the first decade of the 21st century, with many poems taken from books not available in Britain.

While this new anthology has been conceived as a companion volume to *Staying Alive* and *Being Alive*, the power and range of its selections are such that it can be read just as fruitfully on its own. Like its trilogy companions, *Being Human* is a "bridge" anthology, a book designed to make its readers want to read more work by the poets it features, but new readers who come first to *Being Human* should find the many-stranded network of contemporary poetry easier to navigate if they use *Staying Alive* and *Being Alive* as further guides before seeking out individual collections by the hundreds of poets featured in the three books.

When I first had the idea for *Staying Alive*, it was for a diverse and lively book to introduce new readers to contemporary poetry as well as to show existing poetry readers (whose access to international poetry is restricted by the narrowness of British publishing) a wider range of poems from around the world. I had no thoughts then of a sequel, let alone a trilogy, but I also had no idea that these books would be championed so enthusiastically that readers would want a third, companion anthology.

Staying Alive was my response to how poetry was viewed by the general public in a readership survey called *Rhyme and Reason* (Arts Council, 2000). People with limited or no knowledge of modern poetry dismissed it as obscure, elitist, difficult, dull, old-fashioned, silly, superficial or pretentious (just a few of their uninformed epithets!). Modern poetry, according to their comments, was irrelevant and incomprehensible, so they didn't bother with it, not even readers of literary fiction and people interested in other language-based arts, such as theatre, or in film; and not even people who read Shakespeare and the classics. In the jargon, poetry – and modern poetry in particular – had a *negative image*. And according to the uninformed, the modern stuff wasn't even poetry because it didn't rhyme (for a concise account of how rhyme has *never* been essential to poetry, see *Staying Alive*, SA 458-63).

Staying Alive was my attempt to show all those people who love literature, traditional poetry and other arts that contemporary poetry *is* relevant to their own lives; and that much of it is lively, imaginative and accessible to intelligent readers who might not have given it much of a chance before. And that didn't involve "dumbing down" but choosing lucid poems to entice new readers. There's no conflict here between public "access" and artistic excellence. As Edmund White wrote of *Staying Alive*: 'Usually if you say a book is "inspirational" that means it's New Agey and soft at the center. This astonishingly rich anthology, by contrast, shows that what is edgy, authentic and provocative can awaken the spirit and make its readers quicken with consciousness.' All three anthologies include being *inhuman*, as witnessed by Carolyn Forché: 'There is nothing one man will not do to another' (BH 321).

Staying Alive is still being discovered by new readers. Ten years on I'm still receiving letters, postcards and e-mails expressing people's appreciation, all saying how much *Staying Alive* had helped or stimulated them and fired up their interest in poetry.

Talismanic poems were a popular feature of *Staying Alive* and *Being Alive*, notably Mary Oliver's 'Wild Geese' (SA 28). These are the kinds of poems that people keep in their wallets, on fridges and noticeboards; poems copied to friends and read on special occasions. Such has been the appeal of *Staying Alive* and *Being Alive* that many readers have written not only to express their appreciation of these books, but also to share poems which have been important in their own lives. *Being Human* draws on this highly unusual publisher's mailbag, including many talismanic personal survival poems suggested by readers from all walks of life, along with others named by writers at readings and in newspaper articles and blogs. Examples of these include, in particular, poems by Robert Frost, Jane Hirshfield, Langston Hughes and Rilke. One poem even served as an actual talisman for its author: Brian Turner kept a copy of 'Here, Bullet' (BH 329) in his breast pocket while he was serving with the US Army in Iraq.

Adrian Mitchell's 'Human Beings' (BH 25) was voted the poem that most people would like to see launched into space in a National Poetry Day poll in 2005. Mitchell called it 'a poem for peace... about the joy of being human'. Like many of the poems in *Being Human*, it is also a celebration of human individuality and diversity. Another characteristic common to these and many other modern poems is the sense of plurality they all embody.

The Irish writer Louis MacNeice is the quintessential poet of flux, openness and possibilities. Many of his poems defend individual freedom and kick against conformism and restrictive ideologies. In 'Snow' (SA 74), he writes that: 'World is crazier and more of it than we think, / Incorrigibly plural. I peel and portion / A tangerine and spit the pips and feel / The drunkenness of things being various.' In 'Entirely' (SA 60), written over half a century ago when the threat was from fascism or communism, MacNeice opposes the fundamentalist view of the world as 'black or white entirely', seeing life as 'a mad weir of tigerish waters / A prism of delight and pain', which is very much the world view expressed throughout *Being Human*, not just in poems on global or social issues but in highly personal love poems, meditations and elegies.

Human understanding and intimacy are created not out of order or perfection but through acceptance of difficulty, inadequacy, imperfection, making do, shortage of time. Alan Dugan's marriage in 'Love Song: I and Thou' (BH 486) is a house in which 'Nothing is plumb, level, or square: / the studs are bowed, the joists / are shaky by nature, no piece fits / any other piece without a gap / or pinch', while Jaan Kaplinski's untitled poem (BH 182) begins with the line 'The washing never gets done' and continues: 'The furnace never gets heated. / Books never get read. / Life is never completed.' Yehuda Amichai's 'A Man in His Life' (BH 183) concludes: 'A man doesn't have time in his life / to have time for everything.' In the extract from her long poem 'Shape of Time' (BH 22), Doris Kareva writes: 'You have been given the world. / See what there is to see. / ...everyone / must have time for the self – / for mirth and laziness / time to be human', while Dennis O'Driscoll's 'Vigil' (BH 38) is one of many poems in the book warning against squandering that time: 'Life is too short to sleep through.' There is a continuing conversation between poets from past and present on many such themes throughout the literary tradition, and I have tried to reflect this in my choice of poems and how I have organised and ordered the selections in *Staying Alive*, *Being Alive* and *Being Human*. The poems in the second section of this book, *The stuff of life*, cover the whole spectrum of that tigerish 'prism of delight and pain', that world we've been given to experience with others, with our one body and one earthly life.

Warnings against wasting that life and denying our hopes or dreams crop up again and again in these poems, notably those by Langston Hughes (including 'What happens to a dream deferred?', BH 179) and Rainer Maria Rilke: 'You must change your life' ('Archaic Torso of Apollo', BH 85).

Rilke's famous caveat has been picked up by numerous poets, including Randall Jarrell in 'The Woman at the Washington Zoo' (BH 144), whose speaker cries: 'You know what I was, / You see what I am: change me, change me!' Mark Doty has said that his poem 'A Green Crab's Shell' was written in response to Rilke's 'Archaic Torso of Apollo', while W.H. Auden's line 'We must love one another or die' in 'September 1, 1939' (SA 359) finds echoes in Philip Larkin's poetry, in 'What will survive of us is love' in 'An Arundel Tomb' (BA 209) and 'we should be kind / While there is still time' in 'The Mower' (BH 436). There are also direct connections between living poets: for example, Robert Lowell wrote his poem 'Skunk Hour' (BH 432) from Maine for Elizabeth Bishop, who responded from Brazil with 'The Armadillo' (BH 433).

As with the previous anthologies, I have "orchestrated" the selections in *Being Human* in such a way as to bring these conversations alive for the reader, so that poems will seem to talk to one another, with themes picked up and developed across a whole series of poems, and not just by writers known to one another. Each poem has its own voice while at the same time speaking from a broad chorus of poems with shared concerns. In this way *Being Human* serves, I hope, as a vocal testament to both the individual and the universal power and relevance of contemporary poetry.

NEIL ASTLEY

1

Being human

Poetry can tell us what human beings are.
It can tell us why we stumble and fall and how,
miraculously, we can stand up.

MAYA ANGELOU

A poem is a human inside talking to a human inside.

DONALD HALL

IN ONE OF HIS POEMS, William Matthews describes a reading he gave to a thousand new cadets at West Point Military Academy, all of whom had been made to read his work beforehand. When he took questions afterwards, one young soldier yelled from the balcony: 'Sir... Why do your poems give / me a headache when I try / to understand them?' And Matthews responds: 'I try to write as well as I can / what it feels to be human,' but acknowledging that they are both 'pained by the same dumb longings', adds: 'I try to say what I don't know / how to say, but of course I can't / get much of it down at all.'

Much of the work in this anthology attempts that difficult task of capturing some sense of 'what it feels to be human'. As T.R. Hummer puts it: 'For poets, poetry is a pure obsession, a sequence of questions which have no answers, of demands that have no satisfaction other than the satisfaction of obsession itself.' Poetry is not a vehicle for ideas. Like music, what it offers us is a particular auditory experience, that of reading and hearing the poem itself, engaging thought and feeling by drawing on the full resources of human language.

Reading poetry is usually a solitary experience, but its effect is communal, as David Constantine has said: 'It connects the reader, across gender, race, culture, time and space with other possible ways of being human; it does not fuse and merge us; on the contrary, on the ground of common humanity, it points up difference and variety.'

T.S. Eliot's poetry includes quotations from many classic poems, often in the original language, expressing the universality of particular human experiences. His epigraph to 'The Love Song of J. Alfred Prufrock' (34) is from Dante's *Inferno*. 'If I thought my answer were given / to anyone who would ever return to the world, / this flame would stand still without moving any further. / But since never from this abyss / has anyone ever returned alive, if what I hear is true, / without fear of infamy I answer you.' (Robert & Jean Hollander, Princeton Dante Project)

from Shape of Time

You aren't better than anyone.
You aren't worse than anyone.
You have been given the world.
See what there is to see.

Protect what is around you,
hold who is there beside you.
All creatures in their own way
are funny –

and fragile.

*

The question isn't
how to be in style
but
how to live in truth
in the face of all the winds?

With mindfulness, courage,
patience, sympathy –
how to remain brave
when the spirit fails?

*

Idleness is often empowering,
recreating oneself –
just as the moon gradually
grows full once again,
a battery surely and
steadily recharges,
so everything, everyone
must have time for the self –

for mirth and laziness
time to be human.

DORIS KAREVA
translated from the Estonian by Tiina Aleman

Funny

What's it like to be a human
the bird asked

I myself don't know
it's being held prisoner by your skin
while reaching infinity
being a captive of your scrap of time
while touching eternity
being hopelessly uncertain
and helplessly hopeful
being a needle of frost
and a handful of heat
breathing in the air
and choking wordlessly
it's being on fire
with a nest made of ashes
eating bread
while filling up on hunger
it's dying without love
it's loving through death

That's funny said the bird
and flew effortlessly up into the air

ANNA KAMIEŃSKA
translated from the Polish by Stanislav Barańczak & Clare Cavanagh

Humankind

We carry the trust.
It was not imposed on us,
nor are we heedless.

Sometimes the stillness stands in the woods
and lies on the lake. We move like drowned beings
through clouded waters.

Sometimes we wake to spent leaves
blowing about in the yard. A door bangs.
A woman – vigorous – shakes a rug into the wind.

The red dog shudders and rises and listens.
Uncertain light shines the grasses.
Wealth sits in inner rooms, staring.

These are our days.
Walk them.
Fear nothing.

KERRY HARDIE

The Guest House

This being human is a guesthouse.
Every morning a new arrival.

A joy, a depression, a meanness,
some momentary awareness comes
as an unexpected visitor.

Welcome and entertain them all!
Even if they're a crowd of sorrows,
who violently sweep your house
empty of its furniture,
still, treat each guest honorably.
He may be clearing you out
for some new delight.

The dark thought, the shame, the malice,
meet them at the door laughing,
and invite them in.

Be grateful for whoever comes,
because each has been sent
as a guide from beyond.

RUMI
translated from the Persian by Coleman Barks with John Moyne

Human

Side-view of *homo sapiens*
Once bending with arms down
Now matchstick torso striking out,
Stark and upright earthling,
A figure striding, God knows where.
Springy twiglike upside-down Y.
A wishbone. A divining rod.
Hito. Human. *Ein Mensch.*

Naked and maskless.
Here neither female nor male.
A bare-boned biped.

And yet a self-reflecting mind.
At first two downward strokes
Inscribed on bone or tortoise shell,
A bare pictograph.
Bit by bit crisscross of symbols
Living lives of their own,
A pointing out and interplay,
A signal's doubleness.

Grounded sign-maker,
High-minded and down-to-earth.
Our human being.

MICHEAL O'SIADHAIL

Human Beings

　　look at your hands
your beautiful useful hands
　　you're not an ape
　　you're not a parrot

you're not a slow loris
or a smart missile
you're human

not british
not american
not israeli
not palestinian
you're human

not catholic
not protestant
not muslim
not hindu
you're human

we all start human
we end up human
human first
human last
we're human
or we're nothing

nothing but bombs
and poison gas
nothing but guns
and torturers
nothing but slaves
of Greed and War
if we're not human

look at your body
with its amazing systems
of nerve-wires and blood canals
think about your mind
which can think about itself
and the whole universe
look at your face
which can freeze into horror
or melt into love
look at all that life
all that beauty

you're human
they are human
we are human
let's try to be human

dance!

ADRIAN MITCHELL

The Sounds of Earth
(broadcast from Voyager-II to the universe)

First, the most popular sound:
we call it talking – it is also known fondly as
shooting one's mouth off, discussing,
chewing the fat, yammering, blabbing,
conversing, confiding, debating, blabbing,
gossiping, hollering, and yakking.
So here's a whole bunch of jaw creakers.
How come none of you guys out there
don't yap at us – we'd sure like to hear
what you have to say
on the subject of where the hell you are.

For our second selection,
we will now play a medley of music
which you may or may not care for
since as I know myself
music is a very personal thing.
Why not aim a little musical extravaganza earthward?
As I say, we're waiting.

Now for our something-for-everyone finale.
Here's a rush hour traffic jam,
brakes are screeching – horns are blasting.
This is a phone ringing, a keyboard tapping,
and a printer whirring in the background.
I'm very partial to this next example of earth sounds:
a rocking chair creaking back and forth on a porch
accompanied by birds and crickets chirping.

To finish up, we've got a lawn mower,
knitting needles, a hammer, a saw,
a football stadium after a score,
a door shutting, a baby crying
and the ever-popular drone of television
blaring across the airways.

We're equal opportunity down here
so if you're a blob or have three heads
or look like something the cat dragged in –
we won't bat an eyelid.

JULIE O'CALLAGHAN

The Human Species

The human species has given me
the right to be mortal
the duty to be civilised
a conscience
2 eyes that don't always function very well
a nose in the middle of my face
2 feet 2 hands
speech

the human species has given me
my father and mother
some brothers maybe who knows
a whole mess of cousins
and some great-grandfathers
the human species has given me
its 3 faculties
feeling intellect and will
each in moderation
32 teeth 10 fingers a liver
a heart and some other viscera
the human species has given me
what I'm supposed to be satisfied with

RAYMOND QUENEAU
translated from the French by Teo Savory

Here and Human

In the warm room, cushioned by comfort,
Idle at fireside, shawled in lamplight,
I know the cold winter night, but only
As a far intimation, like a memory
Of a dead distress whose ghost has grown genial.

The disc, glossy black as a conjurer's hat,
Revolves. Music is unwound: woodwind,
Strings, a tenor voice singing in a tongue
I do not comprehend or have need to –
'The instrument of egoism mastered by art' –

For what I listen to is unequivocal:
A distillation of romantic love,
Passion outsoaring speech. I understand
And, understanding, I rejoice in my condition:
This sweet accident of being here and human.

Later, as I lie in the dark, the echoes
Recede, the blind cat of sleep purrs close
But does not curl. Beyond the window
The hill is hunched under his grey cape
Like a watchman. I cannot hear his breathing.

Silence is a starless sky on the ceiling
Till shock slashes, stillness is gashed
By a dazzle of noise chilling the air
Like lightning. It is an animal screech,
Raucous, clawing: surely the language of terror.

But I misread it, deceived. It is the sound
Of passionate love, a vixen's mating call.
It lingers hurtful, a stink in the ear,
But soon it begins to fade. I breathe deep,
Feeling the startled fur settle and smooth. Then I sleep.

VERNON SCANNELL

29

Being Human,

Though all the force to hold the parts together
And service love reversed, turned negative,
Fountained in self-destroying flames
And rained ash in volcanic weather;
We are still here where you left us
With our own kind: unstable strangers
Trembling in the sound waves of meaningless
Eloquence. They say we live.
They say, as they rise on the horizon
And come toward us dividing and dividing,
That we must save; that we must solve; transcend
Cohesive and repelling flesh, protoplasm, particles, and survive.
I do not doubt we will; I do not doubt all things are possible.
Even that wildest hope that we may meet beyond the grave.

RUTH STONE

Another Country

She said she loved being a woman.
Her skin pressed mine, my face her hair.
And I a man? Just being human
Can sometimes be too much to bear:

The hands remember what they held,
The tongue recalls the salt-sweet skin.
Who was it said that 'her hair smelled
Like a country I could be happy in'?

It's not in human form that I
Have leave to stray in that domain
But only now as the swept sky
Or a thin fall of cold sweet rain.

STEPHEN EDGAR

Happiness

My hair is happy
and my skin is happy.
My skin quivers with happiness.

I breathe happiness instead of air,
slowly and deeply,
as a man who avoided a mortal danger.

Tears roll down my face,
I do not know it.
I forget I still have a face.
My skin is singing,
I shiver.

I feel time's duration
as it felt in the hour of death.
As if my sense of time alone were grasping the world,
as if existence were time only.
Immersed in terrifying
magnificence
I feel every second of happiness, as it arrives,
fills up, bursts into flower
according to its own natural way,
unhurried as a fruit,
astounding as a deity.

Now
I begin to scream.
I am screaming. I leave my body.
I do not know whether I am human anymore,
how could anyone know that, screaming with happiness.
Yet one dies from such screaming,
thus I am dying from happiness.
On my face there are probably no more tears,
my skin probably does not sing by now.
I don't know whether I still have a skin,
from me to my skin
is too far to know.

Soon I will go.
I do not shiver any longer,

I do not breathe any longer.
I don't know whether I still have
something to breathe with.

I feel time's duration,
how perfectly I feel time's duration.

I sink
I sink into time.

ANNA SWIR
translated by Czeslaw Milosz & Leonard Nathan

To Cease
(for Samuel Beckett)

*To cease
to be human.*

To be
a rock down
which rain pours,
a granite jaw
slowly discoloured.

Or a statue
sporting a giant's beard
of verdigris or rust
in some forgotten
village square.

A tree worn
by the prevailing winds
to a diagram of
tangled branches:
gnarled, sapless, alone.

To cease
to be human
and let birds soil
your skull, animals rest
in the crook of your arm.

To become
an object, honoured
or not, as the occasion demands;
while time bends you slowly
back to the ground.

JOHN MONTAGUE

Ars Poetica #100: I Believe

Poetry, I tell my students,
is idiosyncratic. Poetry

is where we are ourselves
(though Sterling Brown said

'Every "I" is a dramatic "I"'),
digging in the clam flats

for the shell that snaps,
emptying the proverbial pocketbook.

Poetry is what you find
in the dirt in the corner,

overhear on the bus, God
in the details, the only way

to get from here to there.
Poetry (and now my voice is rising)

is not all love, love, love,
and I'm sorry the dog died.

Poetry (here I hear myself loudest)
is the human voice,

and are we not of interest to each other?

ELIZABETH ALEXANDER

The Love Song of J. Alfred Prufrock

S'io credessi che mia risposta fosse
a persona che mai tornasse al mondo,
questa fiamma staria senza più scosse.
Ma per ciò che giammai di questo fondo
non tornò vivo alcun, s'i'odo il vero,
senza tema d'infamia ti rispondo.

Let us go then, you and I,
When the evening is spread out against the sky
Like a patient etherised upon a table;
Let us go, through certain half-deserted streets,
The muttering retreats
Of restless nights in one-night cheap hotels
And sawdust restaurants with oyster-shells:
Streets that follow like a tedious argument
Of insidious intent
To lead you to an overwhelming question...
Oh, do not ask, 'What is it?'
Let us go and make our visit.

In the room the women come and go
Talking of Michelangelo.

The yellow fog that rubs its back upon the window-panes,
The yellow smoke that rubs its muzzle on the window-panes,
Licked its tongue into the corners of the evening,
Lingered upon the pools that stand in drains,
Let fall upon its back the soot that falls from chimneys,
Slipped by the terrace, made a sudden leap,
And seeing that it was a soft October night,
Curled once about the house, and fell asleep.

And indeed there will be time
For the yellow smoke that slides along the street
Rubbing its back upon the window-panes;
There will be time, there will be time
To prepare a face to meet the faces that you meet;
There will be time to murder and create,
And time for all the works and days of hands
That lift and drop a question on your plate;

Time for you and time for me,
And time yet for a hundred indecisions,
And for a hundred visions and revisions,
Before the taking of a toast and tea.

In the room the women come and go
Talking of Michelangelo.

And indeed there will be time
To wonder, 'Do I dare?' and, 'Do I dare?'
Time to turn back and descend the stair,
With a bald spot in the middle of my hair –
(They will say: 'How his hair is growing thin!')
My morning coat, my collar mounting firmly to the chin,
My necktie rich and modest, but asserted by a simple pin –
(They will say: 'But how his arms and legs are thin!')
Do I dare
Disturb the universe?
In a minute there is time
For decisions and revisions which a minute will reverse.

For I have known them all already, known them all –
Have known the evenings, mornings, afternoons,
I have measured out my life with coffee spoons;
I know the voices dying with a dying fall
Beneath the music from a farther room.
    So how should I presume?

And I have known the eyes already, known them all –
The eyes that fix you in a formulated phrase,
And when I am formulated, sprawling on a pin,
When I am pinned and wriggling on the wall,
Then how should I begin
To spit out all the butt-ends of my days and ways?
    And how should I presume?

And I have known the arms already, known them all –
Arms that are braceleted and white and bare
(But in the lamplight, downed with light brown hair!)
Is it perfume from a dress
That makes me so digress?
Arms that lie along a table, or wrap about a shawl.

And should I then presume?
And how should I begin?

     .   .   .   .   .

Shall I say, I have gone at dusk through narrow streets
And watched the smoke that rises from the pipes
Of lonely men in shirt-sleeves, leaning out of windows?...

I should have been a pair of ragged claws
Scuttling across the floors of silent seas.

     .   .   .   .   .

And the afternoon, the evening, sleeps so peacefully!
Smoothed by long fingers,
Asleep...tired...or it malingers,
Stretched on the floor, here beside you and me.
Should I, after tea and cakes and ices,
Have the strength to force the moment to its crisis?
But though I have wept and fasted, wept and prayed,
Though I have seen my head (grown slightly bald) brought in upon
       a platter,
I am no prophet – and here's no great matter;
I have seen the moment of my greatness flicker,
And I have seen the eternal Footman hold my coat, and snicker,
And in short, I was afraid.

And would it have been worth it, after all,
After the cups, the marmalade, the tea,
Among the porcelain, among some talk of you and me,
Would it have been worth while,
To have bitten off the matter with a smile,
To have squeezed the universe into a ball
To roll it towards some overwhelming question,
To say: 'I am Lazarus, come from the dead,
Come back to tell you all, I shall tell you all' –
If one, settling a pillow by her head,
     Should say: 'That is not what I meant at all.
     That is not it, at all.'

And would it have been worth it, after all,
Would it have been worth while,
After the sunsets and the dooryards and the sprinkled streets,

After the novels, after the teacups, after the skirts that trail along
    the floor –
And this, and so much more? –
It is impossible to say just what I mean!
But as if a magic lantern threw the nerves in patterns on a screen:
Would it have been worth while
If one, settling a pillow or throwing off a shawl,
And turning toward the window, should say:
    'That is not it at all,
    That is not what I meant at all.'

    .   .   .   .   .

    No! I am not Prince Hamlet, nor was meant to be;
Am an attendant lord, one that will do
To swell a progress, start a scene or two,
Advise the prince; no doubt, an easy tool,
Deferential, glad to be of use,
Politic, cautious, and meticulous;
Full of high sentence, but a bit obtuse;
At times, indeed, almost ridiculous –
Almost, at times, the Fool.

    I grow old... I grow old...
I shall wear the bottoms of my trousers rolled.

    Shall I part my hair behind? Do I dare to eat a peach?
I shall wear white flannel trousers, and walk upon the beach.
I have heard the mermaids singing, each to each.

I do not think that they will sing to me.

I have seen them riding seaward on the waves
Combing the white hair of the waves blown back
When the wind blows the water white and black.

We have lingered in the chambers of the sea
By sea-girls wreathed with seaweed red and brown
Till human voices wake us, and we drown.

T.S. ELIOT

Vigil

Life is too short to sleep through.
Stay up late, wait until the sea of traffic ebbs,
until noise has drained from the world
like blood from the cheeks of the full moon.
Everyone else around you has succumbed:
they lie like tranquillised pets on a vet's table;
they languish on hospital trolleys and friends' couches,
on iron beds in hostels for the homeless,
under feather duvets at tourist B&Bs.
The radio, devoid of listeners to confide in,
turns repetitious. You are your own voice-over.
You are alone in the bone-weary tower
of your bleary-eyed, blinking lighthouse,
watching the spillage of tide on the shingle inlet.
You are the single-minded one who hears
time shaking from the clock's fingertips
like drops, who watches its hands
chop years into diced seconds,
who knows that when the church bell
tolls at 2 or 3 it tolls unmistakably for you.
You are the sole hand on deck when
temperatures plummet and the hull
of an iceberg is jostling for prominence.
Your confidential number is the life-line
where the sedated long-distance voices
of despair hold out muzzily for an answer.
You are the emergency services' driver
ready to dive into action at the first
warning signs of birth or death.
You spot the crack in night's façade
even before the red-eyed businessman
on look-out from his transatlantic seat.
You are the only reliable witness to when
the light is separated from the darkness,
who has learned to see the dark in its true
colours, who has not squandered your life.

DENNIS O'DRISCOLL

2

The stuff of life

Every poem is rooted in imaginative awe. Poetry can do a hundred
and one things, delight, sadden, disturb, amuse, instruct – it may
express every possible shade of emotion, and describe every con-
ceivable kind of event, but there is only one thing that all poetry
must do; it must praise all it can for being and for happening.

W.H. AUDEN

THE STUFF OF LIFE covers the whole spectrum of this 'mad weir of tigerish
waters / A prism of delight and pain' (Louis MacNeice, *see* Introduction, 19),
this one world we've been given to experience with others, starting with a
playful series of poems offering different views and provocative definitions of
knowledge, belief and what that world has to offer, from factual to fanciful.

Zimbabwean writer and onetime mineworker Julius Chingono sadly died as
this book was going to press. His poem 'As I Go' (45) depicts a life stripped
to its essentials: 'I pick up my life / as I go.' This is followed by Thomas A.
Clark's praise of walking, a universal human activity too often taken for granted:
'Early one morning, any morning, we can set out, with the least possible bag-
gage, and discover the world' (46). Other poems then take us on further jour-
neys, focussing on both the essentials and difficulties of that 'prism of delight
and pain': mortality and continuity, sorrow and pleasure, food and family,
bread and water; then light, colour and all the 'Things I Didn't Know I Loved'
(Nâzim Hikmet / Linda Pastan, 76-80).

Mark Doty has said that his poem 'A Green Crab's Shell' (85) was written
in response to the opening of Rilke's 'Archaic Torso of Apollo' (85). In an
online talk on Rilke's sonnet, he discusses its surprising ending: 'You must
change your life' (*see* Introduction, BH 20). 'Having read this poem hundreds
of times,' he says, 'I remain startled by that final gesture. I feel something
has taken place that I am and am not prepared for... It's interesting that it's
an experience of standing before a figure of a god, but in the 20th century.
This god is broken, this god's head isn't there. The speaker tries to make a
connection. Attempts to link himself to that source, even broken or lost, of
authority, power, vision... When we confront a great work of art, a great
work of the spirit, we feel something, but how difficult, how impossible it is
to say what it is... It's very difficult to say rationally why the experience of
beauty or spiritual power produces this strong sensation. The poem makes
the leap for us that's like the experience, I think, of seeing the work of art.'

What I Believe

I believe there is no justice,
but that cottongrass and bunchberry
grow on the mountain.

I believe that a scorpion's sting
will kill a man,
but that his wife will remarry.

I believe that, the older we get,
the weaker the body,
but the stronger the soul.

I believe that if you roll over at night
in an empty bed,
the air consoles you.

I believe that no one is spared
the darkness,
and no one gets all of it.

I believe we all drown eventually
in a sea of our making,
but that the land belongs to someone else.

I believe in destiny.
And I believe in free will.

I believe that, when all
the clocks break,
time goes on without them.

And I believe that whatever
pulls us under,
will do so gently.

so as not to disturb anyone,
so as not to interfere
with what we believe in.

MICHAEL BLUMENTHAL

What Do I Really Believe?

I believe that Benedictine
tastes like a meteor;

I believe that antitheses and hyperboles
dilate like slowly eaten fruit;

I believe that when a man takes long, deep breaths
he is trying not to prematurely ejaculate;

that tangerines are oranges, and full of juice,
and do not move unless they are being carried;

that the idea of repelling the rabbits
with moth flakes was not a success;

that abbatoirs binge
on Santa Gertrudis bulls;

that if I meet someone I like,
I start to do it unconsciously;

that a prisoner is painting the bars of his cell sky-blue,
and a tall giraffe is living in a summer-house in Maine;

that Beethoven was so deaf
he thought he was a painter;

that giant slugs
can be bigger than chihuahuas;

that I always seem to get
the wrong end of the stick;

that I love you very much,
but it doesn't seem to make the slightest difference;

that it's all very well
but why don't you love me too?

that there ought to be a law against chihuahuas,
that no one has to groom a giant slug.

SELIMA HILL

What Is Worth Knowing?

That Van Gogh's ear, set free
wanted to meet the powerful nose
of Nevsky Avenue.
That Spain has decided to help
NATO. That Spring is supposed to begin
on the 21st of March.
That if you put too much salt in the *keema*
just add a few bananas.
That although the Dutch were the first
to help the people of Nicaragua they don't say much
about their history with Indonesia.
That Van Gogh collected Japanese prints.
That the Japanese considered
the Dutch to be red-haired barbarians.
That Van Gogh's ear remains full of questions
it wants to ask the nose of Nevsky Avenue.
That the vaccinations for cholera, typhoid and yellow fever
are no good – they must be improved.
That red, green and yellow are the most
auspicious colours.
That turmeric and chilli powder are good
disinfectants. Yellow and red.
That often Spring doesn't come
until May. But in some places
it's there in January.
That Van Gogh's ear left him because
it wanted to become a snail.
That east and west
meet only in the north and south – but never
in the east or west.
That in March 1986 Darwinism is being
reintroduced in American schools.
That there's a difference
between pigeons and doves, although
a ring-dove is a wood-pigeon.
That the most pleasant thing is to have a fever
of at least 101 – because then the dreams aren't
merely dreams but facts.
That during a fever the soul comes out
for fresh air, that during a fever the soul bothers

to speak to you.
That tigers are courageous and generous-hearted
and never attack unless provoked –
but leopards,
leopards are malicious and bad-tempered.
That buffaloes too,
water-buffaloes that is, have a short temper.
That a red sky at night is a good sign for sailors,
for sailors...what is worth knowing?
What is worth knowing?

SUJATA BHATT

Anniversary

What I believe in, now,
is woodwork and sea-grass,
the blond light on country roads and occasional
glimpses of the smaller birds of prey;

or lying awake at night, with a lamp still lit
in one of the lower rooms, to feel the darkness
gather like a fleece
above the stairs,

as if the house would happily reveal
its ghosts: umbrellas dripping in the hall
and rain tracked in from forty years ago
to other mirrors, other kitchen chairs.

Old conversations echo in our hands
and voices, all our lives
continuous and ready to be told
in words and gestures: unrecorded love

and what we take for love, on nights like this,
the cellar locked, the albums put away,
and some blind creature circling in the roof,
its throat plucked clean, its feathers smudged with clay.

JOHN BURNSIDE

The Answer

Debasement is the password of the base,
Nobility the epitaph of the noble.
See how the gilded sky is covered
With the drifting twisted shadows of the dead.

The Ice Age is over now,
Why is there ice everywhere?
The Cape of Good Hope has been discovered,
Why do a thousand sails contest the Dead Sea?

I came into this world
Bringing only paper, rope, a shadow,
To proclaim before the judgment
The voice that has been judged:

Let me tell you, world,
I – do – not – believe!
If a thousand challengers lie beneath your feet,
Count me as number thousand and one.

I don't believe the sky is blue;
I don't believe in thunder's echoes;
I don't believe that dreams are false;
I don't believe that death has no revenge.

If the sea is destined to breach the dikes
Let all the brackish water pour into my heart;
If the land is destined to rise
Let humanity choose a peak for existence again.

A new conjunction and glimmering stars
Adorn the unobstructed sky now:
They are the pictographs from five thousand years,
They are the watchful eyes of future generations.

BEI DAO
translated from the Chinese by Bonnie S. McDougall

As I Go

My pot is an old paint container
I do not know
who bought it
I do not know
whose house it decorated
I picked up the empty tin
in Cemetery Lane.
My lamp, a paraffin lamp
is an empty 280ml bottle
labelled 40 per cent alcohol
I picked up the bottle in a trash bin.
My cup
is an old jam tin
I do not know who enjoyed the sweetness
I found the tin
in a storm-water drain.
My plate is a motor car hub-cap cover
I do not know
whose car it belonged to
I found a boy wheeling it, playing with it
My house is built
from plastic over cardboard
I found the plastic being blown by the wind
It's simple
I pick up my life
as I go.

JULIUS CHINGONO

In Praise of Walking

Early one morning, any morning, we can set out, with the least possible baggage, and discover the world.

It is quite possible to refuse all the coercion, violence, property, triviality, to simply walk away.

That something exists outside ourselves and our preoccupations, so near, so readily available, is our greatest blessing.

Walking is the human way of getting about.

Always, everywhere, people have walked, veining the earth with paths, visible and invisible, symmetrical and meandering.

There are walks on which we tread in the footsteps of others, walks on which we strike out entirely for ourselves.

A journey implies a destination, so many miles to be consumed, while a walk is its own measure, complete at every point along the way.

There are things we will never see, unless we walk to them.

Walking is a mobile form of waiting.

What I take with me, what I leave behind, are of less importance than what I discover along the way.

To be completely lost is a good thing on a walk.

The most distant places seem most accessible once one is on the road.

Convictions, directions, opinions, are of less importance than sensible shoes.

In the course of a walk, we usually find out something about our companion, and this is true even when we travel alone.

When I spend a day talking I feel exhausted, when I spend it walking I am pleasantly tired.

The pace of a walk will determine the number and variety of things to be encountered, from the broad outlines of a mountain range to a tit's nest among the lichen, and the quality of attention that will be brought to bear upon them.

A rock outcrop, a hedge, a fallen tree, anything that turns us out of our way, is an excellent thing on a walk.

Wrong turnings, doubling back, pauses and digressions, all contribute to the dislocation of a persistent self-interest.

Everything we meet is equally important or unimportant.

The most lonely places are the most lovely.

Walking is egalitarian and democratic; we do not become experts at walking and one side of the road is as good as another.

Walking is not so much romantic as reasonable.

The line of a walk is articulate in itself, a kind of statement.

Pools, walls, solitary trees, are natural halting places.

We lose the flavour of walking if it becomes too rare or too extraordinary, if it turns into an expedition; rather it should be quite ordinary, unexceptional, just what we do.

Daily walking, in all weathers, in every season, becomes a sort of ground or continuum upon which the least emphatic occurrences are registered clearly.

A stick of ash or blackthorn, through long use, will adjust itself to the palm.

Of the many ways through a landscape, we can choose, on each occasion, only one, and the project of the walk will be to remain responsive, adequate, to the consequences of the choice we have made, to confirm the chosen way rather than refuse the others.

One continues on a long walk not by effort of will but through fidelity.

Storm clouds, rain, hail, when we have survived these we seem to have taken on some of the solidity of rocks and trees.

A day, from dawn to dusk, is the natural span of a walk.

A dull walk is not without value.

To walk for hours on a clear night is the largest experience we can have.

For the right understanding of a landscape, information must come to the intelligence from all the senses.

Looking, singing, resting, breathing, are all complementary to walking.

Climbing uphill, the horizon grows wider; descending, the hills gather round.

We can take a walk which is a sampling of different airs: the invigorating air of the heights; the filtered air of a pine forest; the rich air over ploughed earth.

We can walk between two places and in so doing establish a link
between them, bring them into a warmth of contact, like introducing
two friends.

There are walks on which I lose myself, walks which return me to
myself again.

Is there anything that is better than to be out, walking, in the
clear air?

THOMAS A. CLARK

Train Ride

All things come to an end;
small calves in Arkansas,
the bend of the muddy river.
Do all things come to an end?
No, they go on forever.
They go on forever, the swamp,
the vine-choked cypress, the oaks
rattling last year's leaves,
the thump of the rails, the kite,
the still white stilted heron.
All things come to an end.
The red clay bank, the spread hawk,
the bodies riding this train,
the stalled truck, pale sunlight, the talk;
the talk goes on forever,
the wide dry field of geese,
a man stopped near his porch
to watch. Release, release;
between cold death and a fever,
send what you will, I will listen.
All things come to an end.
No, they go on forever.

RUTH STONE

The Road Between Here and There

Here I heard the snorting of hogs trying to re-enter the underearth.
Here I came into the curve too fast, on ice, and touched the brake pedal
and sailed into the pasture.
Here I stopped the car and snoozed while two small children crawled all
over me.
Here I reread *Moby Dick*, skipping big chunks, skimming others, in a
single day, while Maud and Fergus fished.
Here I abandoned the car because of a clonk in the motor and hitchhiked
(which in those days in Vermont meant walking the whole way with
a limp) all the way to a garage, where I passed the afternoon with ex-
loggers who had stopped by to oil the joints of their artificial limbs
and talk.
Here a barn burned down to the snow. 'Friction,' one of the ex-loggers said.
'Friction?' 'Yup, the mortgage, rubbin' against the insurance policy.'
Here I went eighty but was in no danger of arrest, for I was blessed –
speeding, trying to get home to see my children before they slept.
Here I bought speckled brown eggs with bits of straw shitted to them.
Here I brought home in the back seat two piglets who rummaged inside
the burlap sack like pregnancy itself.
Here I heard again on the car radio Handel's concerto transcribed for
harp and lute, which Inés played to me the first time, making me
want to drive after it and hear it forever.
Here I sat on a boulder by the winter-steaming river and put my head in
my hands and considered time – which is next to nothing, merely what
vanishes, and yet can make one's elbows nearly pierce one's thighs.
Here I forgot how to sing in the old way and listened to frogs at dusk.
Here the local fortune teller took my hand and said, 'What is still possible
is inspired work, faithfulness to a few, and a last love, which, being
last, will be like looking up and seeing the parachute opening up in
a shower of gold.'
Here is the chimney standing up by itself and falling down, which tells
you you approach the end of the road between here and there.
Here I arrive there.
Here I must turn around and go back and on the way back look carefully
to left and to right.
For when the spaces along the road between here and there are all used
up, that's it.

GALWAY KINNELL

The Sofas, Fogs and Cinemas

I have lived it, and lived it,
My nervous, luxury civilisation,
My sugar-loving nerves have battered me to pieces.
...Their idea of literature is hopeless.
Make them drink their own poetry!
Let them eat their gross novel, full of mud.

It's quiet; just the fresh, chilly weather...and he
Gets up from his dead bedroom, and comes in here
And digs himself into the sofa.
He stays there up to two hours in the hole – and talks
– Straight into the large subjects, he faces up to *everything*
It's......damnably depressing.
(That great lavatory coat...the cigarillo burning
In the little dish...And when he calls out: 'Ha!'
Madness! – you no longer possess your own furniture.)

On my bad days (and I'm being broken
At this very moment) I speak of my ambitions...and he
Becomes intensely gloomy, with the look of something jugged,
Morose, sour, mouldering away, with lockjaw...

I grow coarser; and more modern (*I*, who am driven mad
By my ideas; who go nowhere;
Who dare not leave my frontdoor, lest an idea...)
All right. I admit everything, everything!

Oh yes, the opera (Ah, but the cinema)
He particularly enjoys it, enjoys it *horribly*, when someone's ill
At the last minute; and they specially fly in
A new, gigantic, Dutch soprano. He wants to help her
With her arias.   Old goat! Blasphemer!
He wants to help her with her arias!

No, I...go to the cinema,
I particularly like it when the fog is thick, the street
Is like a hole in an old coat, and the light is brown as laudanum,
...the fogs! the fogs! The cinemas
Where the criminal shadow-literature flickers over our faces,
The screen is spread out like a thundercloud – that bangs
And splashes you with acid...or lies derelict, with lighted waters in it,

51

And in the silence, drips and crackles – taciturn, luxurious.
...The drugged and battered Philistines
Are all around you in the auditorium...

And he...is somewhere else, in his dead bedroom clothes,
He wants to make me think his thoughts
And they will be *enormous*, dull – (just the sort
To keep away from).
...when I see that cigarillo, when I see it...smoking
And he wants to face the international situation...
Lunatic rages! Blackness! Suffocation!

– All this sitting about in cafés to calm down
Simply wears me out. And their idea of literature!
The idiotic cut of the stanzas; the novels, full up, gross.

I have lived it, and I know too much.
My café-nerves are breaking me
With black, exhausting information.

ROSEMARY TONKS

To Go to Lvov

To go to Lvov. Which station
for Lvov, if not in a dream, at dawn, when dew
gleams on a suitcase, when express
trains and bullet trains are being born. To leave
in haste for Lvov, night or day, in September
or in March. But only if Lvov exists,
if it is to be found within the frontiers and not just
in my new passport, if lances of trees
– of poplar and ash – still breathe aloud
like Indians, and if streams mumble
their dark Esperanto, and grass snakes like soft signs
in the Russian language disappear
into thickets. To pack and set off, to leave
without a trace, at noon, to vanish
like fainting maidens. And burdocks, green
armies of burdocks, and below, under the canvas
of a Venetian café, the snails converse
about eternity. But the cathedral rises,

you remember, so straight, as straight
as Sunday and white napkins and a bucket
full of raspberries standing on the floor, and
my desire which wasn't born yet,
only gardens and weeds and the amber
of Queen Anne cherries, and indecent Fredro.
There was always too much of Lvov, no one could
comprehend its boroughs, hear
the murmur of each stone scorched
by the sun, at night the Orthodox church's silence was unlike
that of the cathedral, the Jesuits
baptised plants, leaf by leaf, but they grew,
grew so mindlessly, and joy hovered
everywhere, in hallways and in coffee mills
revolving by themselves, in blue
teapots, in starch, which was the first
formalist, in drops of rain and in the thorns
of roses. Frozen forsythia yellowed by the window.
The bells pealed and the air vibrated, the cornets
of nuns sailed like schooners near
the theatre, there was so much of the world that
it had to do encores over and over,
the audience was in frenzy and didn't want
to leave the house. My aunts couldn't have known
yet that I'd resurrect them,
and lived so trustfully; so singly;
servants, clean and ironed, ran for
fresh cream, inside the houses
a bit of anger and great expectation, Brzozowski
came as a visiting lecturer, one of my
uncles kept writing a poem entitled *Why*,
dedicated to the Almighty, and there was too much
of Lvov, it brimmed the container,
it burst glasses, overflowed
each pond, lake, smoked through every
chimney, turned into fire, storm,
laughed with lightning, grew meek,
returned home, read the New Testament,
slept on a sofa beside the Carpathian rug,
there was too much of Lvov, and now
there isn't any, it grew relentlessly
and the scissors cut it, chilly gardeners
as always in May, without mercy,

without love, ah, wait till warm June
comes with soft ferns, boundless
fields of summer, i.e., the reality.
But scissors cut it, along the line and through
the fibre, tailors, gardeners, censors
cut the body and the wreaths, pruning shears worked
diligently, as in a child's cutout
along the dotted line of a roe deer or a swan.
Scissors, penknives, and razor blades scratched,
cut, and shortened the voluptuous dresses
of prelates, of squares and houses, and trees
fell soundlessly, as in a jungle,
and the cathedral trembled, people bade goodbye
without handkerchiefs, no tears, such a dry
mouth, I won't see you anymore, so much death
awaits you, why must every city
become Jerusalem and every man a Jew,
and now in a hurry just
pack, always, each day,
and go breathless, go to Lvov, after all
it exists, quiet and pure as
a peach. It is everywhere.

ADAM ZAGAJEWSKI
translated from the Polish by Renata Gorczynski

A Brief for the Defense

Sorrow everywhere. Slaughter everywhere. If babies
are not starving someplace, they are starving
somewhere else. With flies in their nostrils.
But we enjoy our lives because that's what God wants.
Otherwise the mornings before summer dawn would not
be made so fine. The Bengal tiger would not
be fashioned so miraculously well. The poor women
at the fountain are laughing together between
the suffering they have known and the awfulness
in their future, smiling and laughing while somebody
in the village is very sick. There is laughter
every day in the terrible streets of Calcutta,

and the women laugh in the cages of Bombay.
If we deny our happiness, resist our satisfaction,
we lessen the importance of their deprivation.
We must risk delight. We can do without pleasure,
but not delight. Not enjoyment. We must have
the stubbornness to accept our gladness in the ruthless
furnace of this world. To make injustice the only
measure of our attention is to praise the Devil.
If the locomotive of the Lord runs us down,
we should give thanks that the end had magnitude.
We must admit there will be music despite everything.
We stand at the prow again of a small ship
anchored late at night in the tiny port
looking over to the sleeping island: the waterfront
is three shuttered cafés and one naked light burning.
To hear the faint sound of oars in the silence as a rowboat
comes slowly out and then goes back is truly worth
all the years of sorrow that are to come.

JACK GILBERT

Burlap Sack

A person is full of sorrow
the way a burlap sack is full of stones or sand.
We say, 'Hand me the sack,'
but we get the weight.
Heavier if left out in the rain.
To think that the sand or stones are the self is an error.
To think that grief is the self is an error.
Self carries grief as a pack mule carries the side bags,
being careful between the trees to leave extra room.
The mule is not the load of ropes and nails and axes.
The self is not the miner nor builder nor driver.
What would it be to take the bride
and leave behind the heavy dowry?
To let the thin-ribbed mule browse in tall grasses,
its long ears waggling like the tails of two happy dogs?

JANE HIRSHFIELD

Table

A man filled with the gladness of living
Put his keys on the table,
Put flowers in a copper bowl there.
He put his eggs and milk on the table.
He put there the light that came in through the window,
Sound of a bicycle, sound of a spinning wheel.
The softness of bread and weather he put there.
On the table the man put
Things that happened in his mind.
What he wanted to do in life,
He put that there.
Those he loved, those he didn't love,
The man put them on the table too.
Three times three make nine:
The man put nine on the table.
He was next to the window next to the sky;
He reached out and placed on the table endlessness.
So many days he had wanted to drink a beer!
He put on the table the pouring of that beer.
He placed there his sleep and his wakefulness;
His hunger and his fullness he put there.

Now that's what I call a table!
It didn't complain at all about the load.
It wobbled once or twice, then stood firm.
The man kept piling things on.

EDIP CANSEVER
translated from the Turkish by Julia Clare Tillinghast & Richard Tillinghast

Table Laid

I laid my linen on the hill of night.
    The moon came up on my left,
The sun sank on my right.
    Perched on a star the heavenly peacock
Opened his fan and rose-red light

Fell on my flask, I drank,
Out of this world with every swallow.
Time unlived grows old
Like unworn robes in a locked chest.
Clearly my days were hollow
Through and through,
Numbered as the flickerings of a candle.

OKTAY RIFAT
translated from the Turkish by Ruth Christie

The great tablecloth

When they were called to the table,
the tyrants came rushing
with their temporary ladies,
it was fine to watch the women pass
like wasps with big bosoms
followed by those pale
and unfortunate public tigers.

The peasant in the field ate
his poor quota of bread,
he was alone, it was late,
he was surrounded by wheat,
but he had no more bread,
he ate it with grim teeth,
looking at it with hard eyes.

In the blue hour of eating,
the infinite hour of the roast,
the poet abandons his lyre,
takes up his knife and fork,
puts his glass on the table,
and the fishermen attend
the little sea of the soup bowl.
Burning potatoes protest
among the tongues of oil.
The lamb is gold on its coals
and the onion undresses.

It is sad to eat in dinner clothes,
like eating in a coffin,
but eating in convents
is like eating underground.
Eating alone is a disappointment,
but not eating matters more,
is hollow and green, has thorns
like a chain of fish hooks
trailing from the heart,
clawing at your insides.

Hunger feels like pincers,
like the bite of crabs,
it burns, burns and has no fire.
Hunger is a cold fire.
Let us sit down soon to eat
with all those who haven't eaten;
let us spread great tablecloths,
put salt in the lakes of the world,
set up planetary bakeries,
tables with strawberries in snow,
and a plate like the moon itself
from which we can all eat.

For now I ask no more
than the justice of eating.

PABLO NERUDA
translated from the Spanish by Alastair Reid

A Long Way from Bread

1

We have come so far from bread.
Rarely do we hear the clatter of the mill wheel;
see the flour in every cranny,
the shaking down of the sack, the chalk on the door,
the rats, the race, the pool,
baking day, and the old loaves:
cob, cottage, plaited, brick.

We have come so far from bread.
Once the crock said 'BREAD'
and the bread was what was there,
and the family's arm went deeper down each day
to find it, and the crust was favoured.

We have come so far from bread.
Terrifying is the breach between wheat and table,
wheat and bread, bread and what goes for bread.
Loaves come now in regiments, so that loaf
is not the word. *Hlaf*
is one of the oldest words we have.

2

I go on about bread
because it was to bread
that Jesus trusted
the meaning he had of himself.
It was an honour for bread
to be the knot in the Lord's handkerchief
reminding him about himself. So,
O bread, breakable;
O bread, given;
O bread, a blessing;
count yourself lucky, bread.

3

Not that I am against wafers,
especially the ones produced under steam
from some hidden nunnery
with our Lord crucified into them.
They are at least unleavened, and fit the hand,
without remainder, but it is still
a long way from bread.
Better for each household to have its own bread,
daily, enough and to spare,
dough the size of a rolled towel,
for feeding angels unawares.
Then if the bread is holy,
all that has to do with bread is holy:
board, knife, cupboard,
so that the gap between all things is closed
in our attention to the bread of the day.

4
I know that
'man cannot live on bread alone'.
I say, let us get the bread right.

DAVID SCOTT

Bread

Someone else cut off my head
In a golden field.
Now I am re-created

By her fingers. This
Moulding is more delicate
Than a first kiss,

More deliberate than her own
Rising up
And lying down,

I am fine
As anything in
This legendary garden

Yet I am nothing till
She runs her fingers through me
And shapes me with her skill.

The form that I shall bear
Grows round and white.
It seems I comfort her

Even as she slits my face
And stabs my chest.
Her feeling for perfection is

Absolute.
So I am glad to go through fire
And come out

Shaped like her dream.
In my way
I am all that can happen to men.
I came to life at her finger-ends.
I will go back into her again.

BRENDAN KENNELLY

Don't Talk to Me about Bread

she kneads
deep into the night
and the whey-coloured dough

springy and easy and yielding to her will

is revenge. Like a rival,
dough toys with her. Black-brown hands in the belly
bringing forth a sigh.

She slaps it, slaps it double with fists
with heel of hand applies the punishment
not meant for bread

and the bitch on the table sighs
and exhales a little spray of flour
a satisfied breath of white

on her hand

mocking the colour
robbing hands of their power
as they go through the motions, kneading...
She listens for the sigh which haunts

from the wrong side of her own door
from this wanton cheat of dough
this whey-faced bitch rising up

in spite of her fight, rising up
her nipples, her belly, rising up
two legs, dear god, in a blackwoman's rage...

Laughing at her, all laughing at her:
giggling bitch, abandoned house, and Man
still promising from afar what men promise...

Hands come to life again: knife
in the hand, the belly ripped open, and she smears

white lard and butter, she sprinkles
a little obeah of flour and curses to stop up the wound.

Then she doubles the bitch up
with cuffs, wrings her like washing
till she's the wrong shape

and the tramp lets out a damp, little sigh
a little hiss of white
enjoying it.

E.A. MARKHAM

Quilts
(for Sally Sellers)

Like a fading piece of cloth
I am a failure

No longer do I cover tables filled with food and laughter
My seams are frayed my hems falling my strength no longer able
To hold the hot and cold

I wish for those first days
When just woven I could keep water
From seeping through
Repelled stains with the tightness of my weave
Dazzled the sunlight with my
Reflection

I grow old though pleased with my memories
The tasks I can no longer complete
Are balanced by the love of the tasks gone past

I offer no apology only
this plea:

When I am frayed and strained and drizzle at the end
Please someone cut a square and put me in a quilt
That I might keep some child warm

And some old person with no one else to talk to
Will hear my whispers

And cuddle
near

NIKKI GIOVANNI

Second-Hand Coat

I feel
in her pockets; she wore nice cotton gloves,
kept a handkerchief box, washed her undies,
ate at the Holiday Inn, had a basement freezer,
belonged to a bridge club.
I think when I wake in the morning
that I have turned into her.
She hangs in the hall downstairs,
a shadow with pulled threads.
I slip her over my arms, skin of a matron.
Where are you? I say to myself, to the orphaned body,
and her coat says,
Get your purse, have you got your keys?

RUTH STONE

Helplessness

Oh, heart,
why can't you learn
that there is nothing to do in the world except live in it?

Why can't you take its deep gifts –
the birds and the cars in the rain;
lost keys and the broken-hearted?

KERRY HARDIE

Don't Give Me the Whole Truth

Don't give me the whole truth,
don't give me the sea for my thirst,
don't give me the sky when I ask for light,
but give me a glint, a dewy wisp, a mote
as the birds bear water-drops from their bathing
and the wind a grain of salt.

OLAV H. HAUGE
translated from the Norwegian by Robin Fulton

'Although the wind'

Although the wind
blows terribly here,
the moonlight also leaks
between the roof planks
of this ruined house.

IZUMI SHIKIBU
translated from the Japanese by Jane Hirshfield & Mariko Aratani

Sir, I Want to Write Poems with Flowers

Sir, you get angry that I write poems with flowers,
you don't know. I hide my scattered body
behind flower curtains.
I sit in the dark, don't turn on the lights.
The wound clock is ringing, ringing until unsprung.
I recall an aching love.
This is the unnecessary sheen of a knife.
I'm the illegal rain kept for years in the clouds.
Once it rains, it'll cost you.
Sir, I'm a basement girl
whose only boss is loneliness
For now I'm solid like plastic vases
but I'm worried. In a while
in your twelve E shoes you'll step
on kids in the garden.
This is not nice, sir.

'Day is night' I'm saying,
casting breadcrumbs to birds.
They'll eat glass shards
in my dream, in a bowl of water,
in technicolor lego blocks.
I'm trying to tell you, you won't listen,
no, I don't think
I can wait till the morning.
One should tell one's dream immediately.

My soul was 14, sir,
it got older in the cold of a marble table.
Prosthetic legs were attached to my soul, delicate and white.
I walked in the city squeaking.
They even whistled at the prosthetic legs.
Meanwhile, an unarmed force in me
made of flowers was besieged,
on the screen *the rustling of organza* was playing.
I tried to slip away, couldn't.
Due to that, sir, writing flower poems
from the angle of my soul I find useful.
Whatever, I remember
all the movies I see,

taking shelter in the endless night of movies.
At *Sophie's Choice* I cried a lot.
If they make a movie called *kissing tetras*
I'll cry there too.
Does one forget the spinning wheel inside,
besides, I'm used to remembering.
'I'm a magpie, sir.'

Sir, there are no more armadas
or sailboats.
I'll burn a large quantity of paper.
A cormorant dove into water,
lost for a while,
even if it reemerges, having swallowed the whole world,
death isn't too large a word, sir.
I know I smell bitter like chrysanthemums.
But do you know the loveliness
of a lonesome love which makes scrambled eggs with sausages
at the stove and eats it?
A rose will tell a rose, if I see it,
but I'm lying
roses aren't much for talking these days, sir.

DIDEM MADAK
translated from the Turkish by Murat Nemet-Nejat

Winter Anemones

The ruby and amethyst eyes of anemones
Glow through me, fiercer than stars.
Flambeaux of earth, their dyes
From age-lost generations burn
Black soil, branches and mosses into light
That does not fail, though winter grip the rocks
To adamant. See, they come now
To lamp me through inscrutable dusk
And down the catacombs of death.

CHARLES BRASCH

Duende

1

The earth is dry and they live wanting.
Each with a small reservoir
Of furious music heavy in the throat.
They drag it out and with nails in their feet
Coax the night into being. Brief believing.
A skirt shimmering with sequins and lies.
And in this night that is not night,
Each word is a wish, each phrase
A shape their bodies ache to fill –

> *I'm going to braid my hair*
> *Braid many colors into my hair*
> *I'll put a long braid in my hair*
> *And write your name there*

They defy gravity to feel tugged back.
The clatter, the mad slap of landing.

2

And not just them. Not just
The ramshackle family, the *tíos*,
Primitos, not just the *bailaor*
Whose heels have notched
And hammered time
So the hours flow in place
Like a tin river, marking
Only what once was.
Not just the voices scraping
Against the river, nor the hands
Nudging them farther, fingers
Like blind birds, palms empty,
Echoing. Not just the women
With sober faces and flowers
In their hair, the ones who dance
As though they're burying
Memory – one last time –
Beneath them.

And I hate to do it here.
To set myself heavily beside them.
Not now that they've proven
The body a myth, parable
For what not even language
Moves quickly enough to name.
If I call it pain, and try to touch it
With my hands, my own life,
It lies still and the music thins,
A pulse felt for through garments.
If I lean into the desire it starts from –
If I lean unbuttoned into the blow
Of loss after loss, love tossed
Into the ecstatic void –
It carries me with it farther,
To chords that stretch and bend
Like light through colored glass.
But it races on, toward shadows
Where the world I know
And the world I fear
Threaten to meet.

3

There is always a road,
The sea, dark hair, *dolor*.

Always a question
Bigger than itself –

> *They say you're leaving Monday*
> *Why can't you leave on Tuesday?*

TRACY K. SMITH

The Thunder Shower

A blink of lightning, then
a rumour, a grumble of white rain
growing in volume, rustling over the ground,
drenching the gravel in a wash of sound.
Drops tap like timpani or shine
like quavers on a line.

It rings on exposed tin,
a suite for water, wind and bin,
plinky Poulenc or strongly groaning Brahms'
rain-strings, a whole string section that describes
the very shapes of thought in warm
self-referential vibes

and spreading ripples. Soon
the whispering roar is a recital.
Jostling rain-crowds, clamorous and vital,
struggle in runnels through the afternoon.
The rhythm becomes a regular beat;
steam rises, body heat –

and now there's city noise,
bits of recorded pop and rock,
the drums, the strident electronic shock,
a vast polyphony, the dense refrain
of wailing siren, truck and train
and incoherent cries.

All human life is there
in the unconfined, continuous crash
whose slow, diffused implosions gather up
car radios and alarms, the honk and beep,
and tiny voices in a crèche
piercing the muggy air.

Squalor and decadence,
the rackety global-franchise rush,
oil wars and water wars, the diatonic
crescendo of a cascading world economy

are audible in the hectic thrash
of this luxurious cadence.

The voice of Baal explodes,
raging and rumbling round the clouds,
frantic to crush the self-sufficient spaces
and re-impose his failed hegemony
in Canaan before moving on
to other simpler places.

At length the twining chords
run thin, a watery sun shines out,
the deluge slowly ceases, the guttural chant
subsides; a thrush sings, and discordant thirds
diminish like an exhausted concert
on the subdominant.

The angry downpour swarms
growling to far-flung fields and farms.
The drains are still alive with trickling water,
a few last drops drip from a broken gutter;
but the storm that created so much fuss
has lost interest in us.

DEREK MAHON

Kinsale

The kind of rain we knew is a thing of the past —
deep-delving, dark, deliberate you would say,
browsing on spire and bogland; but today
our sky-blue slates are steaming in the sun,
our yachts tinkling and dancing in the bay
like racehorses. We contemplate at last
shining windows, a future forbidden to no one.

DEREK MAHON

Daed-traa

I go to the rockpool at the slack of the tide
to mind me what my poetry's for.

It has its ventricles, just like us –
pumping brine, like bull's blood, a syrupy flow.

It has its theatre –
hushed and plush.

It has its Little Shop of Horrors.
It has its crossed and dotted monsters.

It has its cross-eyed beetling Lear.
It has its billowing Monroe.

I go to the rockpool at the slack of the tide
to mind me what my poetry's for.

For monks, it has barnacles
to sweep the broth as it flows, with fans,
grooming every cubic millimetre.

It has its ebb, the easy heft of wrack from rock,
like plastered, feverish locks of hair.

It has its *flodd*.
It has its welling god
with puddled, podgy cheeks and jaw.

It has its holy hiccup.

Its minute's silence

daed-traa.

I go to the rockpool at the slack of the tide
to mind me what my poetry's for.

JEN HADFIELD

Daed-traa: the slack of the tide (Shetland dialect).

Where Water Comes Together with Other Water

I love creeks and the music they make.
And rills, in glades and meadows, before
they have a chance to become creeks.
I may even love them best of all
for their secrecy. I almost forgot
to say something about the source!
Can anything be more wonderful than a spring?
But the big streams have my heart too.
And the places streams flow into rivers.
The open mouths of rivers where they join the sea.
The places where water comes together
with other water. Those places stand out
in my mind like holy places.
But these coastal rivers!
I love them the way some men love horses
or glamorous women. I have a thing
for this cold swift water.
Just looking at it makes my blood run
and my skin tingle. I could sit
and watch these rivers for hours.
Not one of them like any other.
I'm 45 years old today.
Would anyone believe it if I said
I was once 35?
My heart empty and sere at 35!
Five more years had to pass
before it began to flow again.
I'll take all the time I please this afternoon
before leaving my place alongside this river.
It pleases me, loving rivers.
Loving them all the way back
to their source.
Loving everything that increases me.

RAYMOND CARVER

The Local Accent

This river is pronounced by granite drag.
It is a matter of inflection, of knowing what
to emphasise, and what to let drift away,
just as a slipping aspen leaf makes barely a flicker,
one gaffe in the conversation between the current
and the flow; a stifled yawn, a darkness reimbursed;

while, underneath, the thing that falls through shadow
is full of its own occasion. Weighty and dull,
it longs for water, the lacquer and slip of it,
the way it won't allow for brightness on its back,
but flips around to where its fall is a wet-wool,
sodden thing about to break at any moment, and undo.

Something is coming loose like aspen leaves, or froth.
Or maunder, letting itself down like rain into a river
immersed in getting on with what it separates:
the sulk of damp soil; the stiff articulation of the shore,
the giddy vowels sprayed over the drag and ebb
of voices leaking through the rain over the town.

Everything arrives at a standstill under the bridge.
The town grips the river and all the words for elsewhere
or for being there have had their edges worn off
and their meanings powdered to a consonantal darkness
where they dissolve, like happenings, into traffic
and asphalt, or otherwise, in the river and its silt.

This river is pitched so far from the sea
it announces itself in elision, as though everything
unsaid could still bed down in depth and unison,
underwriting words for going on and every other way
in and our of this one place. Excepting the blood-red
trickle of sky, and what it overrides, what slips beneath.

VONA GROARKE

Counting

The river's pulled itself away from us.
We count our losses – a dead fox, a shoe.
The sky yields to what we make of it:
mackerel, cirrous, heaven, blue.

We're of this world but still don't know it.
Such busy inventors we're barely here
with all our dreaming, our factory of gods,
our poor old minds at odds with what's there.

No wonder we've failed.
No wonder it's all adding up:
how what we've taken away
will not come back to us

but be returned at a loss:
this gallon can, this slick black wing.
If there was water here we wouldn't see these things;
we'd throw a stone, we'd count the rings.

GRETA STODDART

Midnight Singer

a song
is a thief who's fled across rooftops
getting away with six colours
and leaving the red hour-hand
on 4 o'clock heaven
4 o'clock detonates
on the rooster's head
and it's 4 o'clock delirium

a song
is an ever hostile tree
across the border

it unleashes that promise
that wolf-pack feeding on tomorrow

a song
is a mirror that knows the body by heart
is the emperor of memory
is the waxen tongue
flame of talk
is the flower garden murtured by myth
is a steam locomotive
bursting into the church

a song
is the death of a singer
his death-night
pressed into black records
singing over and over and over

BEI DAO
translated from the Chinese by David Hinton

Moon

Startled by the moon in the middle of the day,
same blue as the sky, like a crater in it,
for the first time in years I think of the flag
still flying there, of the men whose lives are fastened to it
even though the rest of us have turned away,

and I think of all the places I've been
in love, or happy, where I'll never go again
and probably couldn't find – that linden tree in Boston
I was lying under, watching summer's college kids
lope across the grass on their muscled brown legs,
when I suddenly headed for home.

There are bones inside my body I've never seen.

FRANCES LEVISTON

75

Things I Didn't Know I Loved

it's 1962 March 28th
I'm sitting by the window on the Prague-Berlin train
night is falling
I never knew I liked
night descending like a tired bird on a smoky wet plain
I don't like
comparing nightfall to a tired bird

I didn't know I loved the earth
can someone who hasn't worked the earth love it
I've never worked the earth
it must be my only Platonic love

and here I've loved rivers all this time
whether motionless like this they curl skirting the hills
European hills crowned with chateaus
or whether stretched out flat as far as the eye can see
I know you can't wash in the same river even once
I know the river will bring new lights you'll never see
I know we live slightly longer than a horse but not nearly as long
   as a crow
I know this has troubled people before
      and will trouble those after me
I know all this has been said a thousand times before
      and will be said after me

I didn't know I loved the sky
cloudy or clear
the blue vault Andrei studied on his back at Borodino
in prison I translated both volumes of *War and Peace* into Turkish
I hear voices
not from the blue vault but from the yard
the guards are beating someone again

I didn't know I loved trees
bare beeches near Moscow in Peredelkino
they come upon me in winter noble and modest
beeches are Russian the way poplars are Turkish

'the poplars of Izmir
losing their leaves...
they call me The Knife...
                    lover like a young tree...
I blow stately mansions sky-high'
in the Ilgaz woods in 1920 I tied an embroidered linen handkerchief
        to a pine bough for luck

I never knew I loved roads
even the asphalt kind
Vera's behind the wheel we're driving from Moscow to the Crimea
        Koktebele formerly 'Goktepé ili' in Turkish
the two of us inside a closed box
the world flows past on both sides distant and mute
I was never so close to anyone in my life
bandits stopped me on the red road between Bolu and Geredé
        when I was eighteen
apart from my life I didn't have anything in the wagon they
        could take
and at eighteen our lives are what we value least
I've written this somewhere before
wading through a dark muddy street I'm going to the shadow play
Ramazan night
a paper lantern leading the way
maybe nothing like this ever happened
maybe I read it somewhere an eight-year-old boy going to the
        shadow play
Ramazan night in Istanbul holding his grandfather's hand
        his grandfather has on a fez and is wearing the fur coat
                with a sable collar over his robe
        and there's a lantern in the servant's hand
        and I can't contain myself for joy

flowers come to mind for some reason
poppies cactuses jonquils
in the jonquil garden in Kadikoy Istanbul I kissed Marika
fresh almonds on her breath
I was seventeen
my heart on a swing touched the sky
I didn't know I loved flowers
friends sent me three red carnations in prison

I just remembered the stars
I love them too
whether I'm floored watching them from below
or whether I'm flying at their side

I have some questions for the cosmonauts
were the stars much bigger
did they look like huge jewels on black velvet
                    or apricots on orange
did you feel proud to get closer to the stars
I saw colour photos of the cosmos in *Ogonek* magazine now don't be
        upset comrades but nonfigurative shall we say or abstract
        well some of them looked just like such paintings which is
        to say they were terribly figurative and concrete
my heart was in my mouth looking at them
they are our endless desire to grasp things
seeing them I could even think of death and not feel at all sad
I never knew I loved the cosmos

snow flashes in front of my eyes
both heavy wet steady snow and the dry whirling kind
I didn't know I liked snow

I never knew I loved the sun
even when setting cherry-red as now
in Istanbul too it sometimes sets in postcard colours
but you aren't about to paint it that way

I didn't know I loved the sea
                    except the Sea of Azov
or how much

I didn't know I loved clouds
whether I'm under or up above them
whether they look like giants or shaggy white beasts

moonlight the falsest the most languid the most petit-bourgeois
strikes me
I like it

I didn't know I liked rain
whether it falls like a fine net or splatters against the glass my
     heart leaves me tangled up in a net or trapped inside a
     drop and takes off for uncharted countries I didn't know
     I loved rain but why did I suddenly discover all these
     passions sitting by the window on the Prague-Berlin train
is it because I lit my sixth cigarette
one alone could kill me
is it because I'm half dead from thinking about someone back in
     Moscow
her hair straw-blond eyelashes blue

the train plunges on through the pitch-black night
I never knew I liked the night pitch-black
sparks fly from the engine
I didn't know I loved sparks
I didn't know I loved so many things and I had to wait until sixty to
     find it out sitting by the window on the Prague-Berlin train
     watching the world disappear as if on a journey of no return

[Moscow, *19 April 1962*]

NÂZIM HIKMET
translated from the Turkish by Mutlu Konuk & Randy Blasing

Things I Didn't Know I Loved
(after Nazim Hikmet)

I always knew I loved the sky,
the way it seems solid and insubstantial at the same time;
the way it disappears above us
even as we pursue it in a climbing plane,
like wishes or answers to certain questions – always out of reach;
the way it embodies blue,
even when it is gray.

But I didn't know I loved the clouds,
those shaggy eyebrows glowering
over the face of the sun.
Perhaps I only love the strange shapes clouds can take,

as if they are sketches by an artist
who keeps changing her mind.
Perhaps I love their deceptive softness,
like a bosom I'd like to rest my head against
but never can.

And I know I love the grass, even as I am cutting it as short
as the hair on my grandson's newly barbered head.
I love the way the smell of grass can fill my nostrils
with intimations of youth and lust;
the way it stains my handkerchief with meanings
that never wash out.

Sometimes I love the rain, staccato on the roof,
and always the snow when I am inside looking out
at the blurring around the edges of parked cars
and trees. And I love trees,
in winter when their austere shapes
are like the cutout silhouettes artists sell at fairs
and in May when their branches
are fuzzy with growth, the leaves poking out
like new green horns on a young deer.

But how about the sound of trains,
those drawn-out whistles of longing in the night,
like coyotes made of steam and steel, no color at all,
reminding me of prisoners on chain gangs I've only seen
in movies, defeated men hammering spikes into rails,
the burly guards watching over them?

Those whistles give loneliness and departure a voice.
It is the kind of loneliness I can take in my arms, tasting
of tears that comfort even as they burn, dampening the pillows
and all the feathers of all the geese who were plucked to fill them.

Perhaps I embrace the music of departure – song without lyrics,
so I can learn to love it, though I don't love it now.
For at the end of the story, when sky and clouds and grass,
and even you my love of so many years,
have almost disappeared,
it will be all there is left to love.

LINDA PASTAN

80

The Sunlight on the Garden

The sunlight on the garden
Hardens and grows cold,
We cannot cage the minute
Within its nets of gold,
When all is told
We cannot beg for pardon.

Our freedom as free lances
Advances towards its end;
The earth compels, upon it
Sonnets and birds descend;
And soon, my friend,
We shall have no time for dances.

The sky was good for flying
Defying the church bells
And every evil iron
Siren and what it tells:
The earth compels,
We are dying, Egypt, dying

And not expecting pardon,
Hardened in heart anew,
But glad to have sat under
Thunder and rain with you,
And grateful too
For sunlight on the garden.

LOUIS MacNEICE

Pastoral
(for Ralf Andtbacka, after his Swedish)

A swollen moon is grazing out on the wold.
Deer stand motionless underneath the trees,
cardboard cut-outs, staring, unwieldy.
Where do you linger, my friend? The hour is late,
and already the farmer has taken to his bed. I, though,

81

I lie awake and wait for you. Through the yard
pads black cat Lucifer with soft deliberate tread.
Steaming cattle stand and dream in the byre. Lofts groan
with meat and bread, berries, polished fruit. Spilt grain
lines the trackway verges with gold. And all things
are content, all are at rest, sing their small still song
of contentment, and of rest.

PETER DIDSBURY

The Colours

These the colours of the seasons: gold
for the portal flowering of birth; violet

for shy kisses in a shaded copse, for days
of fast and pleading, for the iris of Van Gogh;

rose, for one long day of joy, for the survival
of sea-thrift on a famished cliff-face ledge;

suburban avenues will be clothed
in the alb of cherry-blossom white;

white and gold the chasuble
of the chestnut tree, and white

for angels flying in to the festival of snow, for virgins
crossing all together the frozen ice-paths of the Alps;

red, for martyrs, for the late-year standing of the dogwood,
the gift of tongues, the long delay of Good Friday

and the blood-stained building-blocks of Gaza;
green, for the ordinary days, *de tempore* labouring,

for past-time, in-between times and times ahead of times;
gold again, for the mind's embossed

portal to the sacrament, and black
for the peaceful, the having-come-through, dead.

JOHN F. DEANE

Blue Field

A flood as the day releases
and the whole snow world
is neither wet nor deep, but primary.
Colour so inherent, it does not fall
but rises from my skin,
the snow, the trees, the road.
This blue isn't built or grown.
It has no tissue, nothing
to touch or taste or bring to mind
a memory, no iris or artery,
no gentian, aconite or anemone,
no slate, plum, oil-spill or gun,
no titanium or turquoise,
no mercury or magnesium,
no phosphorus, sapphire or silver foil,
no duck egg or milk jug,
no chambray, denim or navy,
no indigo, octopus ink, no ink,
no element. The blue moment,
sininen hetki in a language that claims
no relation but greets in passing
picture blue, cyan. Ultraviolet
twilight, higher than the heaven
of swimming or flying – no splash.
A time without clouded objects,
in which you might become the glass
you swallowed through cold.
Light draws back
behind the rim of the eye as it closes.
I keep my distance, as things turn blue
through stillness and distance,
as everything blue is distant.

LAVINIA GREENLAW

On Harlech Beach

Sharpen your eyes looking back from the tide's headland,
and the Lowry figures on the beach could be movable type –
a *p*, pink, *i*, indigo, an *x* running yellow and tan
in pursuit of a flying stop. What an alphabet soup
the bay makes of them, these large fathered families
downloading their daughters and sons, sans serif
and sans grief, on the centrefold page of the sand.

From which a Welsh double *l* is detaching itself –
lovers, hand-linked by a hyphen, weaving with ease
through the ins and outs of the waves' parentheses.
From a distance, how simple they look, how picturesque.
Three dots (an ellipsis in action) rush back and forth –
terriers seeking, retrieving, time-free and care-free
as only dogs in illiterate joyousness can be.

It's a scene to write about. You could walk back
cheering – if not for the human story, for the display
it offers to the pattern-hungry eye –
the bodysway of the lovers, a Frisbee caught
by a bronze torso, striped pigments of cloud and sky
brushed by an appearing, disappearing sun;
prone golden mums and their lucky cartwheeling young.

As if this were a playground raised from the dead for them,
the salvaged remains of old beachheads, suffered and won.
Unremarked by the holiday crowd, two faraway swarms
– I would paint them as shadows in khaki and bloodstained brown –
turn out to be birds; an invasion of scavenging *m*'s
whose squabble of laughter is raucous enough to drown
those boys shouting *king of the castle* as they kick it down.

ANNE STEVENSON

Archaic Torso of Apollo

We cannot know his legendary head
with eyes like ripening fruit. And yet his torso
is still suffused with brilliance from inside,
like a lamp, in which his gaze, now turned to low,

gleams in all its power. Otherwise
the curved breast could not dazzle you so, nor could
a smile run through the placid hips and thighs
to that dark center where procreation flared.

Otherwise this stone would seem defaced
beneath the translucent cascade of the shoulders
and would not glisten like a wild beast's fur:

would not, from all the borders of itself,
burst like a star: for here there is no place
that does not see you. You must change your life.

RAINER MARIA RILKE
translated from the German by Stephen Mitchell

A Green Crab's Shell

Not, exactly, green:
closer to bronze
preserved in kind brine,

something retrieved
from a Greco-Roman wreck,
patinated and oddly

muscular. We cannot
know what his fantastic
legs were like –

though evidence
suggests eight
complexly folded

scuttling works
of armament, crowned
by the foreclaws'

gesture of menace
and power. A gull's
gobbled the center,

leaving this chamber
– size of a demitasse –
open to reveal

a shocking, Giotto blue,
Though it smells
of seaweed and ruin,

this little traveling case
comes with such lavish lining!
Imagine breathing

surrounded by
the brilliant rinse
of summer's firmament.

What color is
the underside of skin?
Not so bad, to die,

if we could be opened
into *this* –
if the smallest chambers

of ourselves,
similarly,
revealed some sky.

MARK DOTY

Wasp on Water

The water surface holds, tense,
for a wasp;
this path is a delta, always moving,
like time, that touch
on the deep quietness
in a brief moment.

Brief, this floating-
time; brief
its spinning journey
in ever-coiling labyrinths,
seething uncertainties, flames,
and transparent
complexity.

CORAL BRACHO
translated from the Spanish by Katherine Pierpoint & Tom Boll

Amber

I have an amber ring that
shimmers through the lake's water

I dive, stir up the silt, particles
of minerals loosen and float along

the bottom, just like the oak-blossom bud's
starry hairs floated and were enclosed in the stone

then, during the time of sabre-toothed tigers
and small horses

in the sub-tropical forests with elderberry
and camphor trees here, where we live in houses

You see more clearly underwater
You see more clearly when you are sick

I dive into the cool water, stir up
silt, particles float slowly, minerals

like the oak-blossom bud's starry hairs float
in amber through thirty million years, shimmering

in the lake's water when I dive, everything
is stirred up, gets cloudy, shimmers

TUA FORSSTRÖM
translated from the Swedish by Stina Katchadourian

The Weighing

The heart's reasons
seen clearly,
even the hardest
will carry
its whip-marks and sadness
and must be forgiven.

As the drought-starved
eland forgives
the drought-starved lion
who finally takes her,
enters willingly then
the life she cannot refuse,
and is lion, is fed,
and does not remember the other.

So few grains of happiness
measured against all the dark
and still the scales balance.

The world asks of us
only the strength we have and we give it.
Then it asks more, and we give it.

JANE HIRSHFIELD

The Layers

I have walked through many lives,
some of them my own,
and I am not who I was,
though some principle of being
abides, from which I struggle
not to stray.
When I look behind,
as I am compelled to look
before I can gather strength
to proceed on my journey,
I see the milestones dwindling
toward the horizon
and the slow fires trailing
from the abandoned camp-sites,
over which scavenger angels
wheel on heavy wings.
Oh, I have made myself a tribe
out of my true affections,
and my tribe is scattered!
How shall the heart be reconciled
to its feast of losses?
In a rising wind
the manic dust of my friends,
those who fell along the way,
bitterly stings my face.
Yet I turn, I turn,
exulting somewhat,
with my will intact to go
wherever I need to go,
and every stone on the road
precious to me.
In my darkest night,
when the moon was covered
and I roamed through wreckage,
a nimbus-clouded voice
directed me:
'Live in the layers,
not on the litter.'
Though I lack the art

to decipher it,
no doubt the next chapter
in my book of transformations
is already written.
I am not done with my changes.

STANLEY KUNITZ

The Way It Is

There's a thread you follow. It goes among
things that change. But it doesn't change.
People wonder about what you are pursuing.
You have to explain about the thread.
But it is hard for others to see.
While you hold it you can't get lost.
Tragedies happen; people get hurt
or die; and you suffer and get old.
Nothing you do can stop time's unfolding.
You don't ever let go of the thread.

WILLIAM STAFFORD

'To be great, be whole...'

To be great, be whole: don't exaggerate
        Or leave out any part of you.
Be complete in each thing. Put all you are
        Into the least of your acts.
So too in each lake, with its lofty life,
        The whole moon shines.

FERNANDO PESSOA
translated from the Portuguese by Richard Zenith

'I drew a line...'

I drew a line:
this far, and no further,
never will I go further than this.

When I went further,
I drew a new line,
and then another line.

The sun was shining
and everywhere I saw people,
hurried and serious,
and everyone was drawing a line,
everyone went further.

TOON TELLEGEN
translated from the Dutch by Judith Wilkinson

The Armful

For every parcel I stoop down to seize
I lose some other off my arms and knees,
And the whole pile is slipping, bottles, buns –
Extremes too hard to comprehend at once,
Yet nothing I should care to leave behind.
With all I have to hold with hand and mind
And heart, if need be, I will do my best
To keep their building balanced at my breast.
I crouch down to prevent them as they fall;
Then sit down in the middle of them all.
I had to drop the armful in the road
And try to stack them in a better load.

ROBERT FROST

'The Whole Mess... Almost

I ran up six flights of stairs
to my small furnished room
opened the window
and began throwing out
those things most important in life

First to go, Truth, squealing like a fink:
'Don't! I'll tell awful things about you!'
'Oh yeah? Well, I've nothing to hide... OUT!'
Then went God, glowering & whimpering in amazement:
'It's not my fault! I'm not the cause of it all!' 'OUT!'
Then Love, cooing bribes: 'You'll never know impotency!
All the girls on *Vogue* covers, all yours!'
I pushed her fat ass out and screamed:
'You always end up a bummer!'
I picked up Faith Hope Charity
all three clinging together:
'Without us you'll surely die!'
'With you I'm going nuts! Goodbye!'

Then Beauty... ah, Beauty –
As I led her to the window
I told her: 'You I loved best in life
...but you're a killer; Beauty kills!'
Not really meaning to drop her
I immediately ran downstairs
getting there just in time to catch her
'You saved me!' she cried
I put her down and told her: 'Move on.'

Went back up those six flights
went to the money
there was no money to throw out.
The only thing left in the room was Death
hiding beneath the kitchen sink:
'I'm not real!' It cried
'I'm just a rumor spread by life...'
Laughing I threw it out, kitchen sink and all
and suddenly realised Humor
was all that was left –

All I could do with Humor was to say:
'Out the window with the window!'

GREGORY CORSO

The Skip

I took my life and threw it on the skip,
Reckoning the next-door neighbours wouldn't mind
If my life hitched a lift to the council tip
With their dry rot and rubble. What you find

With skips is – the whole community joins in
Old mattresses appear, doors kind of drift
Along with all that won't fit in the bin
And what the bin-men can't be fished to shift

I threw away my life, and there it lay
And grew quite sodden. 'What a dreadful shame,'
Clucked some old bag and sucked her teeth. 'The way
The young these days...no values....me, I blame...'

But I blamed no one. Quality control
Had loused it up, and that was that. 'Nough said.
I couldn't stick at home. I took a stroll
And passed the skip, and left my life for dead.

Without my life, the beer was just as foul,
The landlord still as filthy as his wife,
The chicken in the basket was an owl,
And no one said: 'Ee, Jim-lad, whur's thee life?'

Well, I got back that night the worse for wear,
But still just capable of single vision;
Looked in the skip; my life – it wasn't there!
Some bugger'd nicked it – *without* my permission.

Okay, so I got angry and began
To shout, and woke the street. Okay, *Okay*!
And I was sick all down the neighbour's van
And I disgraced myself on the par-*kay*.

And then... you know how if you've had a few
You'll wake at dawn, all healthy, like sea breezes,
Raring to go, and thinking: 'Clever you!
You've got away with it.' And then, oh Jesus,

It hits you. Well, that morning, just at six
I woke, got up and looked down at the skip.
There lay my life, still sodden, on the bricks;
There lay my poor old life, arse over tip.

Or was it mine? Still dressed, I went downstairs
And took a long cool look. The truth was dawning.
Someone had just exchanged my life for theirs.
Poor fool, I thought – I should have left a warning.

Some bastard saw my life and thought it nicer
Than what he had. Yet what he'd had seemed fine.
He'd never caught his fingers in the slicer
The way I'd managed in that life of mine.

His life lay glistening in the rain, neglected,
Yet still a decent, an authentic life.
Some people I can think of, I reflected
Would take that thing as soon as you'd say Knife.

It seemed a shame to miss a chance like that.
I brought the life in, dried it by the stove.
It looked so fetching, stretched out on the mat
I tried it on. It fitted, like a glove.

And now, when some local bat drops off the twig
And new folk take the house, and pull up floors
And knock down walls and hire some kind of big
Container (say, a skip) for their old doors,

I'll watch it like a hawk, and every day
I'll make at least – oh – half a dozen trips.
I've furnished an existence in that way.
You'd not believe the things you'd find on skips.

JAMES FENTON

3

Life history

O Rose thou art sick.
The invisible worm,
That flies in the night
In the howling storm:

Has found out thy bed
Of crimson joy:
And his dark secret love
Does thy life destroy.

WILLIAM BLAKE

Let that be the poetry we search for: worn with the hand's obliga-
tions, as by acids, steeped in sweat and in smoke, smelling of lilies
and urine, spattered diversely by the trades that we live by, inside
the law or beyond it. A poetry impure as the clothing we wear, or our
bodies, soup-stained, soiled with our shameful behaviour, our wrinkles
and vigils and dreams, observations and prophecies, declarations
of loathing and love, idylls and beasts, the shocks of encounter,
political loyalties, denial and doubts, affirmations and taxes.

PABLO NERUDA

THIS SECTION follows the path of human life, from birth to old age, with poems
presenting both childhood and adult perspectives. The selection complements
those in *Staying Alive* (5: 'Growing up', SA 169-216) and *Being Alive* (3: 'Family',
BA 107-78)

Natasha Trethewey's 'Mythmaker' (120) connects bedtime stories told by
her father with the myths we tune into throughout our lives. One pervasive
narrative which many poets have drawn upon for its emotional power and
personal resonance is the story of Persephone, daughter of earth goddess
Demeter, who was abducted by Hades and carried off to the underworld.
Tricked into eating pomegranate seeds, she loses her innocence and has to go
back to Hades each autumn, returning to her mother in the spring, a mythical
interpretation of the cycles of life and seasonal change. Eavan Boland's 'The
Pomegranate' (121) is the first of a series of poems in this section relating to
innocence and experience.

A Lost Memory of Delhi

I am not born
it is 1948 and the bus turns
onto a road without name

There on his bicycle
my father
He is younger than I

At Okhla where I get off
I pass my parents
strolling by the Jamuna River

My mother is a recent bride
her sari a blaze of brocade
Silverdust parts her hair

She doesn't see me
The bells of her anklets are distant
like the sound of china from

teashops being lit up with lanterns
And the stars are coming out
ringing with tongues of glass

They go into the house
always faded in photographs
in the family album

but lit up now
with the oil lamp
I saw broken in the attic

I want to tell them I am their son
older much older than they are
I knock keep knocking

but for them the night is quiet
this the night of my being
They don't they won't

hear me they won't hear
my knocking drowning out
the tongues of stars

AGHA SHAHID ALI

I Go Back to May 1937

I see them standing at the formal gates of their colleges,
I see my father strolling out
under the ochre sandstone arch, the
red tiles glinting like bent
plates of blood behind his head, I
see my mother with a few light books at her hip
standing at the pillar made of tiny bricks,
the wrought-iron gate still open behind her, its
sword-tips aglow in the May air,
they are about to graduate, they are about to get married,
they are kids, they are dumb, all they know is they are
innocent, they would never hurt anybody.
I want to go up to them and say Stop,
don't do it – she's the wrong woman,
he's the wrong man, you are going to do things
you cannot imagine you would ever do,
you are going to do bad things to children,
you are going to suffer in ways you have not heard of,
you are going to want to die. I want to go
up to them there in the late May sunlight and say it,
her hungry pretty face turning to me,
her pitiful beautiful untouched body,
his arrogant handsome face turning to me,
his pitiful beautiful untouched body,
but I don't do it. I want to live. I
take them up like the male and female
paper dolls and bang them together
at the hips, like chips of flint, as if to
strike sparks from them, I say
Do what you are going to do, and I will tell about it.

SHARON OLDS

Woman Unborn

I am not born as yet,
five minutes before my birth.
I can still go back
into my unbirth.
Now it's ten minutes before,
now, it's one hour before birth.
I go back,
I run
into my minus life.

I walk through my unbirth as in a tunnel
with bizarre perspectives.
Ten years before,
a hundred and fifty years before,
I walk, my steps thump,
a fantastic journey through epochs
in which there was no me.

How long is my minus life,
nonexistence so much resembles immortality.

Here is Romanticism, where I could have been a spinster,
Here is the Renaissance, where I would have been
an ugly and unloved wife of an evil husband,
The Middle Ages, where I would have carried water in a tavern.

I walk still further,
what an echo,
my steps thump
through my minus life,
through the reverse of life.
I reach Adam and Eve,
nothing is seen anymore, it's dark.
Now my nonexistence dies already
with the trite death of mathematical fiction.
As trite as the death of my existence would have been
had I been really born.

ANNA SWIR
translated by Czesław Miłosz & Leonard Nathan

Upon Seeing an Ultrasound Photo
of an Unborn Child

Tadpole, it's not time yet to nag you
about college (though I have some thoughts
on that), baseball (ditto), or abstract
principles. Enjoy your delicious,
soupy womb-warmth, do some rolls and saults
(it'll be too crowded soon), delight in your early
dreams – which no one will attempt to analyse.
For now: may your toes blossom, your fingers
lengthen, your sexual organs grow (too soon
to tell which yet) sensitive, your teeth
form their buds in their forming jawbone, your already
booming heart expand (literally
now, metaphorically later); O your spine,
eyebrows, nape, knees, fibulae,
lungs, lips... But your soul,
dear child: I don't see it here, when
does that come in, whence? Perhaps God,
and your mother, and even I – we'll all contribute
and you'll learn yourself to coax it
from wherever: your soul, which holds your bones
together and lets you live
on earth. – Fingerling, sidecar, nubbin,
I'm waiting, it's me, Dad,
I'm out here. You already know
where Mom is. I'll see you more directly
upon arrival. You'll recognise
me – I'll be the tall-seeming, delighted
blond guy, and I'll have
your nose.

THOMAS LUX

Infant

In your frowning, fugitive days, small love,
your coracled, ecstatic night,
possessed or at peace, hands clenched
on an unseen rope, or raised in blessing
like the Pope, as your white etched feet
tread sooty rooves of canal tunnels
or lie released, stretched North in sleep –

you seem to me an early saint, a Celt,
eyes fixed on a celestial light, patiently
setting the sextant straight
to follow your godsent map, now
braced against a baffling gale, now
becalmed, fingers barely sculling
through warm muddy tides.

Soon, you will make your way out
of this estuary country, leave
the low farms and fog banks, tack through
the brackish channels and long
reed-clogged rivulets, reach
the last turn, the salt air and river mouth,
the wide grey sea beyond it.

KATE CLANCHY

Crowning

Now that knowing means nothing,
now that you are more born
than being, more awake
than awaited, since I've seen
your hair deep inside mother,

a glimpse, grass in late
winter, early spring, watching
your mother's pursed, throbbing,
purpled power, her pushing
you for one whole hour, two,
almost three, almost out,
maybe never, animal smell
and peat, breath and sweat
and mulch-matter, and at once
you descend, or drive, are driven
by mother's body, by her will
and brilliance, by bowel,
by wanting and your hair
peering as if it could see, and I saw
you storming forth,
taproot, your cap of hair half
in, half out, and wait, hold
it there, the doctors say, and
she squeezing my hand, her face
full of fire, then groaning your face
out like a flower, blood-bloom,
crocussed into air, shoulders
and the long cord still rooting
you to each other, to the other
world, into this afterlife
among us living, the cord
I cut like an iris, pulsing,
then you wet against mother's chest
still purple, not blue, not yet
red, no cry,
warming now, now opening
your eyes midnight
blue in the blue-black dawn.

KEVIN YOUNG

Naming You

We have not snared you
with the net of a name
we have not tamed you

you are energy the one
word that is every word
the sound of the gong

come into the garden
we will sing you
white stars green leaves

such spring-fever
the birds hop and cheep
around your sleepy head

the surge and shining
the rocking of tall trees
in the eager wind

who are you what are you
but the little sister
of this world around you

morning star and sparrow
bluebell smouldering
the attentive yew

*

but the dance of time
the argument of choice
fingers reach out

well the world can wait
we are disciples
and nothing is arbitrary

you are your own word
and cannot grow out of
a careless visitation

you declare yourself
smiling bubble-blower
your eyes gentian blue

lolling by the willow
your bald head askew
like a medieval saint

come home little sister
take your proper place
in this shining garden

dear daughter come home
come home we are here
and listening for your name

KEVIN CROSSLEY-HOLLAND

Patrick I

Patrick, I cannot write
such poems for you as a father might
coming upon your smile,

your mouth half sucking, half sleeping,
your tears shaken from your eyes like sparklers
break up the nightless weeks of your life:

lighthearted, I go to the kitchen
and cook breakfast, aching as you grow hungry.
Mornings are plain as the pages
of books in sedentary schooldays.

If I were eighty and lived next door
hanging my pale chemises on the porch
would I envy or pity my neighbour?

Polished and still as driftwood
she stands smoothing her dahlias;

liquid, leaking,
I cup the baby's head to my shoulder:

the child's a boy and will not share
one day these obstinate, exhausted mornings.

HELEN DUNMORE

The Weighing of the Heart

What does the heart weigh?
More than the pull of your small
hand on mine? More than your head's
light heaviness on my shoulder?

Under the tender pressure of sleep
my old wool jacket becomes
your memory of consolation, comfort,
that ancient sweetness of love and tweed.

Remembering this, watching you,
I lose my place entirely, not knowing
whose the head, whose the sleeve,
whose the big hand and whose the small.

The Ancients measured a good heart
against the slightest puff of down,
in the gleam and glitter of delicate scales.
Like Thoth, we watch and wait.

What does the heart weigh?
Less than your head's tiny burden,
for lighter than a feather is love
and this the Egyptians knew.

MAURA DOOLEY

All the things you are not yet

(for Tess)

Tonight there's a crowd in my head:
all the things you are not yet.
You are words without paper, pages
sighing in summer forests, gardens
where builders stub out their rubble
and plastic oozes its sweat.
All the things you are, you are not yet.

Not yet the lonely window in midwinter
with the whine of tea on an empty stomach,
not yet the heating you can't afford and must wait for,
tamping a coin in on each hour.
Not the gorgeous shush of restaurant doors
and their interiors, always so much smaller.
Not the smell of the newsprint, the blur
on your fingertips – your fame. Not yet

the love you will have for Winter Pearmains
and Chanel No.5 – and then your being unable
to buy both washing-machine and computer
when your baby's due to be born,
and my voice saying, 'I'll get you one'
and you frowning, frowning
at walls and surfaces which are not mine –
all this, not yet. Give me your hand,

that small one without a mark of work on it,
the one that's strange to the washing-up bowl
and doesn't know Fairy Liquid from whiskey.
Not yet the moment of your arrival in taxis
at daring destinations, or your being alone at stations
with the skirts of your fashionable clothes flapping
and no money for the telephone.

Not yet the moment when I can give you nothing
so well-folded it fits in an envelope –
a dull letter you won't reread.

Not yet the moment of your assimilation
in that river flowing westward: river of clothes,
of dreams, an accent unlike my own
saying to someone I don't know: *darling*...

HELEN DUNMORE

Lullaby

Time to rest now; you have had
enough excitement for the time being.

Twilight, then early evening. Fireflies
in the room, flickering here and there, here and there,
and summer's deep sweetness filling the open window.

Don't think of these things anymore.
Listen to my breathing, your own breathing
like the fireflies, each small breath
a flare in which the world appears.

I've sung to you long enough in the summer night.
I'll win you over in the end; the world can't give you
this sustained vision.

You must be taught to love me. Human beings must be
        taught to love
silence and darkness.

LOUISE GLÜCK

The Baby

He who has nothing to hide,
has nothing to show
MARGUERITE DE HAINAUT

My baby is playing in the bath, delighted. I begin
to wash his head and spend some time at this.
Then he begins. When I start to rinse his hair, I
can't find him. I turn around, and there he is
again. I don't understand what is happening, and
grow stern. I scold him. I don't like what he's
doing. The baby laughs, more and more amused,
glimmers for an instant, and vanishes again. My
impatience only makes things worse. He disap-
pears more and more quickly, doesn't even give
me time to protest. Through layers of uneasiness,
I glimpse his mischievous glance; my blindness is
his victory, my jealousy his passion. For a while, I
go on resisting: I don't know how to welcome
impotence. The baby just wants to play. The
game is dazzling and lasts a lifetime.

MARÍA NEGRONI
translated from the Spanish by Anne Twitty

A Little Tooth

Your baby grows a tooth, then two,
and four, and five, then she wants some meat
directly from the bone. It's all

over: she'll learn some words, she'll fall
in love with cretins, dolts, a sweet
talker on his way to jail. And you,

your wife, get old, flyblown, and rue
nothing. You did, you loved, your feet
are sore. It's dusk. Your daughter's tall.

THOMAS LUX

Spinning

I hold my two-year-old son
under his arms and start to twirl.
His feet sway away from me
and the day becomes a blur.
Everything I own is flying into space:
yard toys, sandbox, tools,
garage and house,
and, finally, the years of my life.

When we stop, my son is a grown man,
and I am very old. We stagger
back into each other's arms
one last time, two lost friends
heavy with drink,
remembering the good old days.

KEVIN GRIFFITH

Shoulders

A man crosses the street in rain,
stepping gently, looking two times north and south:
because his son is asleep on his shoulder.

No car must splash him.
No car drive too near to his shadow.

This man carries the world's most sensitive cargo
but he's not marked.
Nowhere does his jacket say FRAGILE,
HANDLE WITH CARE.

His ear fills up with breathing.
He hears the hum of a boy's dream
deep inside him.

We're not going to be able
to live in this world
if we're not willing to do what he's doing
with one another.

The road will only be wide.
The rain will never stop falling.

NAOMI SHIHAB NYE

Man and Derailment

When the man took his son down the ravine
to view, along the opposite bank,
the pileup of a passenger train,
backhoes and cranes, things the child had seen
only in miniature, now huge, hauling
life-size train cars out of the deep ravine,
inside his life-size head the quiet boy
wondered how he would remember the scene
and, once he knew his father better, later,
and later, knew himself better, what it would mean.

DAN CHIASSON

Generations

I go to see my parents,
we chew the rag a bit;
I turn the telly on
and sit and look at it.

Not much gets said:
there doesn't seem much point.
But still they like to have
me hanging round the joint.

I go to see my son,
I'm like a Santa Claus:
he couldn't like me more;
mad about him, of course.

Still years before he learns
to judge, condemn, dismiss.
I stand against the light
and bleed for both of us.

EVAN JONES

Mother to Son

Well, son, I'll tell you:
Life for me ain't been no crystal stair.
It's had tacks in it,
And splinters,
And boards torn up,
And places with no carpet on the floor —
Bare.
But all the time
I'se been a-climbin' on,
And reachin' landin's,
And turnin' corners,
And sometimes goin' in the dark
Where there ain't been no light.
So, boy, don't you turn back.
Don't you set down on the steps.
'Cause you finds it's kinder hard.
Don't you fall now —
For I'se still goin', honey,
I'se still climbin',
And life for me ain't been no crystal stair.

LANGSTON HUGHES

Mother to Son

He was whole evenings
sometimes & pet names,
he was whole breaths
changing into steam –
we'd never leave
the front seat. I'd straddle him
& the odor was black & new
& someone pushing inside.
The radio dial
was a strip of green light
& his fingers turned
my nipples until the music
eased out of me.
He was a palm full
of tiny deaths, desire
spilling cell by cell
& desire swimming up stream.
He was whole years, Son,
& even at this moment,
he walks through your face...
He'd drive me home
& at dawn I'd stand
behind my mother's house
hosing between my thighs.
It was on one of those nights
that you were conceived,
& with me then,
as I fanned my dress
until the water dried.

TERRANCE HAYES

I Am Becoming My Mother

Yellow/brown woman
fingers smelling always of onions

My mother raises rare blooms
and waters them with tea
her birth waters sang like rivers
my mother is now me

My mother had a linen dress
the colour of the sky
and stored lace and damask
tablecloths
to pull shame out of her eye.

I am becoming my mother
brown/yellow woman
fingers smelling always of onions.

LORNA GOODISON

Self-portrait

I resemble everyone
but myself, and sometimes see
in shop-windows,
    despite the well-known laws
    of optics,
the portrait of a stranger,
date unknown,
often signed in a corner
by my father.

A.K. RAMANUJAN

Autobiography

Who is mother
Of more than one
Is not the same
As the mother
Of an only son
Who never became
Anyone's father –
Still only a son
As an old man –
What I have not done
Made me who I am.

SAMUEL MENASHE

The Mothers

are breathing into my left ear.
Their hands brush my shoulder.
I can smell their hardened palms
they are onion, soap and polish.
Their strong fingers, washing the heads of husbands
holding the spines of husbands desperate from war
smoothing the blood slick from the brow of the first born
I can feel their exhausted fingers.
Their smoky hair spikes the hairs along my arm.
Hair which was leaden with stove grease and nicotine,
which came out on brushes in thickets after the last born
their hair spikes me, ratchety as a cough.
My mothers hug me in the hail of wombs.
Red lips of black mothers releasing golden heads
black bushed desert mothers crowning blue scalps of the cold
        countries
head through pelvis, through pelvis, to the mothers with soft fur
        on their breasts
and the mothers who rocked us on four firm limbs, who eased us
        out, humming

in their wordless tongue
back to the mama watching plate-eyed
hooking her tail over my ear like a question
her muzzle streaked with marks we remember
in ochre, berry-stain and kohl.
In her womb, the cell-mother, dreaming of mud.
A pearl passed from daughter to daughter
riding in the one who rides my shoulder.
I feel her long loving tongue on my cheek,
smell her musk between my legs.

REBECCA EDWARDS

The Fathers

All over the city, women in restaurants,
cafés, bars, wait for their fathers.
The women sip coffee, or wine, pretend to read.
Some fathers arrive promptly, smiling –
dressed as policemen, or in flannel pyjamas.
Sometimes the father is a priest
in a cassock stained with candle wax.
One or two have pockets gritty with sand
from Cornish holidays. One father
flourishes a fledgling sparrow, damp
and frightened, from an ironed handkerchief.
One wears a taffeta dress, fishnets and stilettos,
rubs the stubble under his make-up.
They bring spaniels, Shetland ponies, anacondas,
they bring yellowed photographs
whose edges curl like wilting cabbages.
One father has blue ghosts of numbers
inked on his wrist. There are times the fathers
have been dead or absent for so long
the women hardly recognise them; some
talk rapidly in Polish or Greek and the women
shift on their chairs. A few sign cheques,
others blag a tenner. One smells of wood-shavings
and presents the woman with a dolls' house.

They might tell the women *You're getting fat*
or Put some meat on your bones, girl.
Some women leave arm in arm with their fathers,
huddled against the cold air, and window shop
for turquoise sequinned slippers or angelfish
hanging like jewels in bright tanks. Others
part with a kiss that misses a cheek – lint
left on coats, and buttons done up wrong.

CATHERINE SMITH

Grandchildren

It's not just feasible at the moment
one daughter tells me.
What with Seamus still robbing banks
and ramming garda vans when he gets emotional
on a fish-free Friday in February.

Maybe the other daughter could deliver.
She thinks not, not at the moment anyway
while Thomas still has a few tattoos to get,
to cover any remaining signs that might link him
with the rest of us.

Just now a B52 bomber flies over
on its way from Shannon
to make a gulf in some nation's genealogy.

The shadow it places on all our notions is crystal clear
and for a split of a second helping
it juxtaposes the pecking order.
Now bank robbers and tattooers
have as much or as little standing
as popes and princes
and grandchildren become another lonely utterance
impossible to pronounce.

RITA ANN HIGGINS

Delicious Babies

Because of spring there are babies everywhere,
sweet or sulky, irascible or full of the milk of human kindness.
Yum, yum! Delicious babies!
Babies with the soft skins of babies, cheeks
of such tit-bit pinkness, tickle-able babies, tasty babies,
mouth-watering babies.

The pads of their hands! The rounds
of their knees! Their good smells of bathtime
and new clothes and gobbled rusks!
Even their discarded nappies are worthy of them, reveal their powers.
Legions and hosts of babies! Babies bold as lions, sighing babies,
tricksy babies, omniscient babies, babies using a plain language

of reasonable demands and courteous acceptance.
Others have the habit of loud contradiction,
can empty a railway carriage (though their displeasing howls
cheer up childless women).
Look at this baby, sitting bolt upright in his buggy!
Consider his lofty unsmiling acknowledgement of our adulation,

look at the elfin golfer's hat flattering his fluffy hair!
Look next at this very smallest of babies
tightly wrapped in a foppery of blankets.
In his high promenading pram he sleeps sumptuously,
only a nose, his father's, a white bonnet and a wink
of eyelid showing.

All babies are manic-serene, all babies are mine,
all babies are edible, the boys taste best.
I feed on them, nectareous are my babies,
manna, confiture, my sweet groceries.

I smack my lips,
deep in my belly the egg ripens,
makes the windows shake,
another ovum-quake
moves earth, sky and me...

Bring me more babies! Let me have them for breakfast,
lunch and tea! Let me feast, let my honey-banquet babies
go on forever, fresh deliveries night and day!

PENELOPE SHUTTLE

She Leaves Me

She betrays me, she leaves me.
She pushes me out of herself, and leaves me.
She offers herself to feed on, and leaves me.
She rocks me and she leaves me.
Wipes my bottom, combs my hair,
caresses the soles of my feet, but leaves me.
My nose drinks in her fragrance, how she hugs me:
she says, 'I'll never leave you!' And she leaves me.
She tricks me: smiling, whispers 'Don't be scared!'
I *am* scared, and I'm cold, and yet she leaves me.
She lies down on the bed with me at evening,
but soon enough she slips away and leaves me.
She is so big, so warm, alive, a nest,
she kisses me, and hums to me, and leaves me.
She presses sweets into my open palms
and 'There you are, eat now,' she says, and leaves me.
I cry and howl and press her frame to mine;
I can hold her, hit her too; and yet she leaves me.
She shuts the door, does not look back at all,
I'm nothing when she leaves me.
I wait for her return, a cringing cur:
she then arrives and strokes me, and she leaves me.
I need her – it is death to live without her –
she picks me up to warm me, and she leaves me.
Her arms make up a cage, her lap's a house;
I'd love to go back in there, but she leaves me.
I come to one conclusion: I'm not her:
a stranger, she's a stranger, and she leaves me.

Out there's the world, where someone will be waiting!
For you, there will be someone there to leave.

117

Don't look back. Shut the door. You know
how easy it is to wait, how hard to go.
Some you'll grieve, others will deceive you,
some will wait, others fear your lack,
and some there'll always be who don't come back:
they give you life, but then they die and leave you.

ANNA T. SZABÓ
translated from the Hungarian by Clive Wilmer & George Gömöri

To a Daughter Leaving Home

When I taught you
at eight to ride
a bicycle, loping along
beside you
as you wobbled away
on two round wheels,
my own mouth rounding
in surprise when you pulled
ahead down the curved
path of the park,
I kept waiting
for the thud
of your crash as I
sprinted to catch up,
while you grew
smaller, more breakable
with distance,
pumping, pumping
for your life, screaming
with laughter,
the hair flapping
behind you like a
handkerchief waving
goodbye.

LINDA PASTAN

Small boy

He picked up a pebble
and threw it into the sea.

And another, and another.
He couldn't stop.

He wasn't trying to fill the sea.
He wasn't trying to empty the beach.

He was just throwing away,
nothing else but.

Like a kitten playing
he was practising for the future

when there'll be so many things
he'll want to throw away

if only his fingers will unclench
and let them go.

NORMAN MacCAIG

Monopoly

We sat like slum landlords around the board
buying each other out with fake banknotes,
until we lost more than we could afford,
or ever hope to pay back. Now our seats
are empty – one by one we left the game
to play for real, at first completely lost
in this other world, its building sites, its rain;
but slowly learned the rules and made our own,
stayed out of jail and kept our noses clean.

And now there's only me – sole freeholder
of every empty office space in town,
and from the quayside I can count the cost
each low tide brings – the skeletons and rust
of boats, cars, hats, boots, iron, a terrier.

PAUL FARLEY

Mythmaker

We lived by the words
of gods, mythologies

you'd mold our history to.
How many nights, you,

a young father, squint-eyed
from books and lamplight,

weaving lessons into bedtime –
the story of Icarus wanting

to soar, (like me on my swing set)
not heeding a father's words,

his fall likened to mine.
I'd carry his doom to sleep,

and that of Narcissus too,
his watered face floating

beautiful and tragic above
my head. My own face

a mirrored comfort
you'd pull me from. Late,

when my dreams turned
to nightmare, you were there –

Beowulf to slay Grendel
at my door. The blood on your hands

you'd anoint my head with.
You would have me bold, fearless –

these were things you needed
to teach me. Warning and wisdom.

You couldn't have known
how I'd take your words and shape

them in creation, reinvent you
a thousand times, making you

forever young and invincible.
Not like now. Not like now.

NATASHA TRETHEWEY

The Pomegranate

The only legend I have ever loved is
the story of a daughter lost in hell.
And found and rescued there.
Love and blackmail are the gist of it.
Ceres and Persephone the names.
And the best thing about the legend is
I can enter it anywhere. And have.
As a child in exile in
a city of fogs and strange consonants,
I read it first and at first I was
an exiled child in the crackling dusk of
the underworld, the stars blighted. Later
I walked out in a summer twilight
searching for my daughter at bed-time.

When she came running I was ready
to make any bargain to keep her.
I carried her back past whitebeams
and wasps and honey-scented buddleias.
But I was Ceres then and I knew
winter was in store for every leaf
on every tree on that road.
Was inescapable for each one we passed.
And for me.
                    It is winter
and the stars are hidden.
I climb the stairs and stand where I can see
my child asleep beside her teen magazines,
her can of Coke, her plate of uncut fruit.
The pomegranate! How did I forget it?
She could have come home and been safe
and ended the story and all
our heart-broken searching but she reached
out a hand and plucked a pomegranate.
She put out her hand and pulled down
the French sound for apple and
the noise of stone and the proof
that even in the place of death,
at the heart of legend, in the midst
of rocks full of unshed tears
ready to be diamonds by the time
the story was told, a child can be
hungry. I could warn her. There is still a chance.
The rain is cold. The road is flint-coloured.
The suburb has cars and cable television.
The veiled stars are above ground.
It is another world. But what else
can a mother give her daughter but such
beautiful rifts in time?
If I defer the grief I will diminish the gift.
The legend will be hers as well as mine.
She will enter it. As I have.
She will wake up. She will hold
the papery flushed skin in her hand.
And to her lips. I will say nothing.

EAVAN BOLAND

How to Cut a Pomegranate

'Never,' said my father,
'Never cut a pomegranate
through the heart. It will weep blood.
Treat it delicately, with respect.

Just slit the upper skin across four quarters.
This is a magic fruit,
so when you split it open, be prepared
for the jewels of the world to tumble out,
more precious than garnets,
more lustrous than rubies,
lit as if from inside.
Each jewel contains a living seed.
Separate one crystal.
Hold it up to catch the light.
Inside is a whole universe.
No common jewel can give you this.'

Afterwards, I tried to make necklaces
of pomegranate seeds.
The juice spurted out, bright crimson,
and stained my fingers, then my mouth.

I didn't mind. The juice tasted of gardens
I had never seen, voluptuous
with myrtle, lemon, jasmine,
and alive with parrots' wings.

The pomegranate reminded me
that somewhere I had another home.

IMTIAZ DHARKER

Persephone

Wanting someone who looked natural,
they cast you as Persephone, not thinking
how at regular intervals you were taken

to visit your own mother
under a flaking sky of cream paint
down the echoing corridor
to the long-stay ward, where trees
froze in the black glass
of winter – how you were no stranger
to the clockwork rhythms of figures
moaning and swaying, the mechanical
hands that moved across faces
or scattered things in odd corners,
the hungry hands that flapped after
with their wings of ragged knitting.
Each time you would leave her and return
to birdsong, the urgent green
through frost, the melting grass, the world
you would give her if she would only
recognise you through the heavy doors
your father closed between you. Each week
you rehearsed your flower-steps
with a basket of paper petals
as your teachers smiled down on you, exclaiming
at your sweet face,
at the way you seemed never to see him coming –
as if each last dance were the first dance,
and every mother won over by so little.

SUSAN WICKS

Moonlight: Chickens on the Road

Called out of dream by the pitch and screech,
I awoke to see my mother's hair
set free of its pincurls, springing out
into the still and hurtling air
above the front seat and just as suddenly gone.
The space around us twisted,
and in the instant before the crash
I heard the bubbling of the chickens,
the homely racket they make at all speeds,
signifying calm, resignation, oblivion.

And I listened. All through the slash
and clatter, the rake of steel, shatter of glass,
I listened, and what came
was a blizzard moan in the wind, a wail
of wreckage, severed hoses and lives,
a storm of loose feathers, and in the final
whirl approximating calm, the cluck
and fracas of the birds. I crawled
on hands and knees where a window should
have been and rose uneven

in November dusk. Wind blew
a snow of down, and rows of it quivered along
the shoulder. One thin stream of blood
oozed, flocked in feathers.
This was in the Ozarks, on a road curving miles
around Missouri, and as far as I could
see, no light flickered through the timber,
no mail box leaned the flag
of itself toward pavement, no cars
seemed ever likely to come along.

So I walked, circled the darkening disaster
my life had come to, and cried.
I cried for my family there,
knotted in the snarl of metal and glass;
for the farmer, looking dead, half in
and half out of his windshield; and for myself,
ambling barefoot through the jeweled debris,
glass slitting little blood-stars in my soles,
my arm hung loose at the elbow
and whispering its prophecies of pain.

Around and around the tilted car
and the steaming truck, around the heap
of exploded crates, the smears and small hunks
of chicken and straw. Through
an hour of loneliness and fear
I walked, in the almost black of Ozark night,
the moon just now burning into Missouri. Behind me,
the chickens followed my lead,
some fully upright, pecking

125

the dim pavement for suet or seed,
some half-hobbled by their wounds, worthless wings
fluttering in the effort. The faintest
light turned their feathers phosphorescent,
and as I watched they came on, as though they believed
me some savior, some highwayman
or commando come to save them the last night
of their clucking lives. This, they must have
believed, was the end they'd always heard of,
this the rendering more efficient than the axe,

the execution more anonymous than
a wringing arm. I walked on, no longer crying,
and soon the amiable and distracted chattering came
again, a sound like chuckling, or the backward suck
of hard laughter. And we walked
to the cadence their clucking called,
a small boy towing a cloud around a scene
of death, coming round and round
like a dream, or a mountain road,
like a pincurl, like pulse, like life.

ROBERT WRIGLEY

'My father thought it bloody queer'

My father thought it bloody queer,
the day I rolled home with a ring of silver in my ear
half hidden by a mop of hair. 'You've lost your head.
If that's how easily you're led
you should've had it through your nose instead.'

And even then I hadn't had the nerve to numb
the lobe with ice, then drive a needle through the skin,
then wear a safety-pin. It took a jeweller's gun
to pierce the flesh, and then a friend
to thread the sleeper in, and where it slept
the hole became a sore, became a wound, and wept.

At twenty-nine, it comes as no surprise to hear
my own voice breaking like a tear, released like water,
cried from way back in the spiral of the ear. *If I were you,*
I'd take it out and leave it out next year.

SIMON ARMITAGE

The Drive

My father could not look at me
as we sat in the back of a white sedan
on our way to the police station.
But I looked at him. He was staring
straight ahead through all the years
his son had disappointed him.

News had come through of the boy
who'd fire-bombed the car outside
the Methodist Church. When the detectives
arrived, I was having a family
portrait taken. I saw the suits and ties
in the window, then the doorbell rang.

I smiled into the flash, ran to the bathroom
and vomited my head off. I wanted to make
the Australian team as a fast bowler.
I wanted Frances Clarke to love me.
But instead I'd struck a match and immolated
the minister's new Valiant, my breath

punched out of my lungs by the boom.
I ran behind the Sunday-school buildings
and confessed to the lawn-raking currawongs.
I watched black smoke like useless prayer
gutter into the Sydney sky.
The sirens were a long time coming.

As we pulled into the station carpark,
dead leaves and the two-way static
sounded like years of thrashings: blue
welts across the backs of my legs like
indelible neon, and my mother's weeping
for the times I'd nailed her with insults

to the wall. But now, after breakdowns,
divorce and a distance of eighteen years,
we can talk about the sound a belt makes
as it flies in the bathroom; about
the violent spirit of a teenage son.
My mother kisses my eyes to stop

the sadness we've known from breaking
through. My father tells me about his life
instead of brief reports from the office.
I love them, these parents and strangers,
these friends who appear from time to time,
sharing their names, their blood.

ANTHONY LAWRENCE

Ausculta

(FROM *Dead Mother Poems*)

The drawers in my father's house are empty;
you thought his heart was
but it never was.
You couldn't hear him
and maybe he had a different language
those days.
No one taught him the right words then
or that it was important to use them.
But to you it was, I see that, and
maybe he didn't listen.

Maybe you couldn't hear my brother.
He was small and blond and funny.
He danced for you.

He had a horse on a long green stick,
its name was Trigger.
Do you remember him?
You must remember him.
We loved him so very much.
He made you laugh.
You forgave him everything.

I used to look after him at school.
I was in trouble for that,
hanging around the toilets
to make sure he was ok among the big boys.
The school said you had to stop me,
let him grow up, be independent.
He never forgave me
when I left home at twenty;
nor you, when you did later,
at sixty-four.

He stopped being close to you when he was eleven:
'saw what happened to you,' he says, 'took a step back'.
He wasn't there much at the end.
Maybe he thought you wouldn't notice.
Maybe he was used to that.
He only had to do one thing anyway,
and he was an angel.
One visit made it all ok;
one phone call, one gesture of attention.
One thing from him; never enough from me.

ROBYN ROWLAND

Ausculta: Listen (Latin).

Say You Love Me

What happened earlier I'm not sure of.
Of course he was drunk, but often he was.
His face looked like a ham on a hook above

me – I was pinned to the chair because
he'd hunkered over me with arms like jaws
pried open by the chair arms. 'Do you love

me?' he began to sob. 'Say you love me!'
I held out. I was probably fifteen.
What had happened? Had my mother – had she

said or done something? Or had he just been
drinking too long after work? 'He'll get *mean*,'
my sister hissed, 'just *tell* him.' I brought my knee

up to kick him, but was too scared. Nothing
could have got the words out of me then. Rage
shut me up, yet 'DO YOU?' was beginning

to peel, as of live layers of skin, age
from age from age from him until he gazed
through hysteria as a wet baby thing

repeating, 'Do you love me? Say you do,'
in baby chokes, only loud, for they came
from a man. There wouldn't be a rescue

from my mother, still at work. The same
choking sobs said, 'Love me, love me,' and my game
was breaking down because I couldn't do

anything, not escape into my own
refusal, *I won't, I won't*, not fantasise
a kind, rich father, not fill the narrowed zone,

empty except for confusion until the size
of my fear ballooned as I saw his eyes,
blurred, taurean – my sister screamed – unknown,

unknown to me, a voice rose and levelled
off, 'I love you,' I said. 'Say "*I love you,
Dad!*"' 'I love you, Dad,' I whispered, levelled

by defeat into a cardboard image, untrue,
unbending. I was surprised I could move
as I did to get up, but he stayed, burled

onto the chair – my monstrous fear – she screamed,
my sister, 'Dad, the phone! Go answer it!'
The phone wasn't ringing, yet he seemed

to move toward it, and I ran. He had a fit –
'It's not ringing!' – but I was at the edge of it
as he collapsed into the chair and blamed

both of us at a distance. No, the phone
was not ringing. There was no world out there,
so there we remained, completely alone.

MOLLY PEACOCK

Self Portrait with Fire Ants

To visit you Father, I wear a mask of fire ants.
When I sit waiting for you to explain

why you abandoned me when I was eight
they file in, their red bodies

massing around my eyes, stinging my pupils white
until I'm blind. Then they attack my mouth.

I try to lick them but they climb down my gullet
until an entire swarm stings my stomach,

while you must become a giant anteater,
push your long sticky tongue down my throat,

as you once did to my baby brother,
French-kissing him while he pretended to sleep.

I can't remember what you did to me, but the ants know.

PASCALE PETIT

131

We Remember Your Childhood Well

Nobody hurt you. Nobody turned off the light and argued
with somebody else all night. The bad man on the moors
was only a movie you saw. Nobody locked the door.

Your questions were answered fully. No. That didn't occur.
You couldn't sing anyway, cared less. The moment's a blur, a *Film Fun*
laughing itself to death in the coal fire. Anyone's guess.

Nobody forced you. You wanted to go that day. Begged. You chose
the dress. Here are the pictures, look at you. Look at us all,
smiling and waving, younger. The whole thing is inside your head.

What you recall are impressions; we have the facts. We called the tune.
The secret police of your childhood were older and wiser than you, bigg
than you. Call back the sound of their voices. Boom. Boom. Boom.

Nobody sent you away. That was an extra holiday, with people
you seemed to like. They were firm, there was nothing to fear.
There was none but yourself to blame if it ended in tears.

What does it matter now? No, no, nobody left the skidmarks of sin
on your soul and laid you wide open for Hell. You were loved.
Always. We did what was best. We remember your childhood well.

CAROL ANN DUFFY

Crossing the Frontier

Crossing the frontier they were stopped in time,
Told, quite politely, they would have to wait:
Passports in order, nothing to declare,
And surely holding hands was not a crime;
Until they saw how, ranged across the gate,
All their most formidable friends were there.

Wearing his conscience like a crucifix,
Her father, rampant, nursed the Family Shame;
And, armed with their old-fashioned dinner-gong,
His aunt, who even when they both were six,
Had just to glance towards a childish game
To make them feel that they were doing wrong.

And both their mothers, simply weeping floods,
Her headmistress, his boss, the parish priest,
And the bank manager who cashed their cheques;
The man who sold him his first rubber-goods;
Dog Fido, from whose love-life, shameless beast,
She first observed the basic facts of sex.

They looked as though they had stood there for hours;
For years – perhaps for ever. In the trees
Two furtive birds stopped courting and flew off;
While in the grass beside the road the flowers
Kept up their guilty traffic with the bees.
Nobody stirred. Nobody risked a cough.

Nobody spoke. The minutes ticked away;
The dog scratched idly. Then, as parson bent
And whispered to a guard who hurried in,
The customs-house loudspeakers with a bray
Of raucous and triumphant argument
Broke out the wedding march from *Lohengrin*.

He switched the engine off: 'We must turn back.'
She heard his voice break, though he had to shout
Against a din that made their senses reel,
And felt his hand, so tense in hers, go slack.
But suddenly she laughed and said: 'Get out!
Change seats! Be quick!' and slid behind the wheel.

And drove the car straight at them with a harsh,
Dry crunch that showered both with scraps and chips,
Drove through them; barriers rising let them pass
Drove through and on and on, with Dad's moustache
Beside her twitching still round waxen lips
And Mother's tears still streaming down the glass.

A.D. HOPE

The Makings of You

Almost impossible to do; describing the makings of you
CURTIS MAYFIELD

You will tell no one
of the Christmas day when you sat
alone in your miniscule studio,
raised a forkful of sautéed potato
to your lips, and closed your eyes;

how savouring that mouthful of electric heat
and some farmer's zealous labour, followed
by two hours of reading Neruda and Li-Young
Lee, was your only way of remembering
that life's sack carries pleasure as well as pain.

At that dinner next week you will tell
nothing of how vacuous you felt, nor
will you mention the time when tortured
by your girlfriend's inability to trust you
you drank cheap whiskey and clawed your walls

while singing along to Curtis Mayfield's
the makings of you, as though the song's lush
beauty would save you from depression.
No, you will tell jokes and smile and make
predictably witty and charming comments;

you will tell no one of the day when,
as an ashy-kneed eleven-year-old boy
in boarding school, you surreptitiously
sat on the concrete steps of your classroom
block to pick up a groundnut you had spotted

earlier, cleaned it against your brown shorts
and slipped it in your mouth where you let it sit
for an instant, before you chewed it for six slow
minutes, so you could fool your own stomach
into thinking that life was better than it was.

All these things that make you the man
that you are, you tuck beneath your dark

skin and never share: so nobody really knows
you, although most people say they like you
because of your enigmatic smile.

NII AYIKWEI PARKES

Crossing the Loch

Remember how we rowed toward the cottage
on the sickle-shaped bay,
that one night after the pub
loosed us through its swinging doors
and we pushed across the shingle
till water lipped the sides
as though the loch mouthed 'boat'?

I forgot who rowed. Our jokes hushed.
The oars' splash, creak, and the spill
of the loch reached long into the night.
Out in the race I was scared:
the cold shawl of breeze,
and hunched hills; what the water held
of deadheads, ticking nuclear hulls.

Who rowed, and who kept their peace?
Who hauled salt-air and stars
deep into their lungs, were not reassured;
and who first noticed the loch's
phosphorescence, so, like a twittering nest
washed from the rushes, an astonished
small boat of saints, we watched water shine
on our fingers and oars,
the magic dart of our bow wave?

It was surely foolhardy, such a broad loch, a tide,
but we live – and even have children
to women and men we had yet to meet
that night we set out, calling our own
the sky and salt-water, wounded hills
dark-starred by blaeberries, the glimmering anklets

we wore in the shallows
as we shipped oars and jumped,
to draw the boat safe, high at the cottage shore.

KATHLEEN JAMIE

At Thirty

Whole years I knew only nights: automats
& damp streets, the Lower East Side steep

with narrow rooms where sleepers turn beneath
alien skies. I ran when doorways spoke

rife with smoke & zippers. But it was only the heart's
racketing flywheel stuttering *I want, I want*

until exhaustion, until I was a guest in the yoke
of my body by the last margin of land where the river

mingles with the sea & far off daylight whitens,
a rending & yielding I must kneel before, as

barges loose glittering mineral freight
& behind me façades gleam with pigeons

folding iridescent wings. Their voices echo
in my voice naming what is lost, what remains.

LYNDA HULL

Life History

I got this nose-shaped bruise on my left arm from falling into a
     rack of dolls at Wal-Mart.
This scar on my ring finger came from when I put my hand into
     a beehive when I was two,
a calamity about which I wept into Daddy's lissome clavicle for
     three and a half months.

At for the stretchmarks, don't ask about the stretchmarks. There are men
      who like them,
but men are liars making lairs, body-shaped soul-boats of stretchmark-
      making liquids
and big ideas about the beauty of women. I've been around. I know what
      makes a woman

beautiful. This scar under my eye is from when I played mouse with my cat
      Sebastian.
I am not sure how cats could leave a mark, but with me they do.
It's as though they wish to marry me or say *hello, hello* perpetually.

In photographs of me as a baby, I'm white space all over.
Now in this early fall of my thirty-seventh year there are freckles, moles,
and other assorted blotches. They say it's sun damage, maybe one day will
      be cancer.

Let us wait and see. When you get born, you are as blue as a bad painting
      of Saturn
in the middle of the night. When you're that blue, they might think you
      didn't make it.
They might think you opted out at the last minute, climbing a cable of light

to some spirit world fiesta. But really you're just getting the slow hang of
      gasping.
You're signing up for the Orientation, taking notes via the sluggish
      apparatus of your lungs
while they cut off the cord and take ten names for test drives.

Then you start to breathe. Then you turn pink. The more you wait, the
      pinker you get.
It's not the pink of salmon, and it's not the pink of tongue.
It's not the pink of the sunset of the pink of Matisse's 'Portrait of Madame
      Matisse'

for I-don't-know-how-much money. This pink is the pink of the long
      inhale.
I know because I saw a dead woman who was chiefly dissected,
and she was the color of sand. I looked at her and felt nothing.

I wondered if she was Eskimo. I cut my toe here walking up the stairs.
I knocked my head against the medicine chest and thereby got indented.
My heart sometimes jumps and skips a beat. I don't know how I harmed it,

but I'm sure it was some blunder or another – one of the times
I took a pill, drank tequila, or gave birth against my will. Maybe
    it was when I told Daddy
my crying days were over and took up gulping stones.

But let's assume for the purposes of being accurate
that it was that long ago morning I first attempted speech,
burrowing out of myself like a silky spider, climbing the cliff of
    unremitting self-infliction,

saying you – and you, and you, and you, and you – will one day
    pay for this.

ADRIAN BLEVINS

'the thirty-eighth year...'

the thirty-eighth year
of my life,
plain as bread
round as a cake
an ordinary woman.

an ordinary woman.

i had expected to be
smaller than this,
more beautiful,
wiser in afrikan ways,
more confident,
i had expected
more than this.

i will be forty soon.
my mother once was forty.

my mother died at forty-four,
a woman of sad countenance
leaving behind a girl
awkward as a stork.

138

my mother was thick,
her hair was a jungle and
she was very wise
and beautiful
and sad.

i have dreamed dreams
for you mama
more than once.
i have wrapped me
in your skin
and made you live again

more than once.
i have taken the bones you hardened
and built daughters
and they blossom and promise fruit
like afrikan trees.
i am a woman now.
an ordinary woman.

in the thirty-eighth
year of my life,
surrounded by life,
a perfect picture of
blackness blessed,
i had not expected this
loneliness.

if it is western,
if it is the final
europe in my mind,
if in the middle of my life
i am turning the final turn
into the shining dark
let me come to it whole
and holy
not afraid
not lonely
out of my mother's life
into my own.
into my own.

i had expected more than this.
i had not expected to be
an ordinary woman.

LUCILLE CLIFTON

The Wife Speaks

Being a woman, I am
not more than man nor less
but answer imperatives
of shape and growth. The bone
attests the girl with dolls,
grown up to know the moon
unwind her tides to chafe
the heart. A house designs
my day an artifact
of care to set the hands
of clocks, and hours are round
with asking eyes. Night puts
an ear on silence where
a child may cry. I close
my books and know events
are people, all roads
everywhere walk home
women and men, to take
history under their roofs.
I see Icarus fall
out of the sky, beside
my door, not beautiful,
envy of angels, but feathered
for a bloody death.

MARY STANLEY

Men at Forty

Men at forty
Learn to close softly
The doors to rooms they will not be
Coming back to.

At rest on a stair landing,
They feel it moving
Beneath them now like the deck of a ship,
Though the swell is gentle.

And deep in mirrors
They rediscover
The face of the boy as he practices tying
His father's tie there in secret,

And the face of that father,
Still warm with the mystery of lather.
They are more fathers than sons themselves now.
Something is filling them, something

That is like the twilight sound
Of the crickets, immense,
Filling the woods at the foot of the slope
Behind their mortgaged houses.

DONALD JUSTICE

Mothers and Daughters

The cruel girls we loved
Are over forty,
Their subtle daughters
Have stolen their beauty;

And with a blue stare
Of cool surprise,
They mock their anxious mothers
With their mothers' eyes.

DAVID CAMPBELL

Middle Age

Middle age at last declares itself
As the time when could-have-been
Is not wishful thinking any more,
Is not, say: I could have been at Oxford
If my parents had been richer
Or if the careers mistress had not thought
Exeter was good enough for me.

It is not misunderstanding either
As when at night in the first year of the war
Bombs could have been thunder
And later on in peace
Thunder could have been bombs.
Sights and sounds are more themselves now.

There have been real alternatives.
They have put on weight and yet faded.

Evening walks go past
Where we could have lived:
The coach-house that the mortgage company
Said had too much charm
And not enough rooms.

Everywhere I look it is the same,
The churchyard or the other side of the bed.
The one who is not lying there
Could have been.

PATRICIA BEER

Nel Mezzo del Cammin

No more overcoats; maybe another suit,
A comb or two, and that's my lot.
So the odd poem (two in a good year)
Won't do to make the kind of edifice
I'd hoped to leave. Flush out the fantasy:
The mid-point being passed, the pattern's clear.
This road I had taken for a good byway
Is the main thoroughfare; and even that
Now seems too costly to maintain.
Too many holes to fill; not enough time
To start again. 'I wasn't ready. The sun
Was in my eyes. I thought we weren't counting.'

Soon we'll be counting razorblades and pencils.

BERNARD O'DONOGHUE

Approaching Fifty

Sometimes,
In unwiped bathroom mirrors,
He sees all three faces
Looking at him:

His own,
The grey-haired man's
Whose life policy has matured,
And the mocking youth's
Who paid the first premium.

ARVIND KRISHNA MEHROTRA

The World

I couldn't tell one song from another,
    which bird said what or to whom or for what reason.

The oak tree seemed to be writing something using very few words.
    I couldn't decide which door to open – they looked the same, or what

would happen when I did reach out and turn a knob. I thought I was
    safe, standing there
but my death remembered its date:

only so many summer nights still stood before me, full moon, waning
    moon, October mornings: what to make of them? which door?

I couldn't tell which stars were which or how far away any one of them
    was, or which were still burning or not – their light moving through
    space like a long

late train – and I've lived on this earth so long – 50 winters, 50 springs
    and summers,
and all this time stars in the sky – in daylight

when I couldn't see them, and at night when, most nights I didn't look.

MARIE HOWE

The Woman at the Washington Zoo

The saris go by me from the embassies.

Cloth from the moon. Cloth from another planet.
They look back at the leopard like the leopard.

And I....
          this print of mine, that has kept its color
Alive through so many cleanings; this dull null
Navy I wear to work, and wear from work, and so
To my bed, so to my grave, with no
Complaints, no comment: neither from my chief,

144

The Deputy Chief Assistant, nor his chief –
Only I complain.... this serviceable
Body that no sunlight dyes, no hand suffuses
But, dome-shadowed, withering among columns,
Wavy beneath fountains – small, far-off, shining
In the eyes of animals, these beings trapped
As I am trapped but not, themselves, the trap,
Aging, but without knowledge of their age,
Kept safe here, knowing not of death, for death –
Oh, bars of my own body, open, open!

The world goes by my cage and never sees me.
And there come not to me, as come to these,
The wild beasts, sparrows pecking the llamas' grain,
Pigeons settling on the bears' bread, buzzards
Tearing the meat the flies have clouded....
                                    Vulture,
When you come for the white rat that the foxes left,
Take off the red helmet of your head, the black
Wings that have shadowed me, and step to me as man:
The wild brother at whose feet the white wolves fawn,
To whose hand of power the great lioness
Stalks, purring....
                    You know what I was,
You see what I am: change me, change me!

RANDALL JARRELL

Untitled

If I think *I* have problems
I look in the mirror;
I go to the window, or
ponder the future reduced
to more or less
three pounds of haunted meat.
And it's never
like I always said:
if you don't want something
wish for it...

Lost in the beautiful world
I can no longer perceive
but only, now and then,
imagine
or recall –
First the long sinister youth
and then the dying man
who talks to old friends
teachers, doctors
but they don't understand
the way we feel.

FRANZ WRIGHT

Shave

Observe yourself in the mirror,
unchanged yet strange,
still shaggy with sleep, startled
at seeing your likeness.
These wrinkles, these graying temples
that you've already accepted gracefully
– affable guests who showed up
so suddenly, that you can't quite recall
just when they initially appeared.
They represent the shameless price required
for this fictitious intimacy with the body.
And now, begin to shave.
The blade, once quick and cold, no longer
glides taut on your skin like the pleasant
lickety-split friction of youthful skis:
you're forced to stretch your flabby cheek
with your fingers. Don't despair.
Perhaps if you're shrewd and willfully avoid
the shameful mark of a knick,
you'll forget your alliance with your body
has already begun to dissolve.

FRANCESC PARCERISAS
translated from the Catalan by Cyrus Cassells

Fat Man

How terrible the confession, *We are all dying*.
The way fat weighs us and the heart swells
from too long labouring to make us breathe, slouch
and snore with guttural dreadfulness (the terror
of it). I do not want to die. So absurd
this admission, this effort to confront
the unpredictable odds of our living. But fat
people die quickly – we know this – and I,
too, too solid with the mess of casualness
grow fat with age. So hard to come back.
I stare at my stranger self in hotel mirrors.
I am afraid to meet this stomach-glorious
creature, unable these days to find an angle
of satisfying grace. I am now a circle of errors,
the fat has taken over. Perhaps pride in this
plump existentialism will make it well,
but my child seems too, too small, helplessly
small in my clumsy cumbersome arms.
They, my children, will call me fat,
and I will resent their kindnesses
and compensations for my limp and waddle.
I dream of sweat, the familiar
hint of muscles beneath the inner flesh,
the rib, a round reminder of the body
so vulnerable beneath this cloak of flesh.
I dream of breathing easily when I bend
in two to touch my shoelaces. I dream
of better days when I will leap lightly,
a slender man gambolling in the mirror's face.

KWAME DAWES

147

Self-portrait, Rear View

At first, I do not believe it, in the hotel
triple mirror, that that is my body, in
back, below the waist, and above
the legs – the thing that doesn't stop moving
when I stop moving.
And it doesn't look like just one thing,
or even one big, double thing
– even the word saddlebags has a
smooth, calfskin feel to it,
compared to this compendium
of net string bags shaking our booty of
cellulite, fruits and nuts. Some lumps
look like bonbons translated intact
from chocolate box to buttocks, the curl on top
showing, slightly, through my skin. Once I see what I can
do with this, I do it, high-stepping
to make the rapids of my bottom rush
in ripples like a world wonder. Slowly,
I believe what I am seeing, a 54-year-old
rear end, once a tight end,
high and mighty, almost a chicken butt, now
exhausted, as if tragic. But this is not
an invasion, my cul-de-sac is not being
used to hatch alien cells, ball peens,
gyroscopes, sacks of marbles. It's my hoard
of treasure, my good luck, not to be
dead, yet, though when I flutter
the wing of my ass again, and see,
in a clutch of eggs, each egg,
on its own, as if shell-less, shudder, I wonder
if anyone has ever died
looking in a mirror, of horror. I think I will
not even catch a cold from it.
I will go to school to it, to Butt
Boot Camp, to the video store, where I saw,
in the window, my hero, my workout jelly
role model, my apotheosis: *Killer Buns*.

SHARON OLDS

Getting Older

The first surprise: I like it.
Whatever happens now, some things
that used to terrify have not:

I didn't die young, for instance. Or lose
my only love. My three children
never had to run away from anyone.

Don't tell me this gratitude is complacent.
We all approach the edge of the same blackness
which for me is silent.

Knowing as much sharpens
my delight in January freesia,
hot coffee, winter sunlight. So we say

as we lie close on some gentle occasion:
every day won from such
darkness is a celebration.

ELAINE FEINSTEIN

An Old Woman

An old woman grabs
hold of your sleeve
and tags along.

She wants a fifty paise coin.
She says she will take you
to the horseshoe shrine.

You've seen it already.
She hobbles along anyway
and tightens her grip on your shirt.

She won't let you go.
You know how old women are.
They stick to you like a burr.

You turn around and face her
with an air of finality.
You want to end the farce.

When you hear her say,
'What else can an old woman do
on hills as wretched as these?'

You look right at the sky.
Clear through the bullet holes
she has for her eyes.

And as you look on
the cracks that begin around her eyes
spread beyond her skin.

And the hills crack.
And the temples crack.
And the sky falls

with a plateglass clatter
around the shatter proof crone
who stands alone.

And you are reduced
to so much small change
in her hand.

ARUN KOLATKAR

from After the Operation

I

From a heavenly asylum, shrivelled Mummy,
glare down like a gargoyle at your only son,
who now has white hair and can hardly walk.
I am he who was not I. It's hot in this season
and the acrid reek of my body disturbs me
in a city where the people die on pavements.
That I'm terminally ill hasn't been much help.
There is no reason left for anything to exist.
Goodbye now. Don't try and meddle with this.

Why does your bloated corpse cry out to me
that I took from the hospital, three days dead?
I'd have come before, if the doctors had said.
I couldn't kiss you goodbye, you stank so much.
Or bear to touch you. Anyway, bye-bye, Mumsie.

VII

This city shudders under so many bodies
as would sink most continents. The growth
in my throat's snailsized now, firmly curled,
and suddenly my father comes from death.
He touches my cheek as when I was a child.
'I tried to tell you that it was hell out here,
I tried to say this wasn't a human world.'

The children's eyes that I have often seen
aren't quite what's printed in the magazines.
They may have seen their parents executed
in front of them or, running down the roads,
been raped, whether they were girls or not.
In my time I have been in many countries.
In every one I watched the children's eyes.

V

The bellshaped breasts that I wrung in my hands,
and the eelsmooth bellies under mine, don't heave
nor cries any longer rise from the mouths I knew.
Either I left those bodies or they chose to leave
or our circumstances pushed us countries apart.
I don't know, now, whether they're dead or alive.
But I grieve for them. Though I cannot remember
our awkward dialogues, the cigarettes shared
amidst those rumpled sheets, these women were
all parts of the anagram that spelt my youth.

If they should still be alive, they are grannies now,
living as all the grannies in their worlds must live.
Flaccid breasts, slack bellies, their mouths not sad
but sewn up tight by embittered years, or pensive
with thoughts of unfaithful lovers they once had.

IX

I was good at school, though what I learnt I found
useless for all the rest of my life. But I learnt it
and I learnt to be lonely. Still, I liked my solitude.
Through it, in my own way, I learnt about the world.
At home my mother suffered from clinical insanity.
Her clear eyes became wild. I shrank from her touch.
After some months, strange nurses took her away.
My father did his best for me, but was not a woman.
I developed several masks, and have worn them since.
Sometimes I am not sure which one I have on, or even
what I am underneath. Neither do most others know,
apart from her I love. For thirteen years she has known
what I am, and made me know it. Whether I want to,
except when I am with her, is another matter.

DOM MORAES

152

Golden Mothers Driving West

The inevitable call came from the Alzheimer's nursing home.
Mummy had been sitting there in an armchair for two years
In a top-storey room with two other aged ladies,
Deborah O'Donoghue and Maureen Timoney.
The call was to say that between 3 and 5 A.M.
The three of them had gone missing from the room.
At first it was thought that all three had slipped
Out the window, ajar in the hot, humid night.
But, no, there were no torsos in the flowerbed.
It transpired that a car had also gone missing.
Was it thinkable they had commandeered a car?
At five in the afternoon the police called
To say that a Polish youth in a car wash in Kinnegad
Had washed and hot-waxed a car for three ladies,
All of whom were wearing golden dressing gowns –
Standard issue golden dressing gowns
Worn by all the inmates of the Alzheimer's nursing home.
Why he remembered them was that he was struck
By the fact that all three ladies were laughing
For the ten minutes it took him to wash the car.
'I am surprised,' he stated, 'by laughter.'
At 9 P.M. the car was sighted in Tarmonbarry
On the Roscommon side of the River Shannon,
Parked at the jetty of the Emerald Star marina.
At 9.30 P.M. a female German child was taken
To the police station at Longford by her stepfather.
The eleven-year-old had earlier told her stepfather
In the cabin of their hired six-berth river cruiser
That she had seen three ladies jump from the bridge.
Her stepfather had assumed his daughter imagined it
As she was, he told police, 'a day-dreamer born'.
The girl repeated her story to the police:
How three small, thin, aged ladies with white hair
Had, all at once, together, jumped from the bridge,
Their dressing gowns flying behind them in the breeze.
What colours were the dressing gowns? she was asked.
'They are wearing gold,' she replied.
Wreathed on the weir downstream from the bridge
Police sub-aqua divers retrieved the three bodies,

153

One of whom, of course, was my own emaciated mother,
Whose fingerprints were later found on the wheel of the car.
She had been driving west, west to Westport,
Westport on the west coast of Ireland
In the County of Mayo,
Where she had grown up with her mother and sisters
In the War of Independence and the Civil War,
Driving west to Streamstown three miles outside Westport,
Where on afternoons in September in 1920,
Ignoring the roadblocks and the assassinations,
They used walk down Sunnyside by the sea's edge,
The curlews and the oystercatchers,
The upturned black currachs drying out on the stones,
And picnic on the machair grass above the seaweed,
Under the chestnut trees turning autumn gold
And the fuchsia bleeding like troupes of crimson-tutu'd ballerinas
    in the black hedgerows.
Standing over my mother's carcass in the morgue,
A sheep's skull on a slab,
A girl in her birth-gown blown across the sand,
I shut my eyes:
Thank you, O golden mother,
For giving me a life,
A spear of rain.
After a long life searching for a little boy who lives down the lane
You never found him, but you never gave up;
In your afterlife nightie
You are pirouetting expectantly for the last time.

PAUL DURCAN

Rembrandt's Late Self-Portraits

You are confronted with yourself. Each year
The pouches fill, the skin is uglier.
You give it all unflinchingly. You stare
Into yourself, beyond. Your brush's care
Runs with self-knowledge. Here

Is a humility at one with craft.
There is no arrogance. Pride is apart
From this self-scrutiny. You make light drift
The way you want. Your face is bruised and hurt
But there is still love left.

Love of the art and others. To the last
Experiment went on. You stared beyond
Your age, the times. You also plucked the past
And tempered it. Self-portraits understand,
And old age can divest,

With truthful changes, us of fear of death.
Look, a new anguish. There, the bloated nose,
The sadness and the joy. To paint's to breathe,
And all the darknesses are dared. You chose
What each must reckon with.

ELIZABETH JENNINGS

Old Man Leaves Party

It was clear when I left the party
That though I was over eighty I still had
A beautiful body. The moon shone down as it will
On moments of deep introspection. The wind held its breath.
And look, somebody left a mirror leaning against a tree.
Making sure that I was alone, I took off my shirt.
The flowers of bear grass nodded their moonwashed heads.
I took off my pants and the magpies circled the redwoods.
Down in the valley the creaking river was flowing once more.
How strange that I should stand in the wilds alone with my body.
I know what you are thinking. I was like you once. But now
With so much before me, so many emerald trees, and
Weed-whitened fields, mountains and lakes, how could I not
Be only myself, this dream of flesh, from moment to moment?

MARK STRAND

Still Morning

It appears now that there is only one
age and it knows
nothing of age as the flying birds know
nothing of the air they are flying through
or of the day that bears them up
through themselves
and I am a child before there are words
arms are holding me up in a shadow
voices murmur in a shadow
as I watch one patch of sunlight moving
across the green carpet
in a building
gone long ago and all the voices
silent and each word they said in that time
silent now
while I go on seeing that patch of sunlight

W.S. MERWIN

Salt and Pepper

Here and there
White hairs appear
On my chest—
Age seasons me
Gives me zest—
I am a sage
In the making
Sprinkled, shaking

SAMUEL MENASHE

In Praise of Darkness

Old age (the name that others give it)
can be the time of our greatest bliss.
The animal has died or almost died.
The man and his spirit remain.
I live among vague, luminous shapes
that are not darkness yet.
Buenos Aires,
whose edges disintegrated
into the endless plain,
has gone back to being the Recoleta, the Retiro,
the nondescript streets of the Once,
and the rickety old houses
we still call the South.
In my life there were always too many things.
Democritus of Abdera plucked out his eyes in order to think;
Time has been my Democritus.
This penumbra is slow and does not pain me;
it flows down a gentle slope,
resembling eternity.
My friends have no faces,
women are what they were so many years ago,
these corners could be other corners,
there are no letters on the pages of books.
All this should frighten me,
but it is a sweetness, a return.
Of the generations of texts on earth
I will have read only a few —
the ones that I keep reading in my memory,
reading and transforming.
From South, East, West, and North
the paths converge that have led me
to my secret centre.
Those paths were echoes and footsteps,
women, men, death-throes, resurrections,
days and nights,
dreams and half-wakeful dreams,
every inmost moment of yesterday
and all the yesterdays of the world,
the Dane's staunch sword and the Persian's moon,

the acts of the dead,
shared love, and words,
Emerson and snow, so many things.
Now I can forget them. I reach my centre
my algebra and my key,
my mirror.
Soon I will know who I am.

JORGE LUIS BORGES
translated from the Spanish by Hoyt Rogers

Ignorance

The older I grow, the more ignorant I become,
the longer I live, the less I possess or control.
All I have is a little space, snow-dark
or glittering, never inhabited.
Where is the giver, the guide, the guardian?
I sit in my room and am silent; silence
arrives like a servant to tidy things up
while I wait for the lies to disperse.
And what remains to this dying man
that so well prevents him from dying?
What does he find to say to the four walls?
I hear him talking still, and his words
come in with the dawn, imperfectly understood:

'Love, like fire can only reveal its brightness
on the failure and the beauty of burnt wood.'

DEREK MAHON
version after the French of Philippe Jaccottet

A Quiet Joy

I'm standing in a place where I once loved.
The rain is falling. The rain is my home.

I think words of longing: a landscape
out to the very edge of what's possible.

I remember you waving your hand
as if wiping mist from the windowpane,

and your face, as if enlarged
from an old blurred photo.

Once I committed a terrible wrong
to myself and others.

But the world is beautifully made for doing good
and for resting, like a park bench.

And late in life I discovered
a quiet joy
like a serious disease that's discovered too late:

just a little time left now for quiet joy.

YEHUDA AMICHAI
translated from the Hebrew by Chana Bloch

Voyage

Water opens without end
At the bow of the ship
Rising to descend
Away from it
Days become one
I am who I was

SAMUEL MENASHE

The Niche

The niche narrows
Hones one thin
Until his bones
Disclose him

SAMUEL MENASHE

And Suddenly It's Evening

Each of us is alone on the heart of the earth
pierced by a ray of sun:
and suddenly it's evening.

SALVATORE QUASIMODO
translated from the Italian by Jack Bevan

The Girl

One day life stands
gently smiling like a girl
suddenly on the far side of the stream
and asks
(in her annoying way),

But how did you end up there?

LARS GUSTAFSSON
translated from the Swedish by John Irons

4

About time

Poetry is about time... The oldest theme in poetry is *carpe diem* [seize the day] because poetry is about time running out and then ending in death... Poetry used to be about history – Homer is about history – but once you have other kinds of recording devices besides poetry then the subject of poetry becomes time.

BILLY COLLINS

THE THEMATIC THREAD linking all the poems in *Being Human* is our relationship with time. This section begins with poems on ancestors and inheritance, generations and memory. Julia Copus's 'Raymond at 60' (173) is a *specular* poem, a form invented by her 'where the second half unfolds mirror-like from the first, using the same lines but in reverse order. The result of this discipline should be no more mechanical than a good sonnet or fugue.' The form echoes the way the mind recalls events. 'The Back Seat of My Mother's Car' in *Staying Alive* (SA 202) is another of Copus's specular poems.

Keith Althaus's 'Ladder of Hours' (177) is the first of a series of poems relating to time, mortality and second chances. These include poems warning against wasting the lives we've been given, recalling Rilke's *caveat* in 'Archaic Torso of Apollo' (85): 'You must change your life.' An 'infinite voice' reminds Jorge Luis Borges (180) that he has 'a human body to walk with on the earth', yet 'You have used up the years and they have used up you, / and still, and still, you have not written the poem.' Langston Hughes in 'Harlem [2]' (179) asks 'What happens to a dream deferred', while Stuart Henson's 'The Price' (177) invokes a pause 'to take the measure of what might have been / against the kind of life you settled for. Rodney Jones's 'Salvation Blues' (179) is a lament for people who live 'as though they were not alive'.

Wim Wenders' film *Wings of Desire* (1987) was partly inspired by Rilke's poetry and its angels. Peter Handke wrote the film's recurring 'Song of Childhood' (208), the poetic narrative and much of the dialogue, including the part I've transcribed from the English subtitles (210). The spiritual and the sensual in human life are brought together in this grouping (207-19), followed by other poems evoking stillness and silence, signalling a gentle shift into the seasonal rhythms of a series of poems loosely charting a year of life and lives on earth. 'Earth lets nobody loose; it all / has to be given back,' writes Jaan Kaplinski (244) in a poem which returns us to those ancestors evoked at the beginning of this section (162-65).

161

The Shrine Whose Shape I Am

The shrine whose shape I am
Has a fringe of fire
Flames skirt my skin
There is no Jerusalem but this
Breathed in flesh by shameless love
Built high upon the tides of blood
I believe the Prophets and Blake
And like David I bless myself
With all my might
I know many hills were holy once
But now in the leveled lands to live
Zion ground down must become marrow
Thus in my bones I am the King's son
And through death's domain I go
Making my own procession

SAMUEL MENASHE

Water

I met an ancestor in the lane.
She couldn't stop: she was carrying water.
It slopped and bounced from the stoup against her;
the side of her skirt was dark with the stain,
oozing chillingly down to her shoe.
I stepped aside as she trudged past me,
frowning with effort, shivering slightly
(an icy drop splashed my foot too).
The dress that brushed against me was rough.
She didn't smell the way I smell:
I tasted the grease and smoke in her hair.
Water that's carried is never enough.
She'd a long haul back from the well.

No, I didn't see her. But she was there.

FLEUR ADCOCK

Our Dust

I am your ancestor. You know next to nothing
about me.
There is no reason for you to imagine
the rooms I occupied or my heavy hair.
Not the faint vinegar smell of me. Or
the rubbered damp
of Forrest and I coupling on the landing
en route to our detached day.

You didn't know my weariness, error, incapacity,
I was the poet
of shadow work and towns with quarter-inch
phone books, of failed
roadside zoos. The poet of yard eggs and
sharpening shops,
jobs at the weapons plant and the Maybelline
factory on the penitentiary road.

A poet of spiderwort and jacks-in-the-pulpit,
hollyhocks against the toolshed.
An unsmiling dark blond.
The one with the trowel in her handbag.
I dug up protected and private things.
That sort, I was.
My graves went undecorated and my churches
abandoned. This wasn't planned, but practice.

I was the poet of short-tailed cats and yellow
line paint.
Of satellite dishes and Peterbilt trucks. Red Man
Chewing Tobacco, Triple Hit
Creme Soda. Also of dirt daubers, nightcrawlers,
martin houses, honey, and whetstones
from the Novaculite Uplift.

I had registered dogs 4 sale; rocks, dung
and straw.
I was a poet of hummingbird hives along with
redheaded stepbrothers.

The poet of good walking shoes – a necessity
in vernacular parts – and push mowers.
The rumor that I was once seen sleeping
in a refrigerator box is false (he was a brother
who hated me).
Nor was I the one lunching at the Governor's
mansion.

I didn't work off a grid. Or prime the surface
if I could get off without it. I made
simple music
out of sticks and string. On side B of me,
experimental guitar, night repairs, and suppers
such as this.
You could count on me to make a bad situation
worse like putting liquid makeup over
a passion mark.

I never raised your rent. Or anyone else's by God.
Never said I loved you. The future gave me chills.
I used the medium to say: Arise arise and
come together.
Free your children. Come on everybody. Let's start
with Baltimore.

Believe me I am not being modest when I
admit my life doesn't bear repeating. I
agreed to be the poet of one life,
one death alone. I have seen myself
in the black car. I have seen the retreat
of the black car.

C.D. WRIGHT

Vertical Realities

Waking is an obligation:
three generations open their eyes every morning
inside me.

The first is an old child – my father;
he always chooses his luck and clothes one size too small for him.

Next comes grandfather... In his day, the word 'diagnosis' did not
    exist.
He simply died of misery six months after his wife.
No time was wasted. Above their corpses
rose a factory to make uniforms for dockworkers.

And great-grandfather, if he ever existed,
I don't even know his name. Here my memory goes on hiatus,
my peasant origins cut like the thick and yellow nails
of field-workers.

Three shadows loom like a forest over me
telling me what to do
and what not to do.

You listened to me say 'good morning'
but it was either an elephant pounding on a piano
or the seams coming apart in my father's little jacket.

Indeed, my father, his father, and his father before that
are not trying to change anything
nor do they refuse to change anything; the soap of ephemerality
leaves them feeling fresh and clean.

They only wish to gently touch the world again
through me, the way latex gloves
lovingly touch the evidence
of a crime scene.

LULJETA LLESHANAKU
translated from the Albanian by Henry Israeli & Shpresa Qatipi

In the Waiting Room

In Worcester, Massachusetts,
I went with Aunt Consuelo
to keep her dentist's appointment
and sat and waited for her
in the dentist's waiting room.
It was winter. It got dark
early. The waiting room
was full of grown-up people,
arctics and overcoats,
lamps and magazines.
My aunt was inside
what seemed like a long time
and while I waited and read
the *National Geographic*
(I could read) and carefully
studied the photographs:
the inside of a volcano,
black, and full of ashes;
then it was spilling over
in rivulets of fire.
Osa and Martin Johnson
dressed in riding breeches,
laced boots, and pith helmets.
A dead man slung on a pole
– 'Long Pig,' the caption said.
Babies with pointed heads
wound round and round with string;
black, naked women with necks
wound round and round with wire
like the necks of light bulbs.
Their breasts were horrifying.
I read it right straight through.
I was too shy to stop.
And then I looked at the cover:
the yellow margins, the date.

Suddenly, from inside,
came an *oh!* of pain
– Aunt Consuelo's voice –

not very loud or long.
I wasn't at all surprised;
even then I knew she was
a foolish, timid woman.
I might have been embarrassed,
but wasn't. What took me
completely by surprise
was that it was *me*:
my voice, in my mouth.
Without thinking at all
I was my foolish aunt,
I – we – were falling, falling,
our eyes glued to the cover
of the *National Geographic*,
February, 1918.

I said to myself: three days
and you'll be seven years old.
I was saying it to stop
the sensation of falling off
the round, turning world.
into cold, blue-black space.
But I felt: you are an *I*,
you are an *Elizabeth*,
you are one of *them*.
Why should you be one, too?
I scarcely dared to look
to see what it was I was.
I gave a sidelong glance
– I couldn't look any higher –
at shadowy gray knees,
trousers and skirts and boots
and different pairs of hands
lying under the lamps.
I knew that nothing stranger
had ever happened, that nothing
stranger could ever happen.

Why should I be my aunt,
or me, or anyone?
What similarities –
boots, hands, the family voice

I felt in my throat, or even
the *National Geographic*
and those awful hanging breasts
held us all together
or made us all just one?
How I didn't know any
word for it how 'unlikely'...
How had I come to be here,
like them, and overhear
a cry of pain that could have
got loud and worse but hadn't?

The waiting room was bright
and too hot. It was sliding
beneath a big black wave,
another, and another.

Then I was back in it.
The War was on. Outside,
in Worcester, Massachusetts,
were night and slush and cold,
and it was still the fifth
of February, 1918.

ELIZABETH BISHOP

The Train

The railway embankment to our left
drives a green line through scree and grizzled heather.
A ghost track carries a ghost train
west from Letterkenny to Burtonport.
On one of the slatted wooden seats sits
a serious fourteen-year-old from Tyrone
with fine, straight, reddish hair.
The train huffs and clanks over our heads
across tall, cut-stone pylons
which flank the narrowest part of the road.

She is travelling to Irish college in Ranafast
in nineteen twenty-nine.
The narrow-gauge train steams along so slowly
that she can reach out
and pull leaves off the occasional, passing tree.
Her friend holds her hat out of the window
and swizzles and swizzles it around, absent-mindedly,
until it spins off and lands amid the scree.

My mother does not know that the railway line was built
by men who believed that the train was foreseen
in the prophecies of Colmcille
as a black pig snorting through the gap.
She cannot prophesy, so she does not know
that her father will be dead within three years,
or that she will meet her husband
and will spend her adult life
west of these rounded, granite hills
or that, in seventy-five years time,
one of her daughters will drive her
under this disappeared bridge
and out of Donegal
for the last time.
All she knows is that she is going to Ranafast
and that the train is travelling very slowly.

MOYA CANNON

Ein Leben

In the month of her death, she is standing by the windowframe.
a young woman with a stylish, permanent wave.
She seems to be in a contemplative mood
as she stands there looking out the window.

Through the glass an afternoon cloud of 1934
looks in at her, blurred, slightly out of focus,
but her faithful servant. On the inside
I'm the one looking at her, four years old almost,

holding back my ball, quietly
going out of the photo and growing old,
growing old carefully, quietly,
so as not to frighten her.

DAN PAGIS
translated from the Hebrew by Stephen Mitchell

This Is How Memory Works

You are stepping off a train.
A wet blank night, the smell of cinders.
A gust of steam from the engine swirls
around the hem of your topcoat, around
the hand holding the brown leather valise,
the hand that, a moment ago, slicked back
the hair and then put on the fedora
in front of the mirror with the beveled
edges in the cherrywood compartment.

The girl standing on the platform
in the Forties dress
has curled her hair, she has
nylon stockings – no, silk stockings still.
Her shoulders are touchingly military,
squared by those shoulder pads
and a sweet faith in the Allies.
She is waiting for you.
She can be wearing a hat, if you like.

You see her first.
that's part of the beauty:
you get the pure, eager face,
the lyrical dress, the surprise.
You can have the steam,
the crowded depot, the camel's-hair coat,
real leather and brass clasps on the suitcase;
you can make the lights glow with
strange significance, and the black cars
that pass you are historical yet ordinary.

The girl is yours,
the flowery dress, the walk
to the streetcar, a fried egg sandwich
and a joke about Mussolini.
You can have it all:
you're in *that* world, the only way
you'll ever be there now, hired
for your silent hammer, to nail pictures
to the walls of this mansion
made of thinnest air.

PATRICIA HAMPL

A Sofa in the Forties

All of us on the sofa in a line, kneeling
Behind each other, eldest down to youngest,
Elbows going like pistons, for this was a train

And between the jamb-wall and the bedroom door
Our speed and distance were inestimable.
First we shunted, then we whistled, then

Somebody collected the invisible
For tickets and very gravely punched it
As carriage after carriage under us

Moved faster, *chooka-chook*, the sofa legs
Went giddy and the unreachable ones
Far out on the kitchen floor began to wave.

*

Ghost-train? Death-gondola? The carved, curved ends,
Black leatherette and ornate gauntness of it
Made it seem the sofa had achieved

Flotation. Its castors on tiptoe,
Its braid and fluent backboard gave it airs
Of superannuated pageantry:

When visitors endured it, straight-backed,
When it stood off in its own remoteness,
When the insufficient toys appeared on it

On Christmas mornings, it held out as itself,
Potentially heavenbound, earthbound for sure,
Among things that might add up or let you down.

*

We entered history and ignorance
Under the wireless shelf. *Yippee-i-ay*,
Sang 'The Riders of the Range'. HERE IS THE NEWS,

Said the absolute speaker. Between him and us
A great gulf was fixed where pronunciation
Reigned tyrannically. The aerial wire

Swept from a treetop down in through a hole
Bored in the windowframe. When it moved in wind,
The sway of language and its furtherings

Swept and swayed in us like nets in water
Or the abstract, lonely curve of distant trains
As we entered history and ignorance.

*

We occupied our seats with all our might,
Fit for the uncomfortableness.
Constancy was its own reward already.

Out in front, on the big upholstered arm,
Somebody craned to the side, driver or
Fireman, wiping his dry brow with the air

Of one who had run the gauntlet. We were
The last thing on his mind, it seemed; we sensed
A tunnel coming up where we'd pour through

Like unlit carriages through fields at night,
Our only job to sit, eyes straight ahead,
And be transported and make engine noise.

SEAMUS HEANEY

Raymond, at 60

The 185 from Catford Bridge, the 68 from Euston –
those same buses climbing the hill long into the evening.
This is what stays with him best now, this and watching,
in the ward where Mother had finally died,
the way the rain had fallen on the window –
a soft rain sifting down like iron filings.
The whole of that evening he'd kept his eyes fixed on the rain,
out there in the O of the buses' steel-rimmed headlamps.
Now I am I, he thought, his two dark eyes ablaze – as if he'd found God
the very moment she'd left him. He took off his hat,
and he put his dry lips to her cheek and kissed her,
unsettled by her warmth, the scent of her skin
so unexpected he found himself suddenly
back on Bondway, crushed to her breast, in a gesture
that meant, he knew now, *You are loved.* There he was with her
pulling his bobble-hat over his ears in that finicky way she had.
What was he? Eleven? Twelve? Too old, in any case, for her to be
holding his hand the entire short walk from the house
that first time she'd taken him down to watch the buses.

That first time she'd taken him down to watch the buses,
holding his hand the entire short walk from the house,
what was he? Eleven? Twelve? Too old, in any case, for her to be
pulling his bobble-hat over his ears in that finicky way she had
that meant (he knew now) *You are loved.* There he was with her
back on Bondway, crushed to her breast, in a gesture
so unexpected he found himself suddenly
unsettled by her warmth, the scent of her skin,
and he put his dry lips to her cheek and kissed her.
The very moment she'd left him, he took off his hat.
Now I am I, he thought, his two dark eyes ablaze – as if he'd found God
out there in the O of the buses' steel-rimmed headlamps.
The whole of that evening he'd kept his eyes fixed on the rain,
a soft rain sifting down like iron filings,
the way the rain had fallen on the window
in the ward where Mother had finally died.
This is what stays with him best now, this and watching
those same buses climbing the hill long into the evening:
the 185 from Catford Bridge, the 68 from Euston...

JULIA COPUS

from **Monday in Seven Days**

5

Broken toys were my playthings:
zebras, wind-up Chinese dolls, ice-cream carts
given to me as New Year's presents by my father.
But none was worth keeping whole.
They looked like cakes whose icing had been
                    licked off by a naughty child,

until I broke them, cracked and probed their insides, the tiny
                                        gears, the batteries,
not aware then that I was rehearsing
                    my understanding of freedom.

*

When I first looked at a real painting
I took a few steps backward instinctively
                    on my heels
finding the precise place
where I could explore its depth.

It was different with people:
I built them up,
loved them, but stopped short of loving them fully.
None were as tall as the blue ceiling.
As in an unfinished house, there seemed to be a plastic sheet above
                                        them instead of a roof,
at the beginning of the rainy autumn of my understanding.

LULJETA LLESHANAKU
translated from the Albanian by Henry Israeli & Shpresa Qatipi

The Bend in the Road

This is the place where the child
Felt sick in the car and they pulled over
And waited in the shadow of a house.

A tall tree like a cat's tail waited too.
They opened the windows and breathed
Easily, while nothing moved. Then he was better.

Over twelve years it has become the place
Where you were sick one day on the way to the lake.
You are taller now than us.
The tree is taller, the house is quite covered in
With green creeper, and the bend
In the road is as silent as ever it was on that day.

Piled high, wrapped lightly, like the one cumulus cloud
In a perfect sky, softly packed like the air,
Is all that went on in those years, the absences,
The faces never long absent from thought,
The bodies alive then and the airy space they took up
When we saw them wrapped and sealed by sickness
Guessing the piled weight of sleep
We knew they could not carry for long;
This is the place of their presence: in the tree, in the air.

ÉILEAN NÍ CHUILLEANÁIN

Memory

There is no prophecy, only memory.
What happens tomorrow
has happened a thousand years ago
the same way, to the same end –
and does my ancient memory
say that your false memory
is the history of the featherhearted bird
transformed into a crow atop a marble mountain?
The same woman will be there
on the path to reincarnation
her cage of black hair
her generous and bitter heart
like an amphora full of serpents.

175

There is no prophecy, things happen
as they have before –
death finds you in the same bed
lonely and without sorrow, shadowless
as trees wet with night.

There is no destiny, only laws of biology;
fish splash in water
pine trees breathe on mountains.

LULJETA LLESHANAKU
translated from the Albanian by Luljeta Lleshanaku
with Henry Israeli & Joanna Goodman

Memory

Can it be that
memory is useless,
like a torn web
hanging in the wind?

Sometimes it billows
out, a full high gauze –
like a canopy.

But the air passes
through the rents
and it falls again and flaps
shapeless
like the ghost rag that it is –

hanging at the window
of an empty room.

RUTH STONE

Ladder of Hours

A ladder of hours
leads to the dark.
Midnight's tower
looks down on
where you stood
at noon, poised
on a rung,
wondering
what is this room
that stands outside,
in pure light,
even as the ladder
curves in space
to meet itself,
become a treadmill,
whose blurring bars create
a see-through wall,
on the other side of which,
the room endures, and waits,
though moonlit now.

KEITH ALTHAUS

The Price

Sometimes it catches when the fumes rise up
among the throbbing lights of cars, or as
you look away to dodge eye-contact with
your own reflection in the carriage-glass;
or in a waiting-room a face reminds you
that the colour supplements have lied
and some have pleasure and some pay the price.
Then all the small securities you built
about your house, your desk, your calendar,

are blown like straws; and momentarily,
as if a scent of ivy or the earth
had opened up a childhood door, you pause,
to take the measure of what might have been
against the kind of life you settled for.

STUART HENSON

The Killing of Dreams

They are encoded and are the past,
cannot be implanted in souls or brains,
not by the learning of lists
nor by learning definitions of names:
this is injecting the dream vaccine
which does not make better but makes die
the entities of the mist
that wait in the hollows of our heads.
We graft the cobbled dream
onto the inbuilt dream:
acid on alkali.
Some of us, afraid we lack
the findings of the analyst,
inject the vaccine in
the sanctum of the heart
only to find that it rejects
the artificial part
and leaves us dreamless in the dark.
This, the learning of lists,
this taking water to the well,
this planting of waterweed in streams,
this addiction to the fix
developed by the alchemists of print –
this is the killing of dreams.

MICHAEL HARTNETT

Harlem [2]

What happens to a dream deferred?

Does it dry up
like a raisin in the sun?
Or fester like a sore –
And then run?
Does it stink like rotten meat?
Or crust and sugar over –
like a syrupy sweet?

Maybe it just sags
like a heavy load.

Or does it explode?

LANGSTON HUGHES

Salvation Blues

Many people here expect
the dead are not really dead.
Therefore, they resolve to live
as though they were not alive:

so softly the minor thirds,
so tenderly the major sevenths,
white gospel the elderly virgins
keep treading like chastity

until Franz Liszt, ravager
and destroyer of pianos,
critiques with a thunderstorm:

Remind us there is something
to be dead about. Play like
you are alive, even if it is not true.

RODNEY JONES

Matthew XXV: 30

And cast ye the unprofitable servant into outer darkness:
there shall be weeping and gnashing of teeth.

The first bridge, Constitution Station. At my feet
the shunting trains trace iron labyrinths.
Steam hisses up and up into the night,
which becomes at a stroke the night of the Last Judgment.

From the unseen horizon
and from the very center of my being,
an infinite voice pronounced these things –
things, not words. This is my feeble translation,
time-bound, of what was a single limitless Word:

'Stars, bread, libraries of East and West,
playing-cards, chessboards, galleries, skylights, cellars,
a human body to walk with on the earth,
fingernails, growing at nighttime and in death,
shadows for forgetting, mirrors busily multiplying,
cascades in music, gentlest of all time's shapes.
Borders of Brazil, Uruguay, horses and mornings,
a bronze weight, a copy of the Grettir Saga,
algebra and fire, the charge at Junín in your blood,
days more crowded than Balzac, scent of the honeysuckle,
love and the imminence of love and intolerable remembering,
dreams like buried treasure, generous luck,
and memory itself, where a glance can make men dizzy –
all this was given to you, and with it
the ancient nourishment of heroes –
treachery, defeat, humiliation.
In vain have oceans been squandered on you,
in vain the sun, wonderfully seen through Whitman's eyes.
You have used up the years and they have used up you,
and still, and still, you have not written the poem.'

JORGE LUIS BORGES
translated from the Spanish by Alastair Reid

News of the World

Time had beached him like a stranded whale
on the bleak shores of a big brass bed. The past
sang to him: the sea in a shell. I
was his lookout at the window of the upstairs
room. He'd cup his hand round his ear
when I'd call out to him how many cows
Stinson was grazing on the long acre now.
I'd listen to news of a world he knew
long before I knew there was a world to know.

And so it would go on, with him left
high and dry and out of his element by the tide
and me all eyes for the eyes that always
seemed to be looking beyond me
at things I'd never be able to see.

FRANCIS HARVEY

from Mythistorema

15

Sleep wrapped you in green leaves like a tree
you breathed like a tree in the quiet light
in the limpid spring I looked at your face:
eyelids closed, eyelashes brushing the water.
In the soft grass my fingers found your fingers
I held your pulse a moment
and felt elsewhere your heart's pain.

Under the plane tree, near the water, among laurel
sleep moved you and scattered you
around me, near me, without my being able to touch the whole of you –
one as you were with your silence;
seeing your shadow grow and diminish,
lose itself in the other shadows, in the other
world that let you go yet held you back.

The life that they gave us to live, we lived.
Pity those who wait with such patience
lost in the black laurel under the heavy plane trees
and those, alone, who speak to cisterns and wells
and drown in the voice's circles.
Pity the companion who shared our privation and our sweat
and plunged into the sun like a crow beyond the ruins,
without hope of enjoying our reward.

Give us, outside sleep, serenity.

GEORGE SEFERIS
translated from the Greek by Edmund Keeley & Philip Sherrard

'The washing never gets done...'

The washing never gets done.
The furnace never gets heated.
Books never get read.
Life is never completed.
Life is like a ball which one must continually
catch and hit so that it won't fall.
When the fence is repaired at one end,
it collapses at the other. The roof leaks,
the kitchen door won't close, there are cracks in the foundation,
the torn knees of children's pants...
One can't keep everything in mind. The wonder is
that beside all this one can notice
the spring which is so full of everything
continuing in all directions – into evening clouds,
into the redwing's song and into every
drop of dew on every blade of grass in the meadow,
as far as the eye can see, into the dusk.

JAAN KAPLINSKI
translated from the Estonian by Jaan Kaplinski with Sam Hamill & Riina Tamm

A Man in His Life

A man doesn't have time in his life
to have time for everything.
He doesn't have seasons enough to have
a season for every purpose. Ecclesiastes
was wrong about that.

A man needs to love and to hate at the same moment,
to laugh and cry with the same eyes,
with the same hands to throw stones and to gather them,
to make love in war and war in love.

And to hate and forgive and remember and forget,
to arrange and confuse, to eat and to digest
what history
takes years and years to do.

A man doesn't have time.
When he loses he seeks, when he finds
he forgets, when he forgets he loves, when he loves
he begins to forget.

And his soul is seasoned, his soul
is very professional.
Only his body remains forever
an amateur. It tries and it misses,
gets muddled, doesn't learn a thing,
drunk and blind in its pleasures
and its pains.

He will die as figs die in autumn,
shrivelled and full of himself and sweet,
the leaves growing dry on the ground,
the bare branches pointing to the place
where there's time for everything.

YEHUDA AMICHAI
translated from the Hebrew by Chana Bloch

Carpe Diem

From my study window
    I see you
below in the garden, a hand
    here pruning
or leaning across to snip
    a wayward shoot,

a daub of powder-blue in a
    profusion of green;
then next moment, you are
    no longer there –
only to reappear, this time
    perfectly framed

in dappling sunlight, with
    an armful of ivy
you've trimmed, topped by
    hyacinth blooms,
fragrant survivors of last
    night's frost.

And my heart misses a beat
    at love for you,
knowing a time will come
    when you are
no longer there, nor I here
    to watch you

on a day of such simplicity.
    Meantime let us
make sure we clasp each
    shared moment
in cupped hands, like water
    we dare not spill.

STEWART CONN

Riot Eve

I haven't, thank God, become a perpetrator.
I never caused the death of others, though I must utter these words.
I hold myself back, as the shrewd son of my father.
I see it like this: a lion will attack a gazelle.

We have one life. Why spend it being feebly decent?
We see but one night; we contain others.
I ask myself if this path and all those terrible detours were really
    necessary.
There is a reason for everything, and our catastrophe.

Imagine then that a father returns and doesn't speak about any of this.
He carries me on his shoulders during the long walk in the forest.
Imagine a man – so polite, so clean;
his swiftness, his warmth, his murderous ideas.

Look, nothing in this world is perfect.
This is the condition, now growing darker.
History has shown us: the Black Death, the Borgias...
I await the real wooden anger that shapes me.

The gardens have roared for days.
The wind bends the trees. It is like a sign.
I hear of a palace rising.
It is just after midnight, and I will obey you.

EMMA LEW

Sathyaji
(Lac Jemaye, France)

Dusk, and the boathouse keeper
calls the late, scattered boats
from beyond the curve
in the lake; calls them by name,
Hirondelle! Angelique! George Sand!

Are they real or imagined,
those smudges of black
in the shade of the far bank?
Again his call, carrying, returning.

What's in a name? You are –
in the name I called you by;
its weight and shape hard to convey
except – it lent itself to tenderness,
teasing and respect; closeness
and a certain distance.
Now it's a vessel
for the far-flung
only sure reality of you.

Love draws you back.
In saying your name, I see it
boat-shaped and luminous
stitching the dark,
returned from formless drift
about the world. Let me
recall you. I've words enough –
a sheaf of versions. My pen
engraves you differently each time.

Nothing can be held, or hurried.
Wind casts a shiver on the water;
shallows uncertain in withdrawing light.
A phalarope races its image
and is gone; reflected, relinquished,
discarnate as the distant boats
the boathouse keeper calls and calls,
only a name to summon each of them.

Yet, here they come.

CAROLE SATYAMURTI

Dawn Revisited

Imagine you wake up
with a second chance: The blue jay
hawks his pretty wares
and the oak still stands, spreading
glorious shade. If you don't look back,

the future never happens.
How good to rise in sunlight,
in the prodigal smell of biscuits –
eggs and sausage on the grill.
The whole sky is yours

to write on, blown open
to a blank page. Come on,
shake a leg! You'll never know
who's down there, frying those eggs,
if you don't get up and see.

RITA DOVE

Lava

And what if Heraclitus and Parmenides
are both right
and two worlds exist side by side,
one serene, the other insane; one arrow
thoughtlessly hurtles, another, indulgent,
looks on; the selfsame wave moves and stands still.
Animals all at once come into the world
and leave it, birch leaves dance in the wind
as they fall apart in the cruel, rusty flame.
Lava kills and preserves, the heart beats
and is beaten; there was war, then there wasn't;
Jews died, Jews stay alive, cities are razed,
cities endure, love fades, the kiss everlasting,
the wings of the hawk must be brown,
you're still with me though we're no more,

187

ships sink, sand sings, clouds wander
like wedding veils in tatters.

All's lost. So much brilliance. The hills
gently descend with their long banners of woods.
Moss inches up the stone tower of a church,
its small mouth timidly praising the North.

At dusk, the savage lamp of the jasmine is glowing,
possessed by its own luminescence.
Before a dark canvas in a museum,
eyes narrow like a cat's. Everything's finished.
Riders gallop black horses, a tyrant composes
a sentence of death with grammatical errors.
Youth dissolves
in a day; girls' faces freeze
into medallions, despair turns to rapture
and the hard fruits of stars in the sky
ripen like grapes, and beauty endures, shaken, unperturbed,
and God is and God dies; night returns to us
in the evening, and the dawn is hoary with dew.

ADAM ZAGAJEWSKI
translated from the Polish by Renata Gorczynski,
Benjamin Ivry & C.K. Williams

Could Have

It could have happened.
It had to happen.
It happened earlier. Later.
Nearer. Farther off.
It happened, but not to you.

You were saved because you were the first.
You were saved because you were the last.
Alone. With others.
On the right. The left.
Because it was raining. Because of the shade.
Because the day was sunny.

You were in luck – there was a forest.
You were in luck – there were no trees.
You were in luck – a rake, a hook, a beam, a brake,
a jamb, a turn, a quarter-inch, an instant...
You were in luck – just then a straw went floating by.

As a result, because, although, despite.
What would have happened if a hand, a foot,
within an inch, a hairsbreadth from
an unfortunate coincidence.

So you're here? Still dizzy from another dodge, close shave, reprieve?
One hole in the net and you slipped through?
I couldn't be more shocked or speechless.
Listen,
how your heart pounds inside me.

WISŁAWA SZYMBORSKA
translated from the Polish by Stanisław Barańczak & Clare Cavanagh

Thanks

Thanks for the tree
between me & a sniper's bullet.
I don't know what made the grass
sway seconds before the Viet Cong
raised his soundless rifle.
Some voice always followed,
telling me which foot
to put down first.
Thanks for deflecting the ricochet
against that anarchy of dusk.
I was back in San Francisco
wrapped up in a woman's wild colors,
causing some dark bird's love call
to be shattered by daylight
when my hands reached up
& pulled a branch away
from my face. Thanks
for the vague white flower
that pointed to the gleaming metal

reflecting how it is to be broken
like mist over the grass,
as we played some deadly
game for blind gods.
What made me spot the monarch
writhing on a single thread
tied to a farmer's gate,
holding the day together
like an unfingered guitar string,
is beyond me. Maybe the hills
grew weary & leaned a little in the heat.
Again, thanks for the dud
hand grenade tossed at my feet
outside Chu Lai. I'm still
falling through its silence.
I don't know why the intrepid
sun touched the bayonet,
but I know that something
stood among those lost trees
& moved only when I moved.

YUSEF KOMUNYAKAA

Caught

in a flicker of gunfire (off to one side;
I believe you when you said you never fought);
caught in a war

of three sides and not one
to call your own; and when the dreadful music
stopped, caught

on the wrong side of the line
through Europe that the powers at Yalta ruled;
caught out of place;

caught in the zone, with transport waiting
to a bone mine in the Urals when the deadline fell; caught
wind of that

and walked, walked west and long;
caught out by sunrise in the wrong sort of uniform,
caught sight

of a scarecrow in a turnip field,
gave thanks for its coat and tatty britches; snagged
for a moment

when the snare of history pulled tight
you jerked free, torn somewhat, never quite mended but
not caught.

PHILIP GROSS

Listen

Listen, I have flown through darkness towards joy,
I have put the mossy stones away from me,
and the thorns, the thistles, the brambles.
I have swum upward like a fish

through the black wet earth, the ancient roots
which insanely fight with each other
in a grave which creates a treasure house
of light upward-springing leaves.

Such joy, such joy! Such airy drama
the clouds compose in the heavens,
such interchange of comedies,
disguises, rhymes, dénouements.

I had not believed that the stony heads
would change to actors and actresses,
and that the grooved armour of statues
would rise and walk away

into a resurrection of villages,
townspeople, citizens, dead exiles,
who sing with the salt in their mouths,
winged nightingales of brine.

IAIN CRICHTON SMITH

Meeting Point

Time was away and somewhere else,
There were two glasses and two chairs
And two people with the one pulse
(Somebody stopped the moving stairs):
Time was away and somewhere else.

And they were neither up nor down;
The stream's music did not stop
Flowing through heather, limpid brown,
Although they sat in a coffee shop
And they were neither up nor down.

The bell was silent in the air
Holding its inverted poise –
Between the clang and clang a flower,
A brazen calyx of no noise:
The bell was silent in the air.

The camels crossed the miles of sand
That stretched around the cups and plates;
The desert was their own, they planned
To portion out the stars and dates:
The camels crossed the miles of sand.

Time was away and somewhere else.
The waiter did not come, the clock
Forgot them and the radio waltz
Came out like water from a rock:
Time was away and somewhere else.

Her fingers flicked away the ash
That bloomed again in tropic trees:
Not caring if the markets crash
When they had forests such as these,
Her fingers flicked away the ash.

God or whatever means the Good
Be praised that time can stop like this,
That what the heart has understood
Can verify in the body's peace
God or whatever means the Good.

Time was away and she was here
And life no longer what it was,
The bell was silent in the air
And all the room one glow because
Time was away and she was here.

LOUIS MacNEICE

The Three Fates

At the instant of drowning he invoked the three sisters.
It was a mistake, an aberration, to cry out for
Life everlasting.

He came up like a cork and back to the river-bank,
Put on his clothes in reverse order,
Returned to the house.

He suffered the enormous agonies of passion
Writing poems from the end backwards,
Brushing away tears that had not yet fallen.

Loving her wildly as the day regressed towards morning
He watched her wringing in the garden, growing younger,
Barefoot, straw-hatted.

And when she was gone and the house and the swing and daylight
There was an instant's pause before it began all over,
The reel unrolling towards the river.

ROSEMARY DOBSON

Leaving

She left the hospital quietly at night.
The lights were out and only a skeleton staff
remained in the office on her first-floor ward.

Outside the streets were dark with drizzle
and there were only a few cars around,
making a smooth tearing sound as they passed.

She noticed that the cars were very old, pre-war,
but were shining in good condition anyway
and that the city centre had a human scale,

the sort of scale it used to have when she
first came here with her parents sixty years ago.
The highest objects were the crosses on the spires.

By the time she reached the station the sun was up
and the platform was a rather frightening place
with its cross-currents of adults dressed for work.

A train had just arrived and from its van
men in overalls were unloading wooden crates.
She held her mother's hand as she'd been told to.

The station building hadn't changed a bit.
Its famous row of clocks under the copper dome,
its tiled floors and timber ceilings were all intact.

Moving off, the train whistled and she saw again
the enamel platform sign, cast-iron flamed,
which had cast her mind's image of that number.

It only took a few suburbs before the train
was out in a landscape of fifty-acre farms
where harnessed horses and small grey tractors

both worked the paddocks, and where the roads,
even the main ones back to town, weren't sealed.
Sometimes she saw a farmer waving at the train.

Her carriage creaked and swayed like an old bed.
It seemed to her the further away they went
the more she recognised the farms and little towns.

The home stop, when it came, was feverishly hot
and the light was very harsh. She squinted
with interest at the lack of progress in this town.

It was here as a girl she had first seen life
away from the formality of her parents' farm.
Nothing since had been as new as that look.

The station was as crowded as it had been then.
Most of the population seemed to be there
for it was the railway that kept the town alive.

Soon the train began to take on new passengers.
She waited until she had to give up her place
and then stepped out into the terrible light.

PHILIP HODGINS

Progress

They say that for years Belfast was backwards
and it's great now to see some progress.
So I guess we can look forward to taking boxes
from the earth. I guess that ambulances
will leave the dying back amidst the rubble
to be explosively healed. Given time,
one hundred thousand particles of glass
will create impossible patterns in the air
before coalescing into the clarity
of a window. Through which, a reassembled head
will look out and admire the shy young man
taking his bomb from the building and driving home.

ALAN GILLIS

The mud-spattered recollections of a woman who lived her life backwards

I'll tell you a tale: one morning one morning I lay
in my uncomfortable six-foot small grave,
I lay sulking about a somewhat too short-lit
life both fruitful and dutiful.

It was death it was death like an inbreath fully inhaled
in the grief of the world when at last
there began to emerge a way out, alas
the in-snowing silence made any description difficult.

No eyes no matches and yet mathematically speaking
I could still reach at a stretch a wispish whiteish
last seen outline any way up, which could well be my own
were it only a matter of re-folding.

So I creased I uncreased and the next thing I knew
I was pulled from the ground at the appointed hour
and rushed to the nearest morgue to set out yet again
from the bed to the floor to the door to the air.

And there was the car still there in its last known place
under the rain where I'd left it, my husband etc.
even myself, in retrospect I was still there
still driving back with the past all spread out already in front of me.

What a refreshing whiff with the windows open!
there were the dead leaves twitching and tacking back
to their roosts in the trees and all it required
was a certain minimum level of inattention.

I tell you, for many years from doorway to doorway
and in through a series of rooms I barely noticed
I was humming the same tune twice, I was seeing the same
three children racing towards me getting smaller and smaller.

This tale's like a rose, once opened it
cannot reclose, it continues: one morning
one terrible morning for maybe the hundredth time
they came to insert my third child back inside me.

It was death it was death: from head to foot
I heard myself crack with the effort, I leaned and cried
and a feeling fell on me with a dull clang
that I'd never see my darling daughter again.

Then both my sons, slowly at first
then faster and faster, their limbs retracted inwards
smaller and smaller till all that remained
was a little mound where I didn't quite meet in the middle.

Well either I was or was not either living or dead
in a windowless cubicle of the past, a mere
8.3 light minutes from the present moment when at last
my husband walked oh dear he walked me to church.

All in one brief winter's day, both
braced for confusion with much shy joy,
reversed our vows, unringed our hands
and slid them back in our pockets God knows why.

What then what then I'll tell you what then: one evening
there I stood in the matchbox world of childhood
and saw the stars fall straight through Jimmy's binoculars,
they looked so weird skewered to a fleeting instant.

Then again and again for maybe the hundredth time
they came to insert me feet first back into nothing
complete with all my missing hopes – next morning
there was that same old humming thrum still there.

That same old humming thrumming sound that is either
my tape re-winding again or maybe it's stars
passing through stars coming back to their last known places,
for as far as I know in the end both sounds are the same.

ALICE OSWALD

Pause: Rewind

Nowadays the dead walk and talk
in the wedding video, the camcorded break,

the fuzzed black-and-white of security cameras.
A policeman watches, as two balaclavas

burst, again and again, through the door
of an off-licence, and the old shopkeeper

panics: blunders into a baseball bat;
slumps in his blood. Before things can get

any worse, the young D.C. presses 'pause',
then 'rewind'. And the dark stream flows

into the head again: the old fellow
gets up: the thieves are backing jerkily through

the door, which closes on them. All right;
all tidy. This could get to be a habit:

so many tapes he could whizz backwards.
That bus and bike, speeding to the crossroads,

will not collide: the drunk at the hotel
will stop short of his car: the young girl

will never disappear down the subway
where her rapist waits so patiently.

Pause: rewind. Freeze-frame where you want
the world to stop. The moment before the moment;

before Challenger leaves the launch pad,
before the boat sails or the letter's posted,

before the singer jumps off the bridge,
before you see the face that ends your marriage,

before the pink suit is dyed red,
before a thought is formed or a word said.

SHEENAGH PUGH

The Little Box

The little box grows her first teeth
And her little length grows
Her little width her little emptiness
And everything she has

The little box grows and grows
And now inside her is the cupboard
She was in before

And she grows and grows and grows
And now inside her is the room
And the house and town and land
And the world she was in before

The little box remembers her childhood
And by wishing really hard
Becomes a little box again

Now inside the little box
Is the whole world all teeny-weeny
Easy to slip in your pocket
Easy to steal easy to lose

Look after the little box

VASKO POPA
translated from the Serbian by Anne Pennington & Francis R. Jones

Inside the Apple

You visit me inside the apple.
Together we can hear the knife
paring around and around us, carefully,
so the peel won't tear.

You speak to me. I trust your voice
because it has lumps of hard pain in it
the way real honey
has lumps of wax from the honeycomb.

I touch your lips with my fingers:
that too is a prophetic gesture.
And your lips are red, the way a burnt field
is black.
It's all true.

You visit me inside the apple
and you'll stay with me inside the apple
until the knife finishes its work.

YEHUDA AMICHAI
translated from the Hebrew by Chana Bloch

Life

A child is born
in a broad landscape
half a century later
he's just a dead soldier
and that was him
the man you saw
appear and set down
a heavy sackful of apples
two or three of them rolling out
a noise among those of a world
where the bird sang its song
on the stone threshold.

JEAN FOLLAIN
translated from the French by Jennie Feldman & Stephen Romer

Nothing Is Lost

Nothing is lost. Nothing is so small
that it does not return.
                              Imagine
that as a child on a day like this
you held a newly minted coin and had
the choice of spending it in any way
you wished.
                 Today the coin comes back to you,
the date rubbed out, the ancient mottoes vague,
the portrait covered with the dull shellac
of anything used up, passed on, disposed of
with something else in view, and always worth
a little less each time.
                              Now it returns,
and you will think it unimportant, lose
it in your pocket change as one more thing
that's not worth counting, not worth singling out.
That is the mistake you must avoid today.
You sent it on a journey to yourself.
Now hold it in your hand. Accept it as
the little you have earned today.
                              And realise
that you must choose again but over less.

DANA GIOIA

A Woman's Portrait 1938

The painting conveys her exquisite taste:
ear studs, bracelets, green and yellow *selendang*;
the sash conceals her pregnancy.

The death she is carrying can't be disguised.
The life she carries will grasp and cling on.
Yearning, restlessness and the turmoil of fear
are not recorded in the brush-strokes,

pencil outline of a face
surrendering to the flow of history.

The painting, with its final brilliant gesture,
only fully reveals this face
when it is framed by memory.

TOETI HERATY
translated from the Indoniesian by Carole Satyamurti & Ulrich Kratz

In Santa Maria del Populo

Waiting for when the sun an hour or less
Conveniently oblique makes visible
The painting on one wall of this recess
By Caravaggio, of the Roman School,
I see how shadow in the painting brims
With a real shadow, drowning all shapes out
But a dim horse's haunch and various limbs,
Until the very subject is in doubt.

But evening gives the act, beneath the horse
And one indifferent groom, I see him sprawl,
Foreshortened from the head, with hidden face,
Where he has fallen, Saul becoming Paul.
O wily painter, limiting the scene
From a cacophony of dusty forms
To the one convulsion, what is it you mean
In that wide gesture of the lifting arms?

No Ananias croons a mystery yet,
Casting the pain out under name of sin.
The painter saw what was, an alternate
Candour and secrecy inside the skin.
He painted, elsewhere, that firm insolent
Young whore in Venus' clothes, those pudgy cheats,
Those sharpers; and was strangled, as things went,
For money, by one such picked off the streets.

I turn, hardly enlightened, from the chapel
To the dim interior of the church instead,
In which there kneel already several people,
Mostly old women: each head closeted
In tiny fists holds comfort as it can.
Their poor arms are too tired for more than this
– For the large gesture of solitary man,
Resisting, by embracing, nothingness.

THOM GUNN

Black Moon

For white he used toothpaste,
for red, blood – but only his own
that he hijacked just enough of each day.

For green he crushed basil in a little
olive oil. His yellow was egg yolk,
his black, coal dust dampened with water.

He tried several routes to blue
before stopping at the intersection
of bilberry juice and pounded bluebells.

His brown was his own, too, applied
last thing in the day before the first
Laphraoig, and the stone jug of ale.

He used no other colours, but his tone
was praised by Prince Haisal, no less,
which got him a rake of commissions

and a residency-offer in Kuwait
which he turned down. At home
the Royal Family was less generous

so he painted them all, in a series
that came to be called his brown period,
though this was strictly incorrect.

He never exhibited with other painters,
never drank with them, spoke of them –
never even spat at their work.

A cave in the Orkneys was his last dwelling
and he rode a horse to his studio.
There were no people in these paintings,

which were found piled up on one another
inside the cave, with no sign of him,
and on top was a depiction of a black moon.

MATTHEW SWEENEY

'Life draws a tree'

Life draws a tree
and death draws another one.
Life draws a nest
and death copies it.
Life draws a bird
to live in the nest
and right away death
draws another bird.

A hand that draws nothing
wanders among the drawings
and at times moves one of them.
For example:
a bird of life
occupies death's nest
on the tree that life drew.

Other times
the hand that draws nothing
blots out one drawing of the series.
For example:
the tree of death
holds the nest of death,
but there's no bird in it.

And other times
the hand that draws nothing
itself changes
into an extra image
in the shape of a bird,
in the shape of a tree,
in the shape of a nest.
And then, only then,
nothing's missing and nothing's left over.
For example:
two birds
occupy life's nest
in death's tree.

Or life's tree
holds two nests
with only one bird in them.

Or a single bird
lives in the one nest
on the tree of life
and the tree of death.

ROBERTO JUARROZ
translated from the Spanish by W.S. Merwin

Etching of a Line of Trees
(i.m. John Goodfellow Glenday)

I cut away the careful absence of a hill and a hill grew.
I cut away the fabric of the trees
and the trees stood shivering in the darkness.

When I had burned off the last syllables of wind,
a fresh wind rose and lingered.
But because I could not bring myself

to remove you from that hill,
you are no longer there. How wonderful it is
that neither of us managed to survive

when it was love that surely pulled the burr
and love that gnawed its own shape from the burnished air
and love that shaped that absent wind against a tree.

Some shadow's hands moved with my hands
and everything I touched was turned to darkness
and everything I could not touch was light.

JOHN GLENDAY

The Art of Disappearing

The moon that broke on the fencepost will not hold.
Desire will not hold. Memory will not hold.
The house you grew up in; its eaves; its attic will not hold.
The still lives and the Botticellis will not hold.
The white peaches in the bowl will not hold.
Something is always about to happen.
You get married, you change your name,
and the sun you wore like a scarf on your wrist has vanished.
It is an art, this ever more escaping grasp of things;
imperatives will not still it – no *stay* or *wait* or *keep*
to seize the disappeared and hold it clear, like pain.
So tell the car idling in the street to go on;
tell the skirmish of chesspieces to go on;
tell the scraps of paper, the lines to go on.
It is winter: that means the blossoms are gone,
that means the days are getting shorter.
And the dark water flows endlessly on.

SARAH HOLLAND-BATT

Childhood

School's long anxiety and time slips past
with waiting, in endless dreary things.
O solitude, O heavy spending on and on of time...
And then outside: the streets flash and ring
and on the squares the fountains leap
and the world becomes boundless in the gardens.
And to walk through it all in one's small suit,
so unlike the way others walked and sauntered –:
O wondrous time, O spending on and on of time,
O solitude.

And to look far off into it all:
men and women; men, more men, women
and then children, who are different and bright;
and here a house and now and then a dog
and fear changing places soundlessly with trust –:
O sadness without cause, O dream, O dread,
O endless depth.

And so to play: ball and hoop and handstands
in a garden that keeps softly fading,
and to collide sometimes against grownups
blindly and wildly in the rush of tag,
but at evening quietly, with small, stiff steps
to walk back home, your hand firmly held –:
O ever more escaping grasp of things,
O weight, O fear.

And for hours at the big gray pond
to kneel entranced with a small sailboat;
to neglect it, because other, identical yet
more beautiful sails glide through the rings,
and to have to think about the small pale face
that sinking gazed back out of the pond –:
O childhood, O likeness gliding off...
Where? Where?

RAINER MARIA RILKE
translated from the German by Edward Snow

Song of Childhood

(FROM Wim Wenders' *Wings of Desire*)

When the child was a child
It walked with its arms swinging,
wanted the brook to be a river,
the river to be a torrent,
and this puddle to be the sea.

When the child was a child,
it didn't know that it was a child,
everything was soulful,
and all souls were one.

When the child was a child,
it had no opinion about anything,
had no habits,
it often sat cross-legged,
took off running,
had a cowlick in its hair,
and made no faces when photographed.

When the child was a child,
It was the time for these questions:
Why am I me, and why not you?
Why am I here, and why not there?
When did time begin, and where does space end?
Is life under the sun not just a dream?
Is what I see and hear and smell
not just an illusion of a world before the world?
Given the facts of evil and people.
does evil really exist?
How can it be that I, who I am,
didn't exist before I came to be,
and that, someday, I, who I am,
will no longer be who I am?

When the child was a child,
It choked on spinach, on peas, on rice pudding,
and on steamed cauliflower,
and eats all of those now, and not just because it has to.

When the child was a child,
it awoke once in a strange bed,
and now does so again and again.
Many people, then, seemed beautiful,
and now only a few do, by sheer luck.

It had visualised a clear image of Paradise,
and now can at most guess,
could not conceive of nothingness,
and shudders today at the thought.

When the child was a child,
It played with enthusiasm,
and, now, has just as much excitement as then,
but only when it concerns its work.

When the child was a child,
It was enough for it to eat an apple...bread,
And so it is even now.

When the child was a child,
Berries filled its hand as only berries do,
and do even now,
Fresh walnuts made its tongue raw,
and do even now,
it had, on every mountaintop,
the longing for a higher mountain yet,
and in every city,
the longing for an even greater city,
and that is still so,
It reached for cherries in topmost branches of trees
with an elation it still has today,
has a shyness in front of strangers,
and has that even now.
It awaited the first snow,
And waits that way even now.

When the child was a child,
It threw a stick like a lance against a tree,
And it quivers there still today.

PETER HANDKE

209

Angels talking in *Wings of Desire*
(Dialogue from Wim Wenders' film)

DAMIEL:
When the child was a child...
it was the time of these questions.
Why am I me
and why not you?
Why am I here, and why not there?
When did time begin,
and where does space end?

Isn't life under the sun just a dream?
Isn't what I see, hear, and smell
just a mirage of a world before the world?
Does evil actually exist
and people who are really evil?
How can it be that I, who am I
wasn't there before I was there...
and that sometime I, the one I am
no longer will be the one I am?

[...]

CASSIEL:
Twenty years ago today
a Soviet jet fighter crashed
into the lakes at Spandau.

Fifty years ago there were...
– *The Olympic Games.*

Two hundred years ago,
Blanchard flew over the city in a balloon.
– *Like the fugitives the other day.*

And today
on the Lilienthaler Chaussee,
a man slows down
and looks over his shoulder into space.

At Post Office 44
someone who wants
to put an end to it today
has stuck first-day issue stamps
on his farewell letters.
A different one on each.

Then he spoke English
with an American soldier
for the first time since his schooldays,
fluently.

A prisoner at Plötzensee
just before dashing his head
against the wall...
said, *Now!*

At the Zoo U-Bahn station, the guard,
instead of the station's name
suddenly shouted, 'Tierra del Fuego!'

In the hills, an old man was reading
The Odyssey to a child
and the young listener
stopped blinking his eyes.

And what do you have to tell?

DAMIEL:
A passer-by, in the rain,
folded her umbrella
and was drenched.

A schoolboy
who described to his teacher
how a fern grows out of the earth,
and astounded the teacher.

A blind woman who groped for her watch
feeling my presence.

It's great to live by the spirit,
to testify day by day
for eternity, only what's spiritual
in people's minds.
But sometimes I'm fed up
with my spiritual existence.

Instead of forever hovering above
I'd like to feel a weight grow in me
to end the infinity and to tie me to earth.
I'd like, at each step, each gust of wind,
to be able to say *Now*.
Now and now
and no longer *forever* and *for eternity*.

To sit at the empty place at a card table
and be greeted, even by a nod.

Every time we participated,
it was a pretence.
Wrestling with one
allowing a hip to be put out in pretence
catching a fish in pretence
in pretence sitting at tables
drinking and eating in pretence.
Having lambs roasted and wine
served in the tents out there
in the desert, only in pretence.

No, I don't have to beget a child
or plant a tree
but it would be nice
coming home after a long day
to feed the cat, like Philip Marlowe
to have a fever
and blackened fingers from the newspaper
to be excited not only by the mind...
but, at last, by a meal
by the line of a neck
by an ear.

To lie!
Through one's teeth.

As you're walking,
to feel your bones moving along.
At last to guess, instead of always knowing.
To be able to say *Ah* and *Oh* and *Hey*
instead of *Yea* and *Amen.*

CASSIEL:
Yes.
To be able, once in a while,
to enthuse for evil.
To draw all the demons
of the earth from passers-by
and to chase them out into the world!
To be a savage.

DAMIEL:
Or at last to feel how it is
to take off shoes under a table
to wriggle your toes barefoot, like that...

CASSIEL:
Stay alone!
Let things happen! Keep serious!
We can only be savages
in as much as we keep serious.
Do no more than look!
Assemble, testify, preserve!
Remain spirit!
Keep your distance. Keep your word.

PETER HANDKE
English subtitles translated from the German

Cerulean Blue: Footnote on Wim Wenders

Angels do exist. Wim Wenders almost
had them right with that slightly shop-soiled look,
neither pure spirit, nor pure intellect, lost
on some level of their own, their eyes in a book

but raised fatally in a cool engagement,
and there they hold you and you feel looked through
but with a vague and troubling presentiment
at the colour, somewhere between grey and blue

intensifying to clear sky which is
merely a form of seduction, and you sigh,
already smitten, and get on with your business

which is what it always was. You start to count
the coins in your pocket or the spots on someone's tie
but keep losing track of the amount.

*

Just as, for example, you might sit down
at a table and begin to swim in pale smoke.
The sun floats in the window. Whole years drown
in your coffee and you start to remember a joke

without a punch line when an angel rises
from your companion's mouth and calmly hovers
above her head but your self-possession surprises
even you, and the thought of becoming lovers

solidifies like a screen on which is projected
the dream-film of all those other lives which are
not yours, and before you know, you've interjected

some ambiguous remark the angel hears
and sniggers at, then moves off to the bar
with his transparent head and disappears.

GEORGE SZIRTES

Privilege of Being

Many are making love. Up above, the angels
in the unshaken ether and crystal of human longing
are braiding one another's hair, which is strawberry blond
and the texture of cold rivers. They glance

down from time to time at the awkward ecstasy –
it must look to them like featherless birds
splashing in the spring puddle of a bed –
and then one woman, she is about to come,
peels back the man's shut eyelids and says,
look at me, and he does. Or is it the man
tugging the curtain rope in that dark theater?
Anyway, they do, they look at each other;
two beings with evolved eyes, rapacious,
startled, connected at the belly in an unbelievably sweet
lubricious glue, stare at each other,
and the angels are desolate. They hate it. They shudder pathetically
like lithographs of Victorian beggars
with perfect features and alabaster skin hawking rags
in the lewd alleys of the novel.
All of creation is offended by this distress.
It is like the keening sound the moon makes sometimes,
rising. The lovers especially cannot bear it,
it fills them with unspeakable sadness, so that
they close their eyes again and hold each other, each
feeling the mortal singularity of the body
they have enchanted out of death for an hour or so,
and one day, running at sunset, the woman says to the man,
I woke up feeling so sad this morning because I realised
that you could not, as much as I love you,
dear heart, cure my loneliness,
wherewith she touched his cheek to reassure him
that she did not mean to hurt him with this truth.
And the man is not hurt exactly,
he understands that life has limits, that people
die young, fail at love,
fail of their ambitions. He runs beside her, he thinks
of the sadness they have gasped and crooned their way out of
coming, clutching each other with old, invented
forms of grace and clumsy gratitude, ready
to be alone again, or dissatisfied, or merely
companionable like the couples on the summer beach
reading magazine articles about intimacy between the sexes
to themselves, and to each other,
and to the immense, illiterate, consoling angels.

ROBERT HASS

God in France

I would like to be God in France, where no one believes anymore.
No calls on me, I could sit all day in cafés...
SAUL BELLOW

Allah of Islam! Yahweh of the Jews!
   They were calling upon me
All over Paris. Sabbaths, but the Bon Dieu
Had gone missing. I had set myself free
From Friday at the mosque, that pile of shoes,
Those thousands praying, Saturday Torah scrolls
And lit menorahs, Sundays salvaging souls –
From Daubenton, Des Rosiers, Saint Gervais,
To live again in the body, *l'homme moyen sensuel*

Adrift on the everyday. Streetlife, glass cafés
   Were my chosen ground.
Whatever I needed easily could be found
In a few square miles. Massage, phlebotomy,
Thalassal brines and hydrotherapeutics.
Mont-Sainte-Geneviève, with its hermeneutics,
Clichy for hardcore, all the highs and lows
Of pure *bien-être*, like a bird in the hand.
Oh yes, if I wanted a woman, I knew where to go –

And who could deny me? Human, all my horizons
   Were reachable by train
From Austerlitz, Saint Lazare, the Gare de Lyon –
Not that I needed them. Gifted, like Urizen,
With omnipresence, simultaneity,
I could sit here over dinner, and still see
Normandy's apple-belt, or the lightwaves of the South
Collapsing on beaches. None could deny me
The springtime glitter of shad in the rivermouth

Of the long Garonne – that exquisite flesh,
   The bone that sticks in the throats
Of twenty centuries. Ichthyus the fish,
Like Renan's Christ, was dying, dying out
In the boredom of villages, of Proustian spires,
Provincial time, the echo-sounding fleets

Off La Rochelle, the sleep of the Loire,
The happiness that is almost too complete,
The Sunday afternoons that run on Michelin tyres.

Was that terrible? Tell me, was that sad?
 The night of the gods,
Of absences, abscondings, abdications?
Was I to kneel before him, the tramp at the station,
Unpeel his stinking trainers, wash his feet,
Amaze the wage-slaves? In the name of what
Would I drive the midnight circle of philosophers
Out of their TV studios, swivel chairs,
With hempen fire, the rope of castigation?

No. Instead I would sit here, I would wait –
 A dinner, a *café crème*,
A chaser of grog. Whatever else, there was time –
Let Judgement take care of itself. To celebrate –
That was the one imperative. Randomness, flux,
Drew themselves about me as I ate,
Protected by the nearnesses of women, their sex
Blown sheer through summer dresses, loving my food,
My freedom, as they say a man should.

HARRY CLIFTON

A Confession

My Lord, I loved strawberry jam
And the dark sweetness of a woman's body.
Also, well-chilled vodka, herring in olive oil,
Scents, of cinnamon, of cloves.
So what kind of prophet am I? Why should the spirit
Have visited such a man? Many others
Were justly called, and trustworthy.
Who would have trusted me? For they saw
How I empty glasses, throw myself on food,
And glance greedily at the waitress's neck.
Flawed and aware of it. Desiring greatness,
Able to recognise greatness wherever it is,

And yet not quite, only in part, clairvoyant,
I know what was left for smaller men like me:
A feast of brief hopes, a rally of the proud.
A tournament of hunchbacks, literature.

CZESŁAW MIŁOSZ
translated by Czesław Miłosz & Robert Hass

Fruit
(for Czesław Miłosz)

How unattainable life is, it only reveals
its features in memory,
in nonexistence. How unattainable
afternoons, ripe, tumultuous, leaves
bursting with sap; swollen fruit, the rustling
silks of women who pass on the other
side of the street, and the shouts of boys
leaving school. Unattainable. The simplest
apple inscrutable, round.
The crowns of trees shake in warm
currents of air. Unattainably distant mountains.
Intangible rainbows. Huge cliffs of clouds
flowing slowly through the sky. The sumptuous,
unattainable afternoons. My life,
swirling, unattainable, free.

ADAM ZAGAJEWSKI
translated from the Polish by Renata Gorczynski,
Benjamin Ivy & C.K. Williams

A Note

Life is the only way
to get covered in leaves,
catch your breath on the sand,
rise on wings;

to be a dog,
or stroke its warm fur;

to tell pain
from everything it's not;

to squeeze inside events,
dawdle in views,
to seek the least of all possible mistakes.

An extraordinary chance
to remember for a moment
a conversation held
with the lamp switched off;

and if only once
to stumble upon a stone,
end up soaked in one downpour or another,

mislay your keys in the grass;
and to follow a spark on the wind with your eyes;

and to keep on not knowing
something important.

WISŁAWA SZYMBORSKA
translated from the Polish by Stanislav Barańczak & Clare Cavanagh

Callers

It is always a shock when they take off their caps,
Those neighbouring farmers who call at our house.
They have to, of course, to have something to roll
Or to press or to twist in their blunt, nervous hands;
But it makes them instantly vulnerable
With their soft bald spots or thinning forelocks.
They seem at once smaller, and much more vivid:
Leaping out of type to personality.

The smell of their beasts comes in with them,
Faint as the breath of growing things in summer,
Rich, as the days draw in, with cake and hay and dung.

They are ill at ease in the house:
One feels they would like to stamp and snort,
Looking sideways, but have been trained out of it –
As with leaving mucky boots beside the door.

Only small, swarthy men with the friendly smell on them;
Yet walls press close and the room seems cluttered.
I am glad to go and make obligatory tea
As their voices sway, slow with the seasons,
And, ponderously, come to the point.

CHRISTINE EVANS

Poet, Lover, Birdwatcher

To force the pace and never to be still
Is not the way of those who study birds
Or women. The best poets wait for words.
The hunt is not an exercise of will
But patient love relaxing on a hill
To note the movement of a timid wing;
Until the one who knows that she is loved
No longer waits but risks surrendering –
In this the poet finds his moral proved,
Who never spoke before his spirit moved.

The slow movement seems, somehow, to say much more.
To watch the rarer birds, you have to go
Along deserted lanes and where the rivers flow
In silence near the source, or by a shore
Remote and thorny like the heart's dark floor.
And there the women slowly turn around,
Not only flesh and bone but myths of light
With darkness at the core, and sense is found
By poets lost in crooked, restless flight,
The deaf can hear, the blind recover sight.

NISSIM EZEKIEL

Audides

How I loved you, slowness,
the soul's cautious winding through life
which is mountain, which is cloud, which is
dense smoke, shadowy bakery,
cattle going home to farms, dogs barking,
blackness of barns, lamp roaming
as it's swung in the hay under cobwebs:
the soul likewise radiant
being intimate with evening...
Morning signalled by the anvil, the wheel,
pigeons outside the shutters, the wisp of sadness
fading in the presence of hills summoned to my window
so that I can admire, can adore
this world lofted into the colour blue,
– O landscape, you weren't so sure,
O memory, jilted city,
what I breathe is no longer the wind that brought you
the scent of evening, morning's freshness,
and breezes that swirl down powdery lanes,
rolling the feel of forests, enlivening
all that drowsed in my afternoon,
O city who never shut yourself off from the tide
of seasons, who drank long draughts of home,
now a dead city where my poem is alone
with the star and the ungraspable spirit
that hurls its fires, transfixing
the soul forever drunk with life.

HENRI THOMAS
translated from the French by Jennie Feldman & Stephen Romer

Keeping quiet

Now we will count to twelve
and we will all keep still.

For once on the face of the earth
let's not speak in any language,
let's stop for one second,
and not move our arms so much.

It would be an exotic moment
without rush, without engines,
we would all be together
in a sudden strangeness.

Fisherman in the cold sea
would not harm whales
and the man gathering salt
would look at his hurt hands.

Those who prepare green wars,
wars with gas, wars with fire,
victory with no survivors,
would put on clean clothes
and walk about with their brothers
in the shade, doing nothing.

What I want should not be confused
with total inactivity.
Life is what it is about;
I want no truck with death.

If we were not so single-minded
about keeping our lives moving,
and for once could do nothing,
perhaps a huge silence
might interrupt this sadness
of never understanding ourselves
and of threatening ourselves with death.
Perhaps the earth can teach us
as when everything seems dead
and later proves to be alive.

Now I'll count up to twelve
and you keep quiet and I will go.

PABLO NERUDA
translated from the Spanish by Alastair Reid

Quietness

Inside this new love, die.
Your way begins on the other side.
Become the sky.
Take an axe to the prison wall.
Escape.
Walk out like somebody suddenly born into colour.
Do it now.
You're covered with thick cloud.
Slide out the side. Die,
and be quiet. Quietness is the surest sign
that you've died.
Your old life was a frantic running
from silence.

The speechless full moon
comes out now.

RUMI
translated from the Persian by Coleman Barks with John Moyne

Apple Tree in Blossom

See: its stars are not pinned
to unreachable boughs,
the burn of the absolute blue

but float, whisper-close, in wild
aromas. I breathe and see
the universe through its heaven

and the blossom makes a bride of me,
snows on my skin. Marries
me to the world again

the fragrant and the green,
the longed-for return
as grain by crushed grain

the heart's harvest of pain
crumbles. Sourbread
dissolving in blossom, light's kiss.

LYNNE WYCHERLEY

The Oven Bird

There is a singer everyone has heard,
Loud, a mid-summer and a mid-wood bird,
Who makes the solid tree trunks sound again.
He says that leaves are old and that for flowers
Mid-summer is to spring as one to ten.
He says the early petal-fall is past,
When pear and cherry bloom went down in showers
On sunny days a moment overcast;
And comes that other fall we name the fall.
He says the highway dust is over all.
The bird would cease and be as other birds
But that he knows in singing not to sing.
The question that he frames in all but words
Is what to make of a diminished thing.

ROBERT FROST

Flowers
(for Winifred Nicholson)

Flowers,
a dozen or more,
I picked one summer afternoon
from field and hedgerow.
Resting against a wall
I held them up
to hide the sun.
Cell by cell,
exact as dance,

I saw the colour,
structure, purpose
of each flower.
I named them with their secret names.
They flamed in air.

    But, waking
I remember only two
– soapwort and figwort,
the lilac and the brown.
The rest I guess at
but cannot see
– only myself,
almost a ghost upon the road,
without accoutrement,
holding the flowers
as torch and talisman
against the coming dark.

FRANCES HOROVITZ

The Life Around Us
(for David Mitchell and David Hass)

Poplar and oak awake
all night. And through
all weathers of the days of the year.
There is a consciousness
undefined.
Yesterday's twilight, August
almost over, lasted, slowly changing,
until daybreak. Human sounds
were shut behind curtains.
No human saw the night in this garden,
sliding blue into morning.
Only the sightless trees,
without braincells, lived it
and wholly knew it.

DENISE LEVERTOV

Burning the Bracken

When summer stopped, and the last
Lit cloud blazed tawny cumulus
Above the hills, it was the bracken

Answered; its still crests
Contained an autumn's burning.
Then, on an afternoon of promised

Cold, true flames ripped
The ferns. Hurrying fire, low
And pale in the sun, ran

Glittering through them. As
Night fell, the brindle
Flambeaux, full of chattering

We were too far to hear, leapt
To the children's singing.
'Fire on the mountain,' we

Chanted, who went to bed warmed
By joy. But I would know that fires
Die, that the cold sky holds

Uneasily the fronds and floating
Twigs of broken soot, letting
Them fall, fall now, soft

As darkness on this white page.

LESLIE NORRIS

'The trees are bare...'

The trees are bare.
Autumn
leads its fog-horses to the river.

Dogs bark far away, far away.
A small carriage comes from a narrow gate,
alone, driverless, and disappears.

They say ghosts ride like that,
if the heart sleeps under a holly tree.
But ghosts are just memories.

Night comes early.
Soon it'll be winter
deep and cold, like a well.

EEVA-LIISA MANNER
translated from the Swedish by Emily Jeremiah

Song at the Beginning of Autumn

Now watch this autumn that arrives
In smells. All looks like summer still;
Colours are quite unchanged, the air
On green and white serenely thrives.
Heavy the trees with growth and full
The fields. Flowers flourish everywhere.

Proust who collected time within
A child's cake would understand
The ambiguity of this –
Summer still raging while a thin
Column of smoke stirs from the land
Proving that autumn gropes for us.

But every season is a kind
Of rich nostalgia. We give names –
Autumn and summer, winter, spring –
As though to unfasten from the mind
Our moods and give them outward forms.
We want the certain, solid thing.

But I am carried back against
My will into a childhood where
Autumn is bonfires, marble, smoke;
I lean against my window fenced
From evocations in the air.
When I said autumn, autumn broke.

ELIZABETH JENNINGS

The Snakes of September

All summer I heard them
rustling in the shrubbery,
outracing me from tier
to tier in my garden,
a whisper among the viburnums,
a signal flashed from the hedgerow,
a shadow pulsing
in the barberry thicket.
Now that the nights are chill
and the annuals spent,
I should have thought them gone,
in a torpor of blood
slipped to the nether world
before the sickle frost.
Not so. In the deceptive balm
of noon, as if defiant of the curse
that spoiled another garden,
these two appear on show
through a narrow slit
in the dense green brocade

of a north-country spruce,
dangling head-down, entwined
in a brazen love-knot.
I put out my hand and stroke
the fine, dry grit of their skins.
After all,
we are partners in this land,
co-signers of a covenant,
At my touch the wild
braid of creation
trembles.

STANLEY KUNITZ

September Evening: Deer at Big Basin

When they talk about angels in books
I think what they mean is this sudden
arrival: this gift of an alien country
we guessed all along,

and how these deer are moving in the dark,
bound to the silence, finding our scent in their way
and making us strange, making us all that we are
in the fall of the light,

as if we had entered the myth
of one who is risen, and one who is left behind
in the gap that remains,

a story that gives us the questions we wanted to ask,
and a sense of our presence as creatures,
about to be touched.

JOHN BURNSIDE

The Wild Swans at Coole

The trees are in their autumn beauty,
The woodland paths are dry,
Under the October twilight the water
Mirrors a still sky;
Upon the brimming water among the stones
Are nine-and-fifty swans.

The nineteenth autumn has come upon me
Since I first made my count;
I saw, before I had well finished,
All suddenly mount
And scatter wheeling in great broken rings
Upon their clamorous wings.

I have looked upon those brilliant creatures,
And now my heart is sore.
All's changed since I, hearing at twilight,
The first time on this shore,
The bell-beat of their wings above my head,
Trod with a lighter tread.

Unwearied still, lover by lover,
They paddle in the cold
Companionable streams or climb the air;
Their hearts have not grown old;
Passion or conquest, wander where they will,
Attend upon them still.

But now they drift on the still water,
Mysterious, beautiful;
Among what rushes will they build,
By what lake's edge or pool
Delight men's eyes when I awake some day
To find they have flown away?

W.B. YEATS

Autumn

I walk outside the stone wall
Looking into the park at night
As armed trees frisk a windfall
Down paths that lampposts light

SAMUEL MENASHE

Nothing Gold Can Stay

Nature's first green is gold,
Her hardest hue to hold.
Her early leaf's a flower;
But only so an hour.
Then leaf subsides to leaf,
So Eden sank to grief,
So dawn goes down to day
Nothing gold can stay.

ROBERT FROST

Blue Grapes

Eating blue grapes
          near the window
     and looking out
          at the snow-covered valley.
For a moment, the deep world
          gazing back. Then a blue jay
     scatters snow from a bough.
No world, no meeting. Only
          tremors, sweetness
                    on the tongue.

TESS GALLAGHER

A Few Facts

The chiming clock. The girl at her desk sneezing,
The hiss of traffic after rain has sleeked the street.
The chime sounding off the silent library air.
Outside, a kind of monumental after-icy-rain
relenting, something loosening and the ground
going soft, glistening, the water on it taking in
the world, the broad sycamore drawing water
up its roots, the huge trunk sopping it. In the room
the vase of Cremone daisies: yellow, white
and flaming orange. Shoes and books, a lit figure
bent to her work, lifting her shoulders slowly
up and looking out, letting a breath go. Smiling
when the child comes in with a question. Outside,
the spreading yellow maple shedding branches. A cairn
of bulky logs. Birds from dawn to dusk at the feeder:
black flashings across the blank window. The cats
dazzled, feeling the old hunger. Now the child
is posing, an arabesque, by the stove; now she's
wrapped in a rug, reading; now she's sitting up
in bed, a duchess, asking for her cardigan, grinning
at the laden tray – its porridge, milk, tea, striped napkin
in its ring – at light seeping through blue curtains.

EAMON GRENNAN

Trio

Coming up Buchanan Street, quickly, on a sharp winter evening
a young man and two girls, under the Christmas lights –
The young man carries a new guitar in his arms,
the girl on the inside carries a very young baby,
and the girl on the outside carries a chihuahua.
And the three of them are laughing, their breath rises
in a cloud of happiness, and as they pass
the boy says, 'Wait till he sees this but!'

The chihuahua has a tiny Royal Stewart tartan coat like a teapot-holder,
the baby in its white shawl is all bright eyes and mouth like favours
     in a fresh sweet cake,
the guitar swells out under its milky plastic cover, tied at the neck
     with silver tinsel tape and a brisk sprig of mistletoe.
Orphean sprig! Melting baby! Warm chihuahua!
The vale of tears is powerless before you.
Whether Christ is born, or is not born, you
put paid to fate, it abdicates
                under the Christmas lights.
Monsters of the year
go blank, are scattered back,
can't bear this march of three.

– And the three have passed, vanished in the crowd
(yet not vanished, for in their arms they wind
the life of men and beasts, and music,
laughter ringing them round like a guard)
at the end of this winter's day.

EDWIN MORGAN

Canticle

Sometimes when you walk down to the red gate
hearing the scrape-music of your shoes across gravel,
a yellow moon will lift over the hill;
you swing the gate shut and lean on the topmost bar
as if something has been accomplished in the world;
a night wind mistles through the poplar leaves
and all the noise of the universe stills
to an oboe hum, the given note of a perfect
music; there is a vast sky wholly dedicated
to the stars and you know, with certainty,
that all the dead are out, up there, in one
holiday flotilla, and that they celebrate
the fact of a red gate and a yellow moon
that tunes their instruments with you to the symphony.

JOHN F. DEANE

New Year's Poem

The Christmas twigs crispen and needles rattle
Along the window-ledge.
       A solitary pearl
Shed from the necklace spilled at last week's party
Lies in the suety, snow-luminous plainness
Of morning, on the window-ledge beside them.
And all the furniture that circled stately
And hospitable when these rooms were brimmed
With perfumes, furs, and black-and-silver
Crisscross of seasonal conversation, lapses
Into its previous largeness.
       I remember
Anne's rose-sweet gravity, and the stiff grave
Where cold so little can contain;
I mark the queer delightful skull and crossbones
Starlings and sparrows left, taking the crust,
And the long loop of winter wind
Smoothing its arc from dark Arcturus down
To the bricked corner of the drifted courtyard,
And the still window-ledge.
       Gentle and just pleasure
It is, being human, to have won from space
This unchill, habitable interior
Which mirrors quietly the light
Of the snow, and the new year.

MARGARET AVISON

February – not everywhere

Such days, when trees run downwind,
their arms stretched before them.

Such days, when the sun's in a drawer
and the drawer is locked.

When the meadow is dead, is a carpet
thin and shabby, with no pattern

and at bus stops people retract into collars
their faces like fists.

— And when, in a firelit room, a mother looks
at her four seasons, her little boy,

in the centre of everything, with still pools
of shadows and a fire throwing flowers.

NORMAN MacCAIG

April and Silence

Spring lies desolate.
The velvet-dark ditch
crawls by my side
without reflections.

The only thing that shines
is yellow flowers.

I am carried in my shadow
like a violin
in its black case.

The only thing I want to say
glitters out of reach
like the silver
in a pawnbroker's.

TOMAS TRANSTRÖMER
translated from the Swedish by Robin Fulton

Seed

The first warm day of spring
and I step out into the garden from the gloom
of a house where hope had died
to tally the storm damage, to seek what may
have survived. And finding some forgotten
lupins I'd sown from seed last autumn
holding in their fingers a raindrop each
like a peace offering, or a promise,
I am suddenly grateful and would
offer a prayer if I believed in God.
But not believing, I bless the power of seed,
its casual, useful persistence,
and bless the power of sun,
its conspiracy with the underground,
and thank my stars the winter's ended.

PAULA MEEHAN

This Morning

I watched the sun moving round the kitchen,
an early spring sun that strengthened and weakened,
coming and going like an old mind.

I watched like one bedridden for a long time
on their first journey back into the world
who finds it enough to be going on with:

the way the sunlight brought each possession in turn
to its attention and made of it a small still life:

the iron frying-pan gleaming on its hook like an ancient find,
the powdery green cheek of a bruised clementine.

Though more beautiful still was how the light moved on,
letting go each chair and coffee cup without regret

the way my grandmother, in her final year, received me:
neither surprised by my presence, nor distressed by my leaving,
content, though, while I was there.

ESTHER MORGAN

Matins

The sun shines; by the mailbox, leaves
of the divided birch tree folded, pleated like fins.
Underneath, hollow stems of the white daffodils,
        Ice Wings, Cantatrice; dark
leaves of the wild violet. Noah says
depressives hate the spring, imbalance
between the inner and outer world. I make
another case – being depressed, yes, but in a sense passionately
attached to the living tree, my body
actually curled in the split trunk, almost at peace,
        in the evening rain
almost able to feel
sap frothing and rising: Noah says this is
an error of depressives, identifying
with a tree, whereas the happy heart
wanders the garden like a falling leaf, a figure for
the part, not the whole.

LOUISE GLÜCK

What It Is

It is in the smallest leaf – of oak, maple, elm, dogwood, birch
or Chinese redwood. In the way leaves droop in the air
of this rain-laundered time of day, each involuntary drip
a pearl-drop earring. Shadows of barn gable and pin-oak tree
live in print on the avocado green of grass. What it is

is that *Amen* stuck in Macbeth's throat, or the road one
wheatear didn't take, or the child you didn't have the right
time or space to have, all its dark-eyed answers – eyes
glittering behind each twig of the persimmon, fleshlights
igniting every fruitglobe. What it is is ripening, so

inhale the immaculate late afternoon as you pass
through the garden: fruit, dust, moist fungus, a fine distillate
of finality you keep breathing, being in your own way
a part of it, wanting its laden air to leaven your lungs,
letting the heart be a small box of beaten gold that holds

secrets and hopeless promises. It is rife with promise.

EAMON GRENNAN

May
(for Marian)

The blessèd stretch and ease of it –
heart's ease. The hills blue. All the flowering weeds
bursting open. Balm in the air. The birdsong
bouncing back out of the sky. The cattle
lain down in the meadow, forgetting to feed.
The horses swishing their tails.
The yellow flare of furze on the near hill.
And the first cream splatters of blossom
high on the thorns where the day rests longest.

All hardship, hunger, treachery of winter
forgotten.
This unfounded conviction: forgiveness, hope.

KERRY HARDIE

The Old Neighbors

The weather's turned, and the old neighbors creep out
from their crammed rooms to blink in the sun, as if
surprised to find they've lived through another winter.
Though steam heat's left them pale and shrunken
like old root vegetables,
Mr and Mrs Tozzi are already
hard at work on their front-yard mini-Sicily:
a Virgin Mary birdbath, a thicket of roses,
and the only outdoor aloes in Manhattan.
It's the old immigrant story,
the beautiful babies
grown up into foreigners. Nothing's
turned out the way they planned
as sweethearts in the sinks of Palermo. Still,
each waves a dirt-caked hand
in geriatric fellowship with Stanley,
the former tattoo king of the Merchant Marine,
turning the corner with his shaggy collie,
who's hardly three but trots
arthritically in sympathy. It's only
the young who ask if life's worth living,
not Mrs Sansanowitz, who for the last hour
has been inching her way down the sidewalk,
lifting and placing
her new aluminum walker as carefully
as a spider testing its web. On days like these,
I stand for a long time
under the wild gnarled root of the ancient wisteria,
dry twigs that in a week
will manage a feeble shower of purple blossom,
and I believe it: this is all there is,
all history's brought us here to our only life
to find, if anywhere,
our hanging gardens and our street of gold:
cracked stoops, geraniums, fire escapes, these old
stragglers basking in their bit of sun.

KATHA POLLITT

Midsummer, Tobago

Broad sun-stoned beaches.

White heat.
A green river.

A bridge,
scorched yellow palms

from the summer-sleeping house
drowsing through August.

Days I have held,
days I have lost,

days that outgrow, like daughters,
my harbouring arms.

DEREK WALCOTT

So many summers

Beside one loch, a hind's neat skeleton,
Beside another, a boat pulled high and dry:
Two neat geometries drawn in the weather:
Two things already dead and still to die.

I passed them every summer, rod in hand,
Skirting the bright blue or the spitting gray,
And, every summer, saw how the bleached timbers
Gaped wider and the neat ribs fell away.

Time adds one malice to another one —
Now you'd look very close before you knew
If it's the boat that ran, the hind went sailing.
So many summers, and I have lived them too.

NORMAN MacCAIG

Amaryllis

(after Rilke)

You've seen a cat consume a hummingbird,
scoop its beating body from the pyracantha bush
and break its wings with tufted paws
before marshaling it, whole, into its bone-tough throat;
seen a boy, heart racing with cocaine, climb
from a car window in a tumble on the ground,
his search for pleasure ending in skinned palms;
heard a woman's shouts as she is pushed into the police cruiser,
large hand pressing her head into the door,
red lights spinning their tornado in the street.

But of all that will fade; on the table is the amaryllis,
pushing its monstrous body in the air,
requiring no soil to do so, having wound
two seasons' rot into a white and papered bulb,
exacting nutrition from the winter light,
culling from complex chemistry the tints
and fragments that tissue and pause and build
again the pigment and filament.
The flower crescendos toward the light,
though better to say despite it,
gores through gorse and pebble
to form a throat – so breakable – open
with its tender pistils, damp with rosin,
simple in its simple sex, to burn and siphon
itself in air. Tongue of fire, tongue
of earth, the amaryllis is a rudiment
forming its meretricious petals
to trumpet and exclaim.

How you admire it. It vibrates
in the draft, a complex wheel
bitten with cogs, swelling and sexual
though nothing will touch it. You forced it
to spread itself, to cleave and grasp,
remorseless, open to your assignments –
this is availability, this is tenderness,
this red plane is given to the world.

Sometimes the heart breaks. Sometimes
it is not held hostage. The red world
where cells prepare for the unexpected
splays open at the window's ledge.
Be not human you inhuman thing.
No anxious, no foible, no hesitating hand.
Pry with fiber your course through sand.
Point your whole body toward the unknown,
away from the dead.
Be water and light and land –
no contrivance, no gasp, no dream
where there is no head.

MARK WUNDERLICH

Screened Porch

The stars were foolish, they were not worth waiting for.
The moon was shrouded, fragmentary.
Twilight like silt covered the hills.
The great drama of human life was nowhere evident –
but for that, you don't go to nature.

The terrible harrowing story of a human life,
the wild triumph of love: they don't belong
to the summer night, panorama of hills and stars.

We sat on our terraces, our screened porches,
as though we expected to gather, even now,
fresh information or sympathy. The stars
glittered a bit above the landscape, the hills
suffused still with a faint retroactive light.
Darkness. Luminous earth. We stared out, starved for knowledge,
and we felt, in its place, a substitute:
indifference that appeared benign.

Solace of the natural world. Panorama
of the eternal. The stars
were foolish, but somehow soothing. The moon
presented itself as a curved line.

And we continued to project onto the glowing hills
qualities we needed: fortitude, the potential
for spiritual advancement.

Immunity to time, to change. Sensation
of perfect safety, the sense of being
protected from what we loved –

And our intense need was absorbed by the night
and returned as sustenance.

LOUISE GLÜCK

Landscape

Love the land!
Feel the earth-pulse beating
In the earth-shaking Caribbean;
Worship the root-gods swelling
Mighty Silk-Cotton, poui and ginger lily
And the hibiscus trailing our destiny.
The mountain-scape swims sweetly
In the soothing river-light;
Sun panting on tree-top spotlights the caterpillar
Eating a star-apple inside out.
Caress the blue-scape, eyes peeling wide open
The bat suckling a bursting sapodilla.
When the moon is full, the crabs come out to play.
The breadfruit gives birth, bursting into rosy cheeks,
And the murmur from surrounding hills,
Hails the newborn trumpeter;
The sweet voiced bees honey the blossoms
On the shading immortelle
With an enchanting rhythm.

Love the land!
Come back to the ancient castle covered with stars,
Garlanded by birds and threaded in red wood;
The swaying cedar signals all with the melodic bamboo
Calling! calling!

When all the grasses have sprouted
And a spray of sandflies ride the leaves
And ponder the next biting session,
Listen to the night-worm gnawing the cane-root!
Listen to the golden grasshopper chirping
In the magic garden!
Listen to the cricket! Singing in the forest
Where the souls of the ancients chant through dove-calls.

Listen to the soil as it charms its children!
Return to the land!
Reclaim the children!

FAUSTIN CHARLES

'Every dying man...'

Every dying man
is a child:
in trenches, in bed, on a throne, at a loom,
we are tiny and helpless
when black velvet bows our eyes
and the letters slide from the pages.
Earth lets nobody loose: it all
has to be given back – breath, eyes, memory.
We are children when the earth
turns with us through the night towards morning
where there are no voices, no ears, no light, no door,
only darkness and movement
in the soil and its thousands
of mouths, chins, jaws, and limbs
dividing everything so that
no names and no thoughts remain
in the one who is silent lying in the dark
on his right side, head upon knees.
Beside him, his spear, his knife
and his bracelet, and a broken pot.

JAAN KAPLINSKI
translated from the Estonian by Jaan Kaplinski with Sam Hamill

5

Fight to the death

What is born will die,
What has been gathered will be dispersed,
What has been accumulated will be exhausted,
What has been built up will collapse
And what has been high will be brought low.

TRADITIONAL BUDDHIST SCRIPTURE

'FIGHT TO THE DEATH' is a sequence beginning with poems on depression, illness and suicide, followed by poems on death and grief. In many of these the dead are still present in our lives, not just in spirit but 'holding our hands', continuing conversations with those who love them. Ted Hughes continued to write to Sylvia Plath for many years after her suicide in the poems later published as *Birthday Letters* (1988) shortly before his own death: alternating poems by each writer are arranged here to show a dialogue (265-71).

Four authors are represented with groups of related poems. In three poems on the birth, short life and death of a beloved handicapped daughter (257-59), Catalan poet Joan Margarit reminds us that it is not death we have to understand but life. There are five poems (282-84) by Romania's Marin Sorescu from his last book *The Bridge* (1997), a whole collection written from his sickbed over five weeks as he waited for death to take him. He was composing poetry until the day before he died, aged 60, from liver cancer, dictating the final poems to his wife who read them back and made any corrections he wanted.

There are also selections from two books of elegies. The four poems from Christopher Reid's twelve-part elegy 'A Widower's Dozen' (294-97) are from *A Scattering* (2009), mourning the death of his late wife, actress Lucinda Gane. There are three poems (300-02) from Mary Jo Bang's book *Elegy* (2007), written – she has said – to escape from a 'state of exquisite suffering' after the death of her son Michael from an accidental overdose of prescription drugs: 'The other thing for me was this continuing conversation I'm having with my son. We were very close and the idea of not ever speaking to him again was unacceptable. And so this was a way to keep talking.'

This section adds to the selections of poems on sickness, loss, death and mortality in *Staying Alive* (3: 'Dead or alive', 117-30; 10: 'Disappearing acts', 369-412) and *Being Alive* (10: 'Ends and Beginnings', 443-82). I've also edited a separate anthology, *Do Not Go Gentle* (from Bloodaxe), which offers a selection of poems chosen specifically for reading at funerals and memorial services.

Having It Out with Melancholy

If many remedies are prescribed for an illness,
you may be certain that the illness has no cure.
                    A.P. CHEKHOV
                    The Cherry Orchard

1 *From the Nursery*

When I was born, you waited
behind a pile of linen in the nursery,
and when we were alone, you lay down
on top of me, pressing
the bile of desolation into every pore.
And from that day on
everything under the sun and moon
made me sad – even the yellow
wooden beads that slid and spun
along a spindle on my crib.

You taught me to exist without gratitude.
You ruined my manners toward God:
'We're here simply to wait for death;
the pleasures of earth are overrated.'

I only appeared to belong to my mother,
to live among blocks and cotton undershirts
with snaps; among red tin lunch boxes
and report cards in ugly brown slipcases.
I was already yours – the anti-urge,
the mutilator of souls.

2 *Bottles*

Elavil, Ludiomil, Doxepin,
Norpramin, Prozac, Lithium, Xanax,
Wellbutrin, Parnate, Nardil, Zoloft.
The coated ones smell sweet or have
no smell; the powdery ones smell
like the chemistry lab at school
that made me hold my breath.

246

3 Suggestion from a Friend

You wouldn't be so depressed
if you really believed in God.

4 Often

Often I go to bed as soon after dinner
as seems adult
(I mean I try to wait for dark)
in order to push away
from the massive pain in sleep's
frail wicker coracle.

5 Once There Was Light

Once, in my early thirties, I saw
that I was a speck of light in the great
river of light that undulates through time.

I was floating with the whole
human family. We were all colors – those
who are living now, those who have died,
those who are not yet born. For a few

moments I floated, completely calm,
and I no longer hated having to exist.

Like a crow who smells hot blood
you came flying to pull me out
of the glowing stream.
'I'll hold you up. I never let my dear
ones drown!' After that, I wept for days.

6 In and Out

The dog searches until he finds me
upstairs, lies down with a clatter
of elbows, puts his head on my foot.

Sometimes the sound of his breathing
saves my life – in and out, in
and out; a pause, a long sigh....

7 *Pardon*

A piece of burned meat
wears my clothes, speaks
in my voice, dispatches obligations
haltingly, or not at all.
It is tired of trying
to be stouthearted, tired
beyond measure.

We move on to the monoamine
oxidase inhibitors. Day and night
I feel as if I had drunk six cups
of coffee, but the pain stops
abruptly. With the wonder
and bitterness of someone pardoned
for a crime she did not commit
I come back to marriage and friends,
to pink-fringed hollyhocks; come back
to my desk, books, and chair.

8 *Credo*

Pharmaceutical wonders are at work
but I believe only in this moment
of well-being. Unholy ghost,
you are certain to come again.

Coarse, mean, you'll put your feet
on the coffee table, lean back,
and turn me into someone who can't
take the trouble to speak; someone
who can't sleep, or who does nothing
but sleep; can't read, or call
for an appointment for help.

There is nothing I can do
against your coming.
When I awake, I am still with thee.

9 *Wood Thrush*

High on Nardil and June light
I wake at four,

248

waiting greedily for the first
notes of the wood thrush. Easeful air
presses through the screen
with the wild, complex song
of the bird, and I am overcome

by ordinary contentment.
What hurt me so terribly
all my life until this moment?
How I love the small, swiftly
beating heart of the bird
singing in the great maples;
its bright, unequivocal eye.

JANE KENYON

Back

We try a new drug, a new combination
of drugs, and suddenly
I fall into my life again

like a vole picked up by a storm
then dropped three valleys
and two mountains away from home.

I can find my way back. I know
I will recognise the store
where I used to buy milk and gas.

I remember the house and barn,
the rake, the blue cups and plates,
the Russian novels I loved so much,

and the black silk nightgown
that he once thrust
into the toe of my Christmas stocking.

JANE KENYON

Nuptial Song

I got married
I got married to myself
I said yes
a yes that took years to arrive
years of unspeakable suffering
of crying with the rain
of shutting myself in my room
because I – the great love of my existence –
did not call myself
did not write to myself
did not visit myself
and at times
when I'd get the courage to call myself
to say 'hello, am I well?'
I wouldn't come to the phone

I even put myself
on a list of pains-in-the-neck
I didn't want to talk with
because they drove me nuts
because they wouldn't let me alone
because they backed me into corners
because I couldn't stand them

at the end I didn't even pretend
when I asked if I was there

I let myself know
tactfully
that I was fed up with myself

and one day I stopped calling myself
and stopped calling myself

and so much time
went by that I missed me
so I said
how long has it been since I called?
ages

it must be ages
and I called myself and I answered
and I couldn't believe it
because though it's hard to believe
I hadn't healed
I'd only been bleeding
then I said 'hello, it that me?'
It's me, I said, and added:
It's been a long time since we've heard
I from myself or myself from me

would I like to come over?

yes, I said

and we met again
in peace

and I felt good with myself
and myself as well
felt good with me
and so
day after day
I married and I married
and I am together
and not even Death can me part

SUSANA THÉNON
translated from the Spanish by Maria Negroni & Anne Twitty

Plumbing the Deepening Groove

That survival is impossible without repetition
of patterns is platitude – see moon rise or whorls in wolf fur –

but how explain the human need to reenact primal dramas,
even when the act perpetuates a cycle of abuse?

The boy who hides in the tool shed with buckle-shaped welts
rising like figs from his arms will curse his father,

and in turn beat his son. Like a wave anguish rises,
never understands itself before emptying in a fist.

The spurned daughter will seek out lovers who abandon her,
self-will degenerating in the face of what feels familiar.

Childhood, seen in light of recurrence, takes on the heft
of conspiracy, casts a shadow across an entire life,

making it appear that nothing could have happened
differently, that free and easy is the stuff of semblance.

Then of the prerogatives, reclamation is principal,
to appraise the past the way a painter subsumes old canvas

with new layers of paint, each brushstroke unconcerned,
sure, dismantling the contour of what once was realised

so that new forms can emerge to contradict the suggestion
that survival is impossible without repetition.

RAVI SHANKAR

Shrike Tree

Most days back then I would walk by the shrike tree,
a dead hawthorn at the base of a hill.
The shrike had pinned smaller birds on the tree's black thorns
and the sun had stripped them of their feathers.

Some of the dead ones hung at eye level
while some burned holes in the sky overhead.
At least it is honest,
the body apparent
and not rotting in the dirt.

And I, having never seen the shrike at work,
can only imagine how the breasts were driven into the branches.
When I saw him he'd be watching from a different tree
with his mask like Zorro
and the gray cape of his wings.

At first glance he could have been a mockingbird or a jay
if you didn't take note of how his beak was hooked.
If you didn't know the ruthlessness of what he did –
ah, but that is a human judgment.

They are mute, of course, a silence at the center of a bigger silence,
these rawhide ornaments, their bald skulls showing.
And notice how I've slipped into the present tense
as if they were still with me.

Of course they are still with me.

They hang there, desiccating
by the trail where I walked, back when I could walk,
before life pinned me on its thorn.
It is ferocious, life, but it must eat
then leaves us with the artifact.

Which is: these black silhouettes in the midday sun
strict and jagged, like an Asian script.
A tragedy that is not without its glamour.
Not without the runes of the wizened meat.

Because imagine the luck! – to be plucked from the air,
to be drenched and dried in the sun's bright voltage –
well, hard luck is luck, nonetheless.
With a chunk of sky in each eye socket.
And the pierced heart strung up like a pearl.

LUCIA PERILLO

Thinking About Bill, Dead of AIDS

We did not know the first thing about
how blood surrenders to even the smallest threat
when old allergies turn inside out,

the body rescinding all its normal orders
to all defenders of flesh, betraying the head,
pulling its guards back from all its borders.

Thinking of friends afraid to shake your hand,
we think of your hand shaking, your mouth set,
your eyes drained of any reprimand.

Loving, we kissed you, partly to persuade
both you and us, seeing what eyes had said,
that we were loving and were not afraid.

If we had had more, we would have given more.
As it was we stood next to your bed,
stopping, though, to set our smiles at the door.

Not because we were less sure at the last.
Only because, not knowing anything yet,
we didn't know what look would hurt you least.

MILLER WILLIAMS

Faith
(FROM *Atlantis*)

       'I've been having these
awful dreams, each a little different,
though the core's the same –

we're walking in a field,
Wally and Arden and I, a stretch of grass
with a highway running beside it,

or a path in the woods that opens
onto a road. Everything's fine,
then the dog sprints ahead of us,

excited; we're calling but
he's racing down a scent and doesn't hear us,
and that's when he goes

onto the highway. I don't want to describe it.
Sometimes it's brutal and over,
and others he's struck and takes off

so we don't know where he is
or how bad. This wakes me
every night now, and I stay awake;

I'm afraid if I sleep I'll go back
into the dream. It's been six months,
almost exactly, since the doctor wrote

not even a real word
but an acronym, a vacant
four-letter cipher

that draws meanings into itself,
reconstitutes the world.
We tried to say it was just

a word; we tried to admit
it had power and thus to nullify it
by means of our acknowledgement.

I know the current wisdom:
bright hope, the power of wishing you're well.
He's just so tired, though nothing

shows in any tests, Nothing,
the doctor says, detectable;
the doctor doesn't hear what I do,

that trickling, steadily rising nothing
that makes him sleep all day,
vanish into fever's tranced afternoons,

and I swear sometimes
when I put my head to his chest
I can hear the virus humming

like a refrigerator.
Which is what makes me think
you can take your positive attitude

and go straight to hell.
We don't have a future,
we have a dog.
                    Who is he?

Soul without speech,
sheer, tireless faith,
he is that-which-goes-forward,

black muzzle, black paws
scouting what's ahead;
he is where we'll be hit first,

he's the part of us
that's going to get it.
I'm hardly awake on our morning walk

– always just me and Arden now –
and sometimes I am still
in the thrall of the dream,

which is why, when he took a step onto Commercial
before I'd looked both ways,
I screamed his name and grabbed his collar.

And there I was on my knees,
both arms around his neck
and nothing coming,

and when I looked into that bewildered face
I realised I didn't know what it was
I was shouting at,

I didn't know who I was trying to protect.'

MARK DOTY

Dark Night in Balmes Street

Threats and fears fulfilled –
all streets lead to old age –
I go past the clinic where you were born,
twenty-six years ago now, on a dark night
wounded by the light of a corridor.
Here you came, small and defenceless,
to the gentle beach of your smile,
to the difficulties with speech,
to the schools that did not want you,
to the bones' weariness, to the cruel
and obvious calm of the corridors
watched over by silent white coats
with the cold murmur of angels.
Twisted thumbs, a nose like a bird's beak,
the lines in your hand confused:
our own features and those too of the syndrome,
as though you had had another, unknown
mother hidden in the garden.
A far cry from intelligence, from beauty;
now only goodness matters,
the rest are questions of an inhospitable world
from which it is hard to hide ourselves
in rare flights of happiness.

I go back to that dark garden that I was gazing at
from the coffee-machine,
sole companion of those early mornings.
I go back to the blame and the remorse,
old fields of rubble I am still crossing:
my hands refused
to do what I wanted. How I respect
the wisdom of my hands,
that turned against me
and dragged me by my neck towards old age,
forcing me to look at the morning
on which, facing me squarely,
your tenderness just saved you.
Old misunderstanding of what happiness is,
and the world around me, neither friend nor foe:

I gaze at the crowds in the streets,
the building-works, the offices, enquiring
into tears that are lost.

You are the flower, we the branches,
and the gust of wind, stripping your petals,
left us naked, shaking with grief.
I still protect you and passing so close
to the garden, so dark, that summer,
I lean out and see once more that feeble
light from the coffee-machine.
Twenty-six years. And I know that I am happy
and that I've had the life I deserve.
Never could I be something
different from her, chance and fire.
A chance for life, fire
for death, for not even having a tomb.

The eyes in the rear-view mirror

We have both grown accustomed, Joana,
for this slowness,
when you lean on your crutches, and climb out of the car,
to start off a sally of car-horns and their abstract abuse.
Your company makes me happy,
and the smile of a body so far
from what was always called beauty,
that tedious beauty, so far-off.
I have exchanged it for the seductiveness
of tenderness that lights up the gap
that reason left in your face.
And, if I look at myself in the rear-view mirror,
I see a pair of eyes I do not easily recognise,
for in them there shines the love left
by looks, and light, the shadow
of everything I have seen,
and the peace your slowness reflects back to me.
So great is their wealth
that the eyes in the rear-view mirror don't seem to be mine.

Young partridge

It was crouching in a furrow, and when I picked it up,
it felt as though your hand was in mine.
There were patches of dried blood on one wing:
the tiny bones, like ribs,
were shattered by buckshot.
It tried to fly but, trailing the wing,
could scarcely drag itself along the ground
before hiding beneath a stone.
I still feel that warmth in my hand,
because a fragile creature gave meaning
to each of my days. A fragile creature
likewise now beneath a stone.

JOAN MARGARIT
three poems translated from the Catalan by Anna Crowe

Kevin

I don't know where the dead go, Kevin.
The one far place I know
is inside the heavy radio. If I listen late at night,
there's that dark, celestial glow,
heaviness of the cave, the hive.

Music. Someone warms his hands at the fire,
breaking off the arms of chairs,
breaking the brute bodies of beds, burning his comfort
surely to keep alive. Soon he can hardly see,
and so, quietly, he listens: then someone lifts him
and it's some terrible breakfast show.

There are mothers and fathers, Kevin, whom we barely know.
They lift us. Eventually we all shall go
into the dark furniture of the radio.

BILL MANHIRE

What the Doctor Said

He said it doesn't look good
he said it looks bad in fact real bad
he said I counted thirty-two of them on one lung before
I quit counting them
I said I'm glad I wouldn't want to know
about any more being there than that
he said are you a religious man do you kneel down
in forest groves and let yourself ask for help
when you come to a waterfall
mist blowing against your face and arms
do you stop and ask for understanding at those moments
I said not yet but I intend to start today
he said I'm real sorry he said
I wish I had some other kind of news to give you
I said Amen and he said something else
I didn't catch and not knowing what else to do
and not wanting him to have to repeat it
and me to have to fully digest it
I just looked at him
for a minute and he looked back it was then
I jumped up and shook hands with this man who'd just given me
something no one else on earth had ever given me
I may have even thanked him habit being so strong

RAYMOND CARVER

Death Who

The conversation with cancer
begins equitably enough.
You and he are summing each other up,
trading ripostes and *bons mots*
before the soup.
Everything seems ordinary.
There is interest and boredom,
and you've been drinking all afternoon
which could mean that you're depressed

or that you're in good form.
You get each other's measure
and the conversation settles,
subjects divide and increase like cells.
Gradually you realise
that like the background Mozart
all the emotions are involved,
and that you're no longer saying as much.
Put it down to strength of intent.
He's getting aggressive
and you're getting tired. Someone
says he's a conversational bully
but you're fascinated.
He tells you things about yourself,
forgotten things and those not yet found out,
pieces from childhood and the unhealing wound.
It's all there.
Forgetting food, you drink (too much
red wine will encourage nightmares
but that's not a problem now), you marvel.
Isn't he tireless!
A raconteur like something out of Proust.
He blows his cigar smoke into your face
and makes a little joke.
It's actually too much.
You're tired and the more you tire
the more the words are everywhere.
You go and recline on the couch,
but he won't shut up. He follows you there
and makes the cushion uncomfortable for you.
It's so unjust.
Your host is in the kitchen,
all guests have gone
and cancer's got you like conviction
and he's kneeling on your chest,
glaring over you,
pushing a cushion into your face,
talking quietly and automatically,
the words not clear.
He's got you and he's really pushing,
pushing you to death.

PHILIP HODGINS

Tomorrow They Will Carve Me

Death came and stood by me.
I said: I am ready.
I am lying in the surgery clinic in Kraków.
Tomorrow
they will carve me.

There is much strength in me. I can live,
can run, dance, and sing.
All that is in me, but if necessary
I will go.

Today
I make account of my life.
I was a sinner,
I was beating my head against earth,
I implored from the earth and the sky
forgiveness.

I was pretty and ugly,
wise and stupid,
very happy and very unhappy
often I had wings
and would float in air.

I trod a thousand paths in the sun and in snow,
I danced with my friend under the stars.
I saw love
in many human eyes.
I ate with delight
my slice of happiness.

Now I am lying in the surgery clinic in Kraków.
It stands by me.
Tomorrow
they will carve me.
Through the window the trees of May, beautiful like life,
and in me, humility, fear, and peace.

ANNA SWIR
translated by Czesław Miłosz & Leonard Nathan

Procedure

This tea, this cup of tea, made of leaves,
made of the leaves of herbs and absolute

almond blossom, this tea, is the interpreter
of almond, liquid touchstone which lets us
scent its true taste at last and with a bump,

in my case, takes me back to the yellow time
of trouble with blood tests, and cellular
madness, and my presence required

on the slab for surgery, and all that mess
I don't want to comb through here because
it seems, honestly, a trifle now that steam

and scent and strength and steep and infusion
say thank you thank you thank you for the then, and now

JO SHAPCOTT

Process

Just when you give up
the whole process
begins again

and you are as pure
as if you had confessed
and received absolution.

You have done nothing
to deserve it,
you have merely slept

and got up again,
feeling fine
because the morning is fine;

sufficient reason surely
for faith in a process
that can perform such miracles

without assistance from you.
Imagine what it would do
with a little assistance from you!

NISSIM EZEKIEL

The Suicides

It is hard for us to enter
the kind of despair they must have known
and because it is hard we must get in by breaking
the lock if necessary for we have not the key,
though for them there was no lock and the surrounding walls
were supple, receiving as waves, and they drowned
though not lovingly; it is we only
who must enter in this way.

Temptations will beset us, once we are in.
We may want to catalogue what they have stolen.
We may feel suspicion; we may even criticise the décor
of their suicidal despair, may perhaps feel
it was incongruously comfortable.

Knowing the temptations then
let us go in
deep to their despair and their skin and know
they died because words they had spoken
returned always homeless to them.

JANET FRAME

Fever 103°

Pure? What does it mean?
The tongues of hell
Are dull, dull as the triple

Tongues of dull, fat Cerberus
Who wheezes at the gate. Incapable
Of licking clean

The aguey tendon, the sin, the sin.
The tinder cries.
The indelible smell

Of a snuffed candle!
Love, love, the low smokes roll
From me like Isadora's scarves, I'm in a fright

One scarf will catch and anchor in the wheel.
Such yellow sullen smokes
Make their own element. They will not rise,

But trundle round the globe
Choking the aged and the meek,
The weak

Hothouse baby in its crib,
The ghastly orchid
Hanging its hanging garden in the air,

Devilish leopard!
Radiation turned it white
And killed it in an hour.

Greasing the bodies of adulterers
Like Hiroshima ash and eating in.
The sin. The sin.

Darling, all night
I have been flickering, off, on, off, on.
The sheets grow heavy as a lecher's kiss.

Three days. Three nights.
Lemon water, chicken
Water, water make me retch.

I am too pure for you or anyone.
Your body
Hurts me as the world hurts God. I am a lantern —

My head a moon
Of Japanese paper, my gold beaten skin
Infinitely delicate and infinitely expensive.

Does not my heat astound you. And my light.
All by myself I am a huge camellia
Glowing and coming and going, flush on flush.

I think I am going up,
I think I may rise —
The beads of hot metal fly, and I, love, I

Am a pure acetylene
Virgin
Attended by roses,

By kisses, by cherubim,
By whatever these pink things mean.
Not you, nor him

Not him, nor him
(My selves dissolving, old whore petticoats) —
To Paradise.

SYLVIA PLATH

Fever

You had a fever. You had a real ailment.
You had eaten a baddie.
You lay helpless and a little bit crazy

With the fever. You cried for America
And its medicine cupboard. You tossed
On the immovable Spanish galleon of a bed
In the shuttered Spanish house
That the sunstruck outside glare peered into
As into a tomb. 'Help me,' you whispered, 'help me.'

You rambled. You dreamed you were clambering
Into the well-hatch and, waking, you wanted
To clamber into the well-hatch – the all-clear
Short cut to the cool of the water,
The cool of the dark shaft, the best place
To find oblivion from your burning tangle
And the foreign bug. You cried for certain
You were going to die.
                I bustled about.
I was nursemaid. I fancied myself at that.
I liked the crisis of the vital role.
I felt things had become real. Suddenly mother,
As a familiar voice, woke in me.
She arrived with the certain knowledge. I made a huge soup.
Carrots, tomatoes, peppers and onions,
A rainbow stir of steaming elixir. You
Had to become a sluice, a conduit
Of pure vitamin C. I promised you,
This had saved Voltaire from the plague.
I had to saturate you and flush you
With this simmer of essences.
                   I spooned it
Into your helpless, baby-bird gape, gently,
Masterfully, patiently, hour by hour.
I wiped your tear-ruined face, your exhausted face,
All loose with woe and abandon.
I spooned more and you gulped it like life,
Sobbing 'I'm going to die.'
                As I paused
Between your mouthfuls, I stared at the readings
On your dials. Your cry jammed so hard
Over into the red of catastrophe
Left no space for worse. And I thought
How sick is she? Is she exaggerating?
And I recoiled, just a little,

Just for balance, just for symmetry,
Into sceptical patience, a little.
If it can be borne, why make so much of it?
'Come on, now,' I soothed. 'Don't be so scared.
It's only a bug, don't let it run away with you.'

What I was really saying was: 'Stop crying wolf.'
Other thoughts, chilly, familiar thoughts,
Came across the tightrope: 'Stop crying wolf,
Or else I shall not know, I shall not hear
When things get really bad.'
                                        It seemed easy
Watching such thoughts come up in such good time.
Plenty of time to think: 'She is crying
As if the most impossible of all
Horrible things had happened –
Had already happened, was going on
Still happening, with the whole world
Too late to help.' Then the blank thought
Of the anaesthesia that helps creatures
Under the polar ice, and the callous
That eases overwhelmed doctors. A twisting thought
Of the overload of dilemma, the white-out,
That brings baffled planarian worms to a standstill
Where they curl up and die.

You were overloaded. I said nothing.
I said nothing. The stone man made soup.
The burning woman drank it.

TED HUGHES

The Rabbit Catcher

It was a place of force —
The wind gagging my mouth with my own blown hair,
Tearing off my voice, and the sea
Blinding me with its lights, the lives of the dead
Unreeling in it, spreading like oil.

I tasted the malignity of the gorse,
Its black spikes,
The extreme unction of its yellow candle-flowers.
They had an efficiency, a great beauty,
And were extravagant, like torture.

There was only one place to get to.
Simmering, perfumed,
The paths narrowed into the hollow.
And the snares almost effaced themselves —
Zeroes, shutting on nothing,

Set close, like birth pangs.
The absence of shrieks
Made a hole in the hot day, a vacancy.
The glassy light was a clear wall,
The thickets quiet.

I felt a still busyness, an intent.
I felt hands round a tea mug, dull, blunt,
Ringing the white china.
How they awaited him, those little deaths!
They waited like sweethearts. They excited him.

And we, too, had a relationship —
Tight wires between us,
Pegs too deep to uproot, and a mind like a ring
Sliding shut on some quick thing,
The constriction killing me also.

SYLVIA PLATH

Life after Death

What can I tell you that you do not know
Of the life after death?

Your son's eyes, which had unsettled us
With your Slavic Asiatic

269

Epicanthic fold, but would become
So perfectly your eyes,
Became wet jewels,
The hardest substance of the purest pain
As I fed him in his high white chair.
Great hands of grief were wringing and wringing
His wet cloth of face. They wrung out his tears.
But his mouth betrayed you – it accepted
The spoon in my disembodied hand
That reached through from the life that had survived you.

Day by day his sister grew
Paler with the wound
She could not see or touch or feel, as I dressed it
Each day with her blue Breton jacket.

By night I lay awake in my body
The Hanged Man
My neck-nerve uprooted and the tendon
Which fastened the base of my skull
To my left shoulder
Torn from its shoulder-root and cramped into knots –
I fancied the pain could be explained
If I were hanging in the spirit
From a hook under my neck-muscle.
Dropped from life
We three made a deep silence
In our separate cots.

We were comforted by wolves.
Under that February moon and the moon of March
The Zoo had come close.
And in spite of the city
Wolves consoled us. Two or three times each night
For minutes on end
They sang. They had found where we lay.
And the dingos, and the Brazilian-maned wolves –
All lifted their voices together
With the grey Northern pack.

The wolves lifted us in their long voices.
They wound us and enmeshed us
In their wailing for you, their mourning for us,

270

They wove us into their voices. We lay in your death,
In the fallen snow, under falling snow.

As my body sank into the folk-tale
Where the wolves are singing in the forest
For two babes, who have turned, in their sleep,
Into orphans
Beside the corpse of their mother.

TED HUGHES

The Portrait

My mother never forgave my father
for killing himself,
especially at such an awkward time
and in a public park,
that spring
when I was waiting to be born.
She locked his name
in her deepest cabinet
and would not let him out,
though I could hear him thumping.
When I came down from the attic
with the pastel portrait in my hand
of a long-lipped stranger
with a brave moustache
and deep brown level eyes,
she ripped it into shreds
without a single word
and slapped me hard.
In my sixty-fourth year
I can feel my cheek
still burning.

STANLEY KUNITZ

Turn Your Eyes Away

The gendarme came
to tell me you had hung yourself
on the door of a rented room
like an overcoat
like a bathrobe
hung from a hook;
when they forced the door open
your feet pushed against the floor.
Inside your skull
there was no room for us,
your circuits forgot me.
Even in Paris where we never were
I wait for you
knowing you will not come.
I remember your eyes as if I were
someone you had never seen,
a slight frown between your brows
considering me.
How could I have guessed
the plain-spoken stranger in your face,
your body, tagged in a drawer,
attached to nothing, incurious.
My sister, my spouse, you said,
in a place on the other side of the earth
where we lay in a single bed
unable to pull apart
breathing into each other,
the Gideon Bible open to the Song of Songs,
the rush of the El-train
jarring the window.
As if needles were stuck
in the pleasure zones of our brains,
we repeated everything
over and over and over.

RUTH STONE

This Life

My friend tells me
a man in my house jumped off the roof
the roof is the eighth floor of this building
the roof door was locked   how did he manage?
his girlfriend had said   goodbye I'm leaving
he was 22
his mother and father were hurrying
at that very moment
from upstate to help him move out of Brooklyn
they had heard about the girl

the people who usually look up
and call   jump jump   did not see him
the life savers who creep around the back staircases
and reach the roof's edge just in time
never got their chance   he meant it   he wanted
only one person to know

did he imagine that she would grieve
all her young life away   tell everyone
this boy I kind of lived with last year
he died on account of me

my friend was not interested   he said   you're always
inventing stuff   what I want to know   how could he throw
his life away   how do these guys do it
just like that   and here I am fighting this
ferocious insane vindictive virus day and
night   day and night   and for what?   for only
one thing   this life   this life

GRACE PALEY

273

I Feel Drunk All the Time

Jesus it's beautiful!
Great mother of big apples it is a pretty
World!

You're a bastard Mr Death
And I wish you didn't have no look-in here.

I don't know how the rest of you feel,
But I feel drunk all the time

And I wish to hell we didn't have to die.

O you're a merry bastard Mr Death
And I wish you didn't have no hand in this game

Because it's too damn beautiful for anybody to die.

KENNETH PATCHEN

Heart Attack

Throwing his small, blond son
into the air, he begins to feel it,
a slow-motion quivering, some part
broken loose and throbbing with its own pulse,
like the cock's involuntary leaping
toward whatever shadow looms in front.

It is below his left shoulder blade,
a blip regular as radar, and he thinks of wings
and flight, his son's straight soar and fall
out of and into his high-held hands.
He is amused by the quick change
on the boy's little face: from the joy

of release and catch, to the near terror
at apex. It is the same with every throw.

And every throw comes without
his knowing. Nor his son's. Again
and again, the rise and fall, like breathing,
again the joy and fear, squeal and laughter,

until the world becomes a swarm of shapes
around him, and his arms
go leaden and prickled, and he knows
the sound is no longer laughter
but wheezing, knows he holds his son
in his arms and has not let him fly

upward for many long moments now.
He is on his knees, as his son stands,
supporting him, the look in the child's face
something the man has seen before:
not fear, not joy, not even misunderstanding,
but the quick knowledge sons

must come to, at some age
when everything else is put aside –
the knowledge of death, the stench
of mortality – that fraction of an instant
even a child can know, when
his father does not mean to leave, but goes.

ROBERT WRIGLEY

Defying Gravity

Gravity is one of the oldest tricks in the book.
Let go of the book and it abseils to the ground
As if, at the centre of the earth, spins a giant yo-yo
To which everything is attached by an invisible string.

Tear out a page of the book and make an aeroplane.
Launch it. For an instant it seems that you have fashioned
A shape that can outwit air, that has slipped the knot.
But no. The earth turns, the winch tightens, it is wound in.

One of my closest friends is, at the time of writing,
Attempting to defy gravity, and will surely succeed.
Eighteen months ago he was playing rugby,
Now, seven stones lighter, his wife carries him aw-

Kwardly from room to room. Arranges him gently
Upon the sofa for visitors. 'How are things?'
Asks one not wanting to know. Pause. 'Not too bad.'
(Open brackets. Condition inoperable. Close brackets.)

Soon now, the man that I love (not the armful of bones)
Will defy gravity. Freeing himself from the tackle
He will sidestep the opposition and streak down the wing
Towards a dimension as yet unimagined.

Back where the strings are attached there will be a service
And homage paid to the giant yo-yo. A box of leftovers
Will be lowered into a space on loan from the clay.
Then, weighted down, the living will walk wearily away.

ROGER McGOUGH

The Race

When I got to the airport I rushed up to the desk,
bought a ticket, ten minutes later
they told me the flight was cancelled, the doctors
had said my father would not live through the night
and the flight was cancelled. A young man
with a dark brown moustache told me
another airline had a nonstop
leaving in seven minutes. See that
elevator over there, well go
down to the first floor, make a right, you'll
see a yellow bus, get off at the
second Pan Am terminal, I
ran, I who have no sense of direction
raced exactly where he'd told me, a fish
slipping upstream deftly against

the flow of the river. I jumped off that bus with those
bags I had thrown everything into
in five minutes, and ran, the bags
wagged me from side to side as if
to prove I was under the claims of the material,
I ran up to a man with a flower on his breast,
I who always go to the end of the line, I said
Help me. He looked at my ticket, he said
Make a left and then a right, go up the moving stairs and then
run. I lumbered up the moving stairs,
at the top I saw the corridor,
and then I took a deep breath, I said
Goodbye to my body, goodbye to comfort,
I used my legs and heart as if I would
gladly use them up for this,
to touch him again in this life. I ran, and the
bags banged against me, wheeled and coursed
in skewed orbits, I have seen pictures of
women running, their belongings tied
in scarves grasped in their fists, I blessed my
long legs he gave me, my strong
heart I abandoned to its own purpose,
I ran to Gate 17 and they were
just lifting the thick white
lozenge of the door to fit it into
the socket of the plane. Like the one who is not
too rich, I turned sideways and
slipped through the needle's eye, and then
I walked down the aisle toward my father. The jet
was full, and people's hair was shining, they were
smiling, the interior of the plane was filled with a
mist of gold endorphin light,
I wept as people weep when they enter heaven,
in massive relief. We lifted up
gently from one tip of the continent
and did not stop until we set down lightly on the
other edge, I walked into his room
and watched his chest rise slowly
and sink again, all night
I watched him breathe.

SHARON OLDS

At the Bedside

Perhaps it is not, after all,
the whole story which races
through the heads of the dying, with the gloss
of last words in waiting –
but some inconsequential detail
which just happens to have stuck.

Say, for instance, the taste
of a boiled egg eaten, when a child,
in St Austell, by a window looking
out over kaolin mountains.
The sweetness of the yolk against
the tangy bread and butter.

Or the perfect round of apples
at the foot of a tree in Brittany
so scrawny as to make fruit seem
miraculous. It looked as if
it had shed them all at once
as a single golden earth-halo.

Or the view of the old bridge
at Mostar, its high brow
soaring and swooping above
the Neretva. Or the drugging smell
of red valerian, or the feel
of silk rubbed between the fingers.

But perhaps such images are only
the journeys of wishing and warding
for those who wait by the bed,
for whom also it is late,
and who cannot ignore the tut
and sigh of the morphine shunt.

LAWRENCE SAIL

Marginal Jottings on the Prospect of Dying

(FROM *Varieties of Religious Experience*)

It feels like a door in the light
through which the mind might pass at any moment,

arriving like an actor at a scene
you've long rehearsed:

a little market town, perhaps,
with rounds of cheese

and pigeons hung from twine
around the stalls;

a narrow alleyway that looks
familiar, on this rainy afternoon,

the glitter of the lights, the smell of bread,
the windows, with their naked mannequins

contorted and rapt,
like Gray's anatomical drawings;

and, sometimes,
with a little luck or charm,

that inlet on the far side
of the island, where we swam

alone, among the fishes,
in a sea

so clear
we could imagine ourselves healed

and true again
to what we used to know:

the open sky,
the part-song of cicadas.

JOHN BURNSIDE

Antidote to the Fear of Death

Sometimes as an antidote
To fear of death,
I eat the stars.

Those nights, lying on my back,
I suck them from the quenching dark
Till they are all, all inside me,
Pepper hot and sharp.

Sometimes, instead, I stir myself
Into a universe still young,
Still warm as blood:

No outer space, just space,
The light of all the not yet stars
Drifting like a bright mist,
And all of us, and everything
Already there
But unconstrained by form.

And sometimes it's enough
To lie down here on earth
Beside our long ancestral bones:

To walk across the cobble fields
Of our discarded skulls,
Each like a treasure, like a chrysalis,
Thinking: whatever left these husks
Flew off on bright wings.

REBECCA ELSON

Directions for Dying

Eating nothing for days but a forkful of feathers,
you will lie in the soft twin bed of your shadow,
and will see how it whitens like a flowering tree.

At last you will dream, recalling your sorrows,
while the pain fits snugly as a flaming shawl,
while the mice in your bones begin to gnaw free.

You will have time to weave a tent of your breath
before silence rises and falls like a stone bell
and the light deepens in the cave of your eyes.

It is not like entering a mirror nor like closing a door
nor like going to sleep in a hammock of bones.
You may expect what you like. It is nothing like that.

RICHARD BLESSING

The Cinder Path

I know what it means
to choose the cinder path.

You might say death
but I prefer taking

pains with the world.
The signpost ahead

which bears no inscription.
That elm tree withstanding

the terrible heat
of its oily green flame.

ANDREW MOTION

Five poems from *The Bridge* by MARIN SORESCU

translated from the Romanian by Adam J. Sorkin & Lidia Vianu

Pure Pain

I don't feel ill in order to feel better,
I feel ill in order to feel worse.
Like the sea with its green, treacherous waves,
You cannot sound the bottom of pain.

I dive into pure pain,
Essence of scream and despair,
And I return to the surface blue and pale,
Like a diver who lost
His oxygen tank.

To the emperor of fishes, I beg,
Kindly send me your most trustworthy shark
To cut short my passing.

'What hurts the worst'

What hurts the worst
Is that no longer will I be able to
Have contact with books,
To stand in front of my bookcase every morning
As on the shore of the sea
Caressed by secret breezes gently blowing
From the shelves.

Since I'm to be so close by,
O Lord, I hope I won't be denied
The pleasure of reading the stars

Once a week, at least,
According to the schedule posted on a cloud.

Balance Sheet

I have two serious diseases,
A few others, extremely serious,
Plus three more, no less than dreadful
(Every one, I've been assured, is incurable).

Each hurts in its own particular way.
An acute, differentiated pain,
Requiring all my energy
And power of resistance.

In sum they add up to a kind of
Essence of torture and anguish,
Something unimaginable.
I am played like a cursed organ,
Assailed around the clock
By a thousand tempests.

A Ladder to the Sky

A spider's thread
Hangs from the ceiling,
Directly over my bed.

Every day I keep track of
How much closer it descends.
'Look,' I say to myself,
'I'm being sent a ladder to the sky,
Lowered from above.'

I've grown dreadfully thin,
A mere ghost of what I used to be,
Yet I think my body
Is too heavy still
For this delicate ladder.

'Soul, you go ahead.
Shhh! Shhh!'

'So this is it'

So this is it –
The hour.

I don't know what
To do first,
How I'm supposed to behave.

They tell me
I screamed in desperation
For three days at birth.

If it weren't
For these pains, I'd have said
This is a good death.

NOTE: *The Bridge* was Marin Sorescu's last book of poems, all written from his
sickbed over five weeks from October to December 1996 as he waited for death
to take him. The final poems were dictated to his wife.

Breath

People keep telling me you're still here
I can talk to you. Sometimes I believe them.
If breath could mist the mirror you'd appear.

Till I remember the oxygen hissing
from your abandoned mask, making me lightheaded
as I sat, stroked your hand, witnessing

the still blow of morphia winning that last bout,
the long pause, the final angry sigh
as if the world had breathed me out.

PATRICIA POGSON

The pace of change

'Not unconscious, no. The patient's
brain died hours ago.' But look – your skin
is warm to touch; lying back, eyes closed,
you labour fiercely. Something in you
cries out still for struggle, effort:
this is how it is to be alive, to fight
moment by moment to achieve each
rasping, shuddering sob of breath.

I lean down, labouring too, as if by
endlessly repeating names of things
we know I can reverse the tide of blood
they say has taken you. Nothing changes.
Stupidly I try again. Then see at last
the body's terrible sorrow. Poor breath,
that cannot speak a word: how shrewd,
how manifold were once its languages.

LAURIS EDMOND

The Morning After My Death

1

My body is a white thing in the sun, now.
It is not ashamed of itself,
Not anymore. Because today is
The morning after my death.
How little I have to say;
How little desire I have
To say it.

And these flies sleeping on doorsills
And hugging screens; and the child
Who has just run out of the house
After touching my body, who knows,
Suddenly, how heavy a dead man is...

What can the sun do but keep shining?
Even though I don't especially need it
Anymore, it shines on the palm fronds
And makes them look older,
The way someone who writes a letter,
And then tears it up, looks suddenly older.

2

Far off, a band is playing Sousa marches.
And as the conductor, in his sun stained
Uniform, taps his baton for silence, and all
Around him the foliage is getting greener,
Greener, like the end of things,
One of the musicians, resting
His trumpet on his knee, looks around
A moment, before he spits and puts the horn
Into his mouth, counting slowly.

And so I think of the darkness inside the horn,
How no one's breath has been able
To push it out yet, into the air,
How when the concert ends it will still
Be there, like a note so high no one
Can play it, or like the dried blood inside
A dead woman's throat, when the mourners
Listen, and there is nothing left but these flies,
Polished and swarming frankly in the sun.

LARRY LEVIS

My Father's Body

First they take it away,
for now the body belongs to the state.
Then they open it
to see what may have killed it,
and the body had arteriosclerosis
in its heart, for this was an inside job.

Now someone must identify the body
so that the state may have a name
for what it will give away,
and the funeral people come in a stark car
shaped like a coffin with a hood
and take the body away,
for now it belongs to the funeral people
and the body's family buys it back,
though it lies in a box at the crematorium
while the mourners travel and convene.
Then they bring the body to the chapel, as they call it,
of the crematorium, and the body lies in its box
while the mourners enter and sit
and stare at the box, for the box
lies on a pedestal where the altar would be
if this were a chapel.
A rectangular frame with curtains at the sides
rises from the pedestal,
so that the box seems to fill a small stage,
and the stage gives off the familiar
illusion of being a box with one wall torn away
so that we may see into it,
but it's filled with a box we can't see into.
There's music on tape and a man in a robe
speaks for a while and I speak
for a while and then there's a prayer
and then we mourners can hear the whir
of a small motor and curtains slide
across the stage. At least for today,
I think, this is the stage that all the world is,
and another motor hums on
and we mourners realise that behind
the curtains the body is being lowered,
not like Don Giovanni to the flames
but without flourish or song
or the comforts of elaborate plot,
to the basement of the crematorium,
to the mercies of the gas jets
and the balm of the conveyor belt.
The ashes will be scattered,
says a hushed man in a mute suit,
in the Garden of Remembrance,
which is out back.

And what's left of a mild, democratic man
will sift in a heap with the residue of others,
for now they all belong to time.

WILLIAM MATTHEWS

Timer

Gold survives the fire that's hot enough
to make you ashes in a standard urn.
An envelope of coarse official buff
contains your wedding ring which wouldn't burn.

Dad told me I'd to tell them at St James's
that the ring should go in the incinerator.
That 'eternity' inscribed with both their names is
his surety that they'd be together, 'later'.

I signed for the parcelled clothing as the son,
the cardy, apron, pants, bra, dress –

The clerk phoned down: *6-8-8-3-1?*
Has she still her ring on? (Slight pause) *Yes!*

It's on my warm palm now, your burnished ring!

I feel your ashes, head, arms, breasts, womb, legs,
sift through its circle slowly, like that thing
you used to let me watch to time the eggs.

TONY HARRISON

Marked with D.

When the chilled dough of his flesh went in an oven
not unlike those he fuelled all his life,
I thought of his cataracts ablaze with Heaven
and radiant with the sight of his dead wife,

288

light streaming from his mouth to shape her name,
'not Florence and not Flo but always Florrie'.
I thought how his cold tongue burst into flame
but only literally, which makes me sorry,
sorry for his sake there's no Heaven to reach.
I get it all from Earth my daily bread
but he hungered for release from mortal speech
that kept him down, the tongue that weighed like lead.

The baker's man that no one will see rise
and England made to feel like some dull oaf
is smoke, enough to sting one person's eyes
and ash (not unlike flour) for one small loaf.

TONY HARRISON

Only a Small Death

Only a small death, of course,
Not the full ceremony with mourners, a hearse,
Residuary legatees and a beanfeast
After the crematorium. Just a small, fully-
Conscious end.

Never again will you sleep in
This room, see sun rise through glass at this
Familiar angle, never again
Adjust to the shape of this bath, the smell
Of this cupboard.

You have died suddenly. The arrival
Of undertakers informs you of your
Decease. Their muscular detachment dissolves
Bonds between chairs and rooms, shelves
And their books.

The house offers its own valuation
Of the late owner. Dirt appears
In embarrassing contexts. If you were still
Alive, you would feel the need
To apologise.

Casual adjuncts of ordinary
Living, dustbins and drains, the
Unremarkable milkman, haloed in
The otherworldly glare of the last rites,
Achieve reality

Just as you end with them for ever.
Neighbours, paying a deathbed visit,
Acquire the tender resonance of friends,
But die as you go, birth exists on the edge
Of extinction.

The heir, arriving tactlessly early,
Retires till you finish dying. With you go
Archaic patterns of a home you will never
Come home to like an amputation, it will
Haunt you in the grave.

U.A. FANTHORPE

Common and Particular

I like these men and women who have to do with death,
Formal, gentle people whose job it is,
They mind their looks, they use words carefully.

I liked that woman in the sunny room
One after the other receiving such as me
Every working day. She asks the things she must

And thanks me for the answers. Then I don't mind
Entering your particulars in little boxes,
I like the feeling she has seen it all before,

There is a form, there is a way. But also
That no one come to speak up for a shade
Is like the last, I see she knows that too.

I'm glad there is a form to put your details in,
Your dates, the cause. Glad as I am of men
Who'll make a trestle of their strong embrace

And in a slot between two other slots
Do what they have to every working day:
Carry another weight for someone else.

It is common. You are particular.

DAVID CONSTANTINE

What I Learned from My Mother

I learned from my mother how to love
the living, to have plenty of vases on hand
in case you have to rush to the hospital
with peonies cut from the lawn, black ants
still stuck to the buds. I learned to save jars
large enough to hold fruit salad for a whole
grieving household, to cube home-canned pears
and peaches, to slice through maroon grape skins
and flick out the sexual seeds with a knife point.
I learned to attend viewing even if I didn't know
the deceased, to press the moist hands
of the living, to look in their eyes and offer
sympathy, as though I understood loss even then.
I learned that whatever we say means nothing,
what anyone will remember is that we came.
I learned to believe I had the power to ease
awful pains materially like an angel.
Like a doctor, I learned to create
from another's suffering my own usefulness, and once
you know how to do this, you can never refuse.
To every house you enter, you must offer
healing: a chocolate cake you baked yourself,
the blessing of your voice, your chaste touch.

JULIA KASDORF

The House After Her Death

Nothing has changed after my mother's death.
Her portraits are still youthful. My four sisters are still intent on
      keeping the day tied to
its three stalwart rituals: coffee in the mornings, ginger at midday,
      mint in the evenings.
At my family's home you do not need a watch.
The scent will tell you the sun's place in the sky.

Nothing has changed in that house since my mother's death.
My sisters' hands keep busy tidying up the rooms their five
      brothers have left for other rooms
in which their souls will never rest.
They no longer sleep on mattresses spread on the floor,
no longer shiver like addicts while they wait for their morning tea
      and bread.

After my mother's death, nothing has changed in the house.
When we look at Kawthar, our oldest sister, intent on keeping
      even small things whole,
we begin to think that our mother hasn't left the house she built,
      sigh by sigh,
in a white coffin and a body eaten bit by bit
by cancer, for a graveyard to hold the first of the family dead.

Nothing has changed after my mother's death:
the day with its three degrees of latitude,
the tidy rooms awaiting absent sons,
my father's endless marathon racing between ablutions and the
      mosque,
the everlasting nostalgia for the happy days of our poverty.

Everything is still the same,
except for that hand which turns the dust green.

AMJAD NASSER
translated from the Arabic by Khaled Mattawa

Dining

No more in supermarkets will her good taste choose
  Her favourite cheese and lovely things to eat,
Or, hands in murmuring tubs, sigh as her fingers muse
  Over the mundane butter, mundane meat.
Nor round the market stalls of France will Lesley stroll
  Appraising aubergines, *langoustes, patisseries*
And artichokes, or hear the poultry vendors call,
  Watch merchants slicing spokes in wheels of Brie.
My lady loved to cook and dine, but never more
  Across starched linen and the saucy pork
Can we look forward to *Confit de Périgord*.
  How well my lady used her knife and fork!
Happy together – ah, my lady loved to sport
  And love. She loved the good; she loved to laugh
And loved so many things, infallible in art
  That pleased her, water, oil or lithograph,
With her own talent to compose the world in light.
  And it is hard for me to cook my meals
From recipes she used, without that old delight
  Returning, masked in sadness, until it feels
As if I have become a woman hidden in me –
  Familiar with each kitchen-spotted page,
Each stain, each note in her neat hand a sight to spin me
  Into this grief, this kitchen pilgrimage.
O my young wife, how sad I was, yet pleased, to see
  And help you eat the soup that Jenny made
On your last night, who all that day had called for tea,
  And only that, or slept your unafraid,
Serene, courageous sleeps, then woke, and asked for tea –
  'Nothing to eat. Tea. Please' – lucid and polite.
Eunice, Daphne, Cresten, Sandra, how you helped me,
  To feed my girl and keep her kitchen bright.
Know that I shake with gratitude, as, Jenny, when
  My Lesley ate your soup on her last night,
That image of her as she savoured rice and lemon
  Refused all grief, but was alight
  With nature, courage, friendship, appetite.

DOUGLAS DUNN

from A Widower's Dozen

1

Sparse breaths, then none –
and it was done.

Listening and hugging hard,
between mouthings
of sweet next-to-nothings
into her ear –
pillow-talk-cum-prayer –
I never heard
the precise cadence
into silence
that argued the end.
Yet I knew it had happened.

Ultimate calm.

Gingerly, as if
loth to disturb it,
I released my arm
from its stiff vigil athwart
that embattled heart
and raised and righted myself,
the better to observe it.

Kisses followed,
to mouth, cheeks, eyelids, forehead,
and a rigmarole
of unheard farewell
kept up as far
as the click of the door.

After six months, or more,
I observe it still.

5

No imp or devil
but a mere tumour
squatted on her brain.
Without personality
or ill humour,
malignant but not malign,
it set about doing –
not evil,
simply the job
tumours have always done:
establishing faulty
connections, skewing
perceptions, closing down
faculties and functions
one by one.

Hobgoblin, nor foul fiend;
nor even the jobsworth slob
with a slow, sly scheme to rob
my darling of her mind
that I imagined;
just a tumour.

Between which and the neat
gadget with the timer
that eased drugs into her vein
she contrived to maintain
her identity
unimpaired and complete,
resolved to meet
death with all gallantry
and distinction.

7

A warm croissant
and cappuccino
were our morning rite:
alternate bites
of flaking, buttery pith;

then the straw guided
into her mouth
and the coffee making
its hesitant ascent
with puckered sucks
that just as stutteringly subsided.

Tougher work
than playing an oboe,
yet performed with a gusto
that customarily took
more than her fair share.
Not that I was measuring!
Rather, it was a case
of pride and delight
in such simple pleasuring:
the look on her face,
pure, animal appetite.

Therefore, not heart-breaking,
to picture her
across a table
in some quiet French seaside spot,
scanning a cluttered
plateau de fruits de mer
with its full surgical couvert,
and about to clatter
her way through the lot
as slowly as she was able.

9

How bright the wit,
the circumstance-mocking
theatrical badinage, burned.
To a friend concerned
she might be tired
I heard her say,
'Exhausted people
leave the hospice all day,
and I just carry on talking.'

To another, catching
a glimpse of her own
undimmable spirit:
'I'm being radiant
again, aren't I!'

It was inspired,
brave, funny and subtle
of her to interpret
the role of patient
so flat against type –
cheering her nurses,
feeding advice and support
to friends, encouraging
her husband to address his
possible future
with something of her hope.

It's not in his nature,
but he can try.

CHRISTOPHER REID

Memorial

Everywhere she dies. Everywhere I go she dies.
No sunrise, no city square, no lurking beautiful mountain
but has her death in it.
The silence of her dying sounds through
the carousel of language, it's a web
on which laughter stitches itself. How can my hand
clasp another's when between them
is that thick death, that intolerable distance?

She grieves for my grief. Dying, she tells me
that bird dives from the sun, that fish
leaps into it. No crocus is carved more gently
than the way her dying

shapes my mind. But I hear, too,
the other words,
black words that make the sound
of soundlessness, that name the nowhere
she is continuously going into.

Ever since she died
she can't stop dying. She makes me
her elegy. I am a walking masterpiece,
a true fiction
of the ugliness of death.
I am her sad music.

NORMAN MacCAIG

Comparisons

To all light things
I compared her; to
a snowflake, a feather.

I remember she rested
at the dance on my
arm, as a bird

on its nest lest
the eggs break, lest
she lean too heavily

on our love. Snow
melts, feathers
are blown away;

I have let
her ashes down
in me like an anchor.

R.S. THOMAS

Ann

1969

I remember myself most. How, all of a sudden I had one
wife, instead of now and then this love or that.
And how we had to love each other, instead of simply
falling in love sometimes.

I used to sit in bars, boasting about how beautiful you were,
and shy, and brash too, until my women friends would say:
why don't you just go and be in love at home –
and how I still needed to order that one last drink.

I remember how silently you sat sometimes, hugging
your knees; how you wanted to be all sorts of women
for me, if only I'd be there.
And how, too young, I was unable to receive so much.

1971
(for Thomas)

I was better at losing: barely squeezed out
one poetry collection about it. I won
the Flemish Provinces Prize with your death.
I mostly remember I couldn't find my glasses.

They were on the road, next to the car. I found them
first, a new pair, then you.
Thanks to those glasses, I can still see you.
After an eternity, lasting

for a minute or two, a woman pointed to the grass:
look, a child. Oh, yes, we had that too. Quick mouth
to mouth. Tom howling as if murdered. That sounded healthy.

Only then did I realise how silent it had been before.
I thought: what if I tried to cry?
It worked. And that helped a lot in the following days.

HERMAN DE CONINCK
translated from the Flemish by Laure-Anne Bosselaar & Kurt Brown

Three poems from *Elegy* by MARY JO BANG

Landscape with the Fall of Icarus

How could I have failed you like this?
The narrator asks

The object. The object is a box
Of ashes. How could I not have saved you,

A boy made of bone and blood. A boy
Made of a mind. Of years. A hand

And paint on canvas. A marble carving.
How can I not reach where you are

And pull you back. How can I be
And you not. You're forever on the platform

Seeing the pattern of the train door closing.
Then the silver streak of me leaving.

What train was it? The number 6.
What day was it? Wednesday.

We had both admired the miniature mosaics
Stuck on the wall of the Met.

That car should be forever sealed in amber.
That dolorous day should be forever

Embedded in amber.
In garnet. In amber. In opal. In order

To keep going on. And how can it be
That this means nothing to anyone but me now.

You Were You Are Elegy

Fragile like a child is fragile.
Destined not to be forever.
Destined to become other
To mother. Here I am
Sitting on a chair, thinking
About you. Thinking
About how it was
To talk to you.
How sometimes it was wonderful
And sometimes it was awful.
How drugs when drugs were
Undid the good almost entirely
But not entirely
Because good could always be seen
Glimmering like lame glimmers
In the window of a shop
Called Beautiful
Things Never Last Forever.
I loved you. I love you. You were.
And you are. Life is experience.
It's all so simple. Experience is
The chair we sit on.
The sitting. The thinking
Of you where you are a blank
To be filled
In by missing. I loved you.
I love you like I love
All beautiful things.
True beauty is truly seldom.
You were. You are
In May. May now is looking onto
The June that is coming up.
This is how I measure
The year. Everything Was My Fault
Has been the theme of the song
I've been singing,
Even when you've told me to quiet.
I haven't been quiet.
I've been crying. I think you
Have forgiven me. You keep

Putting your hand on my shoulder
When I'm crying.
Thank you for that. And
For the ineffable sense
Of continuance. You were. You are
The brightest thing in the shop window
And the most beautiful seldom I ever saw.

Ode to History

Had she not lain on that bed with a boy
All those years ago, where would they be, she wondered.
She and the child that wouldn't have been but was now
No more. She would know nothing
Of mothering. She would know nothing
Of death. She would know nothing
Of love. The three things she'd been given
To remember. Wake me up, please, she said,
When this life is over. Look at her – It's as if
The windows of night have been sewn to her eyes.

MARY JO BANG

No Time

She left me. What voice
colder than the wind
out of the grave said:
'It is over'? Impalpable,
invisible, she comes
to me still, as she would
do, and I at my reading.
There is a tremor
of light, as of a bird crossing
the sun's path, and I look
up in recognition

of a presence in absence.
Not a word, not a sound,
as she goes her way,
but a scent lingering
which is that of time immolating
itself in love's fire.

R.S. THOMAS

Years go by

Father I say. Dad? You again?
I take your arm, your elbow,
I turn you around in the dark and I say

go back now, you're sleepwalking again,
you're talking out loud again, talking in tongues
and your dream is disturbing my dream.

And none of this is any of your apples,
and even now as the centuries begin to happen
I can say: go away, you and all your violence.

Shush, now, old man.
Time to go back to your seat in the one-and-nines,
to your black bench on the Esplanade,

your name and your dates on a metal plate, back
to your own deckchair on the pier, your very own
kitchen chair tipped back on the red kitchen tiles

and you asleep, your feet up on the brass fender
and the fire banked, your cheek cocked
to the radio set, this is the 9 o'clock news Dad.

It's time. It's long past it.
Time to go back up the long pale corridor
there's no coming back from.

KEN SMITH

Death Is Smaller Than I Thought

My Mother and Father died some years ago
I loved them very much.
When they died my love for them
Did not vanish or fade away.
It stayed just about the same,
Only a sadder colour.
And I can feel their love for me,
Same as it ever was.

Nowadays, in good times or bad,
I sometimes ask my Mother and Father
To walk beside me or to sit with me
So we can talk together
Or be silent.

They always come to me.
I talk to them and listen to them
And think I hear them talk to me.
It's very simple –
Nothing to do with spiritualism
Or religion or mumbo jumbo.

It is imaginary.
It is real.
It is love.

ADRIAN MITCHELL

Darling

You might forget the exact sound of her voice
or how her face looked when sleeping.
You might forget the sound of her quiet weeping
curled into the shape of a half moon,

when smaller than her self, she seemed already to be leaving
before she left, when the blossom was on the trees
and the sun was out, and all seemed good in the world.
I held her hand and sang a song from when I was a girl –

Heel y'ho boys, let her go boys –
and when I stopped singing she had slipped away,
already a slip of a girl again, skipping off,
her heart light, her face almost smiling.

And what I didn't know or couldn't say then
was that she hadn't really gone.
The dead don't go till you do, loved ones.
The dead are still here holding our hands.

JACKIE KAY

The Dead

At night the dead come down to the river to drink.
They unburden themselves of their fears,
their worries for us. They take out the old photographs.
They pat the lines in our hands and tell our futures,
which are cracked and yellow.
Some dead find their way to our houses.
They go up to the attics.
They read the letters they sent us, insatiable
for signs of their love.
They tell each other stories.
They make so much noise
they wake us
as they did when we were children and they stayed up
drinking all night in the kitchen.

SUSAN MITCHELL

No Time

In a rush this weekday morning,
I tap the horn as I speed past the cemetery
where my parents are buried
side by side beneath a slab of smooth granite.

Then, all day, I think of him rising up
to give me that look
of knowing disapproval
while my mother calmly tells him to lie back down.

BILLY COLLINS

Branches

I saw my father and mother standing
in a pond, against sunlight on rushes,
my mother's thin arm reaching
from between the small suns of water-lilies,
and saw that a spider
had strung threads from my father's knees
to glitter out over the water;
that their bleached bones had hardened
in the green on green of circles
and the paired blue wings of dragonflies,
the minute dance of egg-laying.
And I was glad
that they still stood there, sun-dry and reaching,
and I was grateful
that no one had needed to bury them,
shut them out of all that light.

SUSAN WICKS

6

War and survival

When power leads man toward arrogance, poetry reminds him of
his limitations. When power narrows the area of man's concern,
poetry reminds him of the richness and diversity of existence.
When power corrupts, poetry cleanses.

JOHN F. KENNEDY

MANY OF THE WRITERS included in this section fought or suffered in the major
conflicts of the 20th and 21st centuries or under tyrannical regimes. Keith
Douglas (328) was a tank commander in North Africa during the Second World
War and was later killed in action in Normandy. Doug Anderson (328) served
with the US Army in Vietnam and Brian Turner (329, 336) in Bosnia and Iraq.
A copy of Ho Thien's poem 'The Green Beret' (326) is said to have been found
on his body in Vietnam somewhere near the Cambodian border in 1966.

Born in the Warsaw Ghetto, Irena Klepfisz (314) escaped to the Polish
countryside with her mother after her father was killed in the Ghetto Uprising
in 1943 and spent the rest of the war in hiding. Else Lasker-Schüler (358) fled
Nazi Germany and died in Jerusalem in 1945. After losing his family, Paul
Celan (316, 326) survived two years in labour camps; his suicide many years
later is the subject of C.K. Williams's meditation 'Jew on Bridge' (317). Miklós
Radnóti (324) died on a forced march in 1944 (see note, 325). Gyula Illyés
(349) went on the run after the Nazi invasion of Hungary in 1944, and the
following year was elected to the short-lived Hungarian parliament.

Several of the poets were imprisoned for their writing or beliefs for many
years: Nâzim Hikmet (76, 352, 358) in Turkey, Jack Mapanje (356) in Malawi,
Irina Ratushinskaya (355) in Russia, and Heberto Padilla (351) in Cuba. Hikmet
spent much of his life in exile or in prison, his longest period of incarceration
lasting from 1938 to 1950, and like Mapanje and Ratushinskaya he was finally
freed following an international campaign for his release.

Poets writing in response to terrorist atrocities include Michael Longley
on the Northern Irish 'Troubles' (344, 345), New Yorkers X.J. Kennedy and
Deborah Garrison on 9/11 (346, 347), and Australia's Alan Smith (348) on the
Bali bombings (348). Middle East poets include Israel's Yehuda Amichai (159,
183, 199, 331), Aharon Shabtai (337) and Ronny Someck (337); Mourid Barghouti
(334, 336) and Taha Muhammad Ali (338) from Palestine; and two exiled Iraqi
Assyrian writers, Sargon Boulos (362) and Dunya Mikhail (330, 392).

This section extends the selections of poems on war and conflict in *Staying
Alive* (9: 'War and peace', 343-68) and *Being Alive* (9: 'Mad World', 397-442).

What He Thought

(for Fabbio Doplicher)

We were supposed to do a job in Italy
and, full of our feeling for
ourselves (our sense of being
Poets from America) we went
from Rome to Fano, met
the mayor, mulled
a couple matters over (what's
a cheap date, they asked us; what's
flat drink). Among Italian literati

we could recognise our counterparts:
the academic, the apologist,
the arrogant, the amorous,
the brazen and the glib – and there was one

administrator (the conservative), in suit
of regulation gray, who like a good tour guide
with measured pace and uninflected tone narrated
sights and histories the hired van hauled us past.
Of all, he was the most politic and least poetic,
so it seemed. Our last few days in Rome
(when all but three of the New World Bards had flown)
I found a book of poems this
unprepossessing one had written: it was there
in the *pensione* room (a room he'd recommended)
where it must have been abandoned by
the German visitor (was there a bus of *them?*)
to whom he had inscribed and dated it a month before.
I couldn't read Italian, either, so I put the book
back into the wardrobe's dark. We last Americans

were due to leave tomorrow. For our parting evening then
our host chose something in a family restaurant, and there
we sat and chatted, sat and chewed,
till, sensible it was our last
big chance to be poetic, make
our mark, one of us asked

                  'What's poetry?'
Is it the fruits and vegetables and

marketplace of Campo dei Fiori, or
the statue there?' Because I was

the glib one, I identified the answer
instantly, I didn't have to think – 'The truth
is both, it's both,' I blurted out. But that
was easy. That was easiest to say. What followed
taught me something about difficulty,
for our underestimated host spoke out,
all of a sudden, with a rising passion, and he said:

The statute represents Giordano Bruno,
brought to be burned in the public square
because of his offense against
authority, which is to say
the Church. His crime was his belief
the universe does not revolve around
the human being: God is no
fixed point or central government, but rather is
poured in waves through all things. All things
move. 'If God is not the soul itself, He is
the soul of the soul of the world.' Such was
his heresy. The day they brought him
forth to die, they feared he might
incite the crowd (the man was famous
for his eloquence). And so his captors
placed upon his face
an iron mask, in which

he could not speak. That's
how they burned him. That is how
he died: without a word, in front
of everyone.   And poetry –
                         (we'd all
put down our forks by now, to listen to
the man in gray; he went on
softly) –
                         poetry is what

he thought, but did not say.

HEATHER McHUGH

Campo dei Fiori

In Rome on the Campo dei Fiori
baskets of olives and lemons,
cobbles spattered with wine
and the wreckage of flowers.
Vendors cover the trestles
with rose-pink fish;
armfuls of dark grapes
heaped on peach-down.

On this same square
they burned Giordano Bruno.
Henchmen kindled the pyre
close-pressed by the mob.
Before the flames had died
the taverns were full again,
baskets of olives and lemons
again on the vendors' shoulders.

I thought of the Campo dei Fiori
in Warsaw by the sky-carousel
one clear spring evening
to the strains of a carnival tune.
The bright melody drowned
the salvos from the ghetto wall,
and couples were flying
high in the cloudless sky.

At times wind from the burning
would drift dark kites along
and riders on the carousel
caught petals in midair.
That same hot wind
blew open the skirts of the girls
and the crowds were laughing
on that beautiful Warsaw Sunday.

Someone will read as moral
that the people of Rome or Warsaw
haggle, laugh, make love
as they pass by the martyrs' pyres.
Someone else will read
of the passing of things human,
of the oblivion
born before the flames have died.

But that day I thought only
of the loneliness of the dying,
of how, when Giordano
climbed to his burning
he could not find
in any human tongue
words for mankind,
mankind who live on.

Already they were back at their wine
or peddled their white starfish,
baskets of olives and lemons
they had shouldered to the fair,
and he already distanced
as if centuries had passed
while they paused just a moment
for his flying in the fire.

Those dying here, the lonely
forgotten by the world,
our tongue becomes for them
the language of an ancient planet.
Until, when all is legend
and many years have passed,
on a new Campo dei Fiori
rage will kindle at a poet's word.

[*Warsaw, 1943*]

CZESŁAW MIŁOSZ
translated by Louis Iribarne & David Brooks

The Fall of Rome

(for Cyril Connolly)

The piers are pummelled by the waves;
In a lonely field the rain
Lashes an abandoned train;
Outlaws fill the mountain caves.

Fantastic grow the evening gowns;
Agents of the Fisc pursue
Absconding tax-defaulters through
The sewers of provincial towns.

Private rites of magic send
The temple prostitutes to sleep;
All the literati keep
An imaginary friend.

Cerebrotonic Cato may
Extol the Ancient Disciplines,
But the muscle-bound Marines
Mutiny for food and pay.

Caesar's double-bed is warm
As an unimportant clerk
Writes *I DO NOT LIKE MY WORK*
On a pink official form.

Unendowed with wealth or pity,
Little birds with scarlet legs,
Sitting on their speckled eggs,
Eye each flu-infected city.

Altogether elsewhere, vast
Herds of reindeer move across
Miles and miles of golden moss,
Silently and very fast.

[*January 1947*]

W.H. AUDEN

'More Light! More Light!'

(for Heinrich Blücher and Hannah Arendt)

Composed in the Tower before his execution
These moving verses, and being brought at that time
Painfully to the stake, submitted, declaring thus:
'I implore my God to witness that I have made no crime.'

Nor was he forsaken of courage, but the death was horrible,
The sack of gunpowder failing to ignite.
His legs were blistered sticks on which the black sap
Bubbled and burst as he howled for the Kindly Light.

And that was but one, and by no means one of the worst;
Permitted at least his pitiful dignity;
And such as were by made prayers in the name of Christ,
That shall judge all men, for his soul's tranquillity.

We move now to outside a German wood.
Three men are there commanded to dig a hole
In which the two Jews are ordered to lie down
And be buried alive by the third, who is a Pole.

Not light from the shrine at Weimar beyond the hill
Nor light from heaven appeared. But he did refuse.
A Lüger settled back deeply in its glove.
He was ordered to change places with the Jews.

Much casual death had drained away their souls.
The thick dirt mounted toward the quivering chin.
When only the head was exposed the order came
To dig him out again and to get back in.

No light, no light in the blue Polish eye.
When he finished a riding boot packed down the earth.
The Lüger hovered lightly in its glove.
He was shot in the belly and in three hours bled to death.

No prayers or incense rose up in those hours
Which grew to be years, and every day came mute
Ghosts from the ovens, sifting through crisp air,
And settled upon his eyes in a black soot.

ANTHONY HECHT

313

Dedications to *Bashert*

These words are dedicated to those who died

These words are dedicated to those who died
because they had no love and felt alone in the world
because they were afraid to be alone and tried to stick it out
because they could not ask
because they were shunned
because they were sick and their bodies could not resist the disease
because they played it safe
because they had no connections
because they had no faith
because they felt they did not belong and wanted to die

These words are dedicated to those who died
because they were loners and liked it
because they acquired friends and drew others to them
because they took risks
because they were stubborn and refused to give up
because they asked for too much

These words are dedicated to those who died
because a card was lost and a number was skipped
because a bed was denied
because a place was filled and no other place was left

These words are dedicated to those who died
because someone did not follow through
because someone was overworked and forgot
because someone left everything to God
because someone was late
because someone did not arrive at all
because someone told them to wait and they just couldn't any longer
These words are dedicated to those who died
because death is a punishment
because death is a reward
because death is the final rest
because death is eternal rage

These words are dedicated to those who died

Bashert

These words are dedicated to those who survived

These words are dedicated to those who survived
because their second grade teacher gave them books
because they did not draw attention to themselves and got lost in
    the shuffle
because they knew someone who knew someone else who could
help them and bumped into them on a corner on a Thursday
    afternoon
because they played it safe
because they were lucky

These words are dedicated to those who survived
because they knew how to cut corners
because they drew attention to themselves and always got picked
because they took risks
because they had no principles and were hard

These words are dedicated to those who survived
because they refused to give up and defied statistics
because they had faith and trusted in God
because they expected the worst and were always prepared
because they were angry
because they could ask
because they mooched off others and saved their strength
because they endured humiliation
because they turned the other cheek
because they looked the other way

The words are dedicated to those who survived
because life is a wilderness and they were savage
because life is an awakening and they were alert
because life is a flowering and they blossomed
because life is a struggle and they struggled
because life is a gift and they were free to accept it
The words are dedicated to those who survived

Bashert

IRENA KLEPFISZ

ba-shert (Yiddish): inevitable, (pre)destined.

315

Deathfugue

Black milk of daybreak we drink it at evening
we drink it at midday and morning we drink it at night
we drink and we drink
we shovel a grave in the air where you won't lie too cramped
A man lives in the house he plays with his vipers he writes
he writes when it grows dark to Deutschland your golden hair
      Margareta
he writes it and steps out of doors and the stars are all sparkling he
      whistles his hounds to stay close
he whistles his Jews into rows has them shovel a grave in the ground
he commands us play up for the dance

Black milk of daybreak we drink you at night
we drink you at morning and midday we drink you at evening
we drink and we drink
A man lives in the house he plays with his vipers he writes
he writes when it grows dark to Deutschland your golden hair
      Margareta
Your ashen hair Shulamith we shovel a grave in the air
      where you won't lie too cramped

He shouts dig this earth deeper you lot there you others sing up
      and play
he grabs for the rod in his belt he swings it his eyes are so blue
stick your spades deeper you lot there you others play on for the
      dancing

Black milk of daybreak we drink you at night
we drink you at midday and morning we drink you at evening
we drink and we drink
a man lives in the house your goldenes Haar Margareta
your aschenes Haar Shulamith he plays with his vipers

*   *   *

He shouts play death more sweetly this Death is a master from
      Deutschland
he shouts scrape your strings darker you'll rise up as smoke to the sky
you'll then have a grave in the clouds where you won't lie too
      cramped

Black milk of daybreak we drink you at night
we drink you at midday Death is a master aus Deutschland
we drink you at evening and morning we drink and we drink
this Death is ein Meister aus Deutschland his eye it is blue
he shoots you with shot made of lead shoots you level and true
a man lives in the house your goldenes Haar Margarete
he looses his hounds on us grants us a grave in the air
he plays with his vipers and daydreams der Tod ist ein Meister aus
      Deutschland

dein goldenes Haar Margarete
dein aschenes Haar Sulamith

PAUL CELAN
translated from the German by John Felstiner

Jew on Bridge

Raskolnikov hasn't slept. For days. In his brain, something like white.
A wave stopped in mid-leap. Thick, slow, white. Or maybe it's brain.
Brain in his brain. Old woman's brain on the filthy floor of his brain.

His destiny's closing in. He's on his way, we're given to think, though
he'll have to go first through much suffering, to punishment, then
      redemption.
Love, too. Punishment, love, redemption; it's all mixed up in his brain.

Can't I go back to my garret, to my filthy oil-cloth couch, and just sleep?
That squalid neighborhood where he lived. I was there. Whores, beggars,
derelict men with flattened noses: the police break their noses on purpose.

Poor crumpled things. He can't, though, go back to his filthy garret.
Rather this fitful perambulation. Now we come to a bridge on the Neva.
Could you see the sea from there then? I think I saw it from there.

Then, on the bridge, hanging out of the plot like an arm from a car,
no more function than that in the plot, car, window, arm, even less,
there, on the bridge, purposeless, plotless, not even a couch of his own:
      Jew.

On page something or other, chapter something, Raskolnikov sees JEW.
And takes a moment, a break, you might say, from his plot, from his fate,
his doom, to hate him, the Jew, loathe, despise, want him not *there*.

Jew. Not as in Chekhov's ensemble of Jews wailing for a wedding.
Not Chekhov, dear Chekhov. Dostoevsky instead, whom I esteemed
beyond almost all who ever scraped with a pen, but who won't give the Jew,

miserable Jew, the right to be short, tall, thin or fat Jew: just Jew.
Something to distract you from your shuttering tunnel of fate, your
    memory,
consciousness, loathing, self-loathing, knowing the slug you are.

What's the Jew doing anyway on that bridge on the beautiful Neva?
Maybe he's Paul, as in Celan. Antschel-Celan, who went over the rail of
    a bridge.
Oh my *Todesfugue*, Celan is thinking. The river's not the Neva, but the
    Seine.

It's the bridge on the Seine where Jew-poet Celan is preparing himself.
My *Deathfugue*. My black milk of daybreak. Death-master from Germany.
Dein goldenes Haar Marguerite. Dein aschenes Haar Sulamith. Aschenes-
    Antschel.

Was it sunrise, too, as when Raskolnikov, sleepless, was crossing his bridge?
Perhaps sleepless is why Raskolnikov hates this Jew, this Celan, this
    Antschel.
If not, maybe he'd love him. Won't he love the prisoners in his camp?

Won't he love and forgive and cherish the poor girl he's been tormenting?
Christian forgiveness all over the place, like brain on your boot.
Though you mustn't forgive, in your plot, Jew on bridge; *Deathfugue* on
    bridge.

Celan-Antschel goes over the rail. As have many others before him.
There used to be nets down near Boulogne to snare the debris, the bodies,
of prostitutes, bankrupts, sterile young wives, gamblers, and naturally Jews.

Celan was so sick of the *Deathfugue* he'd no longer let it be printed.
In the tape of him reading, his voice is songful and fervent, like a cantor's.
When he presented the poem to some artists, they hated the way he
    recited.

His parents had died in the camps. Of typhus the father. Mama probably
  gun.
Celan-Antschel, had escaped. He'd tried to convince them to come, too.
Was that part of it, on the bridge? Was that he wrote in German part, too?

He stood on the bridge over the Seine, looked into the black milk of
  dying,
Jew on bridge, and hauled himself over the rail. *Dein aschenes Haar...*
Dostoevsky's Jew, though, is still there. On page something or other.

He must be waiting to see where destiny's plotting will take him. It won't.
He'll just have to wait there forever. Jew on bridge, hanging out of the
  plot.
I try to imagine what he would look like. My father? Grandfathers?
  Greats?

Does he wear black? Would he be like one of those hairy Hasids
where Catherine buys metal for her jewelry, in their black suits and hats,
even in summer, shvitzing, in the heat? Crackpots, I think. They depress
me.

Do I need forgiveness for my depression? My being depressed like a Jew?
All right then: how Jewish am I? What portion of who I am is a Jew?
I don't want vague definitions, qualifications, here on the bridge of the
  Jew.

I want certainty, science: everything you are, do, think; think, do, are,
is precisely twenty-two percent Jewish. Or six-and-a-half. Some nice prime.
Your suffering is Jewish. Your resistant, resilient pleasure in living, too,

can be tracked to some Jew on some bridge on page something or other
in some city, some village, some shtetl, some festering *shvitz* of a slum,
with Jews with black hats or not, on their undershirts fringes or not.

Raskolnikov, slouching, shoulders hunched, hands in his pockets,
stinking from all those sleepless nights on his couch, clothes almost rotting,
slouching and stinking and shivering and muttering to himself, plods on

past the Jew on the bridge, who's dressed perhaps like anyone else –
coat, hat, scarf, boots – whatever. Our hero would recognise him
by his repulsive, repellent Jew-face daring to hang out in the air.

My father's name also was Paul. As in Celan. His father's name: Benjamin.
As in Walter. Who flung himself from life, too, with vials of morphine.
In some hotel from which he could have reached safety but declined to.

Chose not to. Make it across. Though in fact none of us makes it across.
Aren't we all in that same shitty hotel on that bridge in the shittiest
    world?
What was he thinking, namesake of my grandpa? Benjamin, Walter,
    knew all.

Past, future, all. He could see perfectly clearly the death he'd miss out on.
You're in a room. Dark. You're naked. Crushed on all sides by others
    naked.
Flesh-knobs. Hairy or smooth. Sweating against you. *Shvitzing* against
    you.

Benjamin would have played it all out in his mind like a fugue. *Death-
    fugue*.
The sweating, the stinking. And that moment you know you're going to
    die,
and the moment past that, which, if you're Benjamin, Walter, not grandpa,

you know already by heart: the searing through you you realise is your
    grief,
for humans, all humans, their world and their cosmos and oil-cloth stars.
All of it worse than your fear and grief for your own minor death.

So, gulp down the morphine quickly, because of your shame for the
    humans,
what humans can do to each other. Benjamin, grandfather, Walter;
Paul, father, Celan: all the names that ever existed wiped out in shame.

Celan on his bridge. Raskolnikov muttering Dostoevsky under his breath.
Jew on bridge. Raskolnikov-Dostoevsky still in my breath. Under my
    breath.
Black milk of daybreak. *Aschenes Haar*. Antschel-Celan. Ash. Breath.

C.K. WILLIAMS

The Visitor

In Spanish he whispers there is no time left.
It is the sound of scythes arcing in wheat,
the ache of some field song in Salvador.
The wind along the prison, cautious
as Francisco's hands on the inside, touching
the walls as he walks, it is his wife's breath
slipping into his cell each night while he
imagines his hand to be hers. It is a small country.

There is nothing one man will not do to another.

CAROLYN FORCHÉ

I Am Your Waiter Tonight and My Name Is Dmitri

Is, more or less, the title of a poem by John Ashbery and has
No investment in the fact that you can get an adolescent
Of the human species to do almost anything (and when adolescence
In the human species ends is what The Fat Man in *The Maltese
    Falcon*
Calls 'a nice question, sir, a very nice question indeed')
Which is why they are tromping down a road in Fallujah
In combat gear and a hundred and fifteen degrees of heat
This morning and why a young woman is strapping
Twenty pounds of explosives to her mortal body in Jerusalem.
Dulce et decorum est pro patria mori. Have I mentioned
That the other law of human nature is that human beings
Will do anything they see someone else do and someone
Will do almost anything? There is probably a waiter
In this country so clueless he wears a T-shirt in the gym
That says Da Meat Tree. Not our protagonist. American amnesia
Is such that he may very well be the great-grandson
Of the elder Karamazov brother who fled to the Middle West
With his girlfriend Grushenka – he never killed his father,
It isn't true that he killed his father – but his religion

Was that woman's honey-colored head, an ideal tangible
Enough to die for, and he lived for it: in Buffalo,
New York, or Sandusky, Ohio. He never learned much English,
But he slept beside her in the night until she was an old woman
Who still knew her way to the Russian pharmacist
In a Chicago suburb where she could buy sachets of the herbs
Of the Russian summer that her coarse white nightgown
Smelled of as he fell asleep, though he smoked Turkish cigarettes
And could hardly smell. Grushenka got two boys out of her body,
One was born in 1894, the other in 1896,
The elder having died in the mud at the Battle of the Somme
From a piece of shrapnel manufactured by Alfred Nobel.
Metal traveling at that speed works amazing transformations
On the tissues of the human intestine; the other son worked
          construction
The year his mother died. If they could have, they would have,
If not filled, half-filled her coffin with the petals
Of buckwheat flowers from which Crimean bees made the honey
Bought in the honey market in St Petersburg (not far
From the place where Raskolnikov, himself an adolescent male,
Couldn't kill the old moneylender without killing her saintly sister,
But killed her nevertheless in a fit of guilt and reasoning
Which went something like this: since the world
Evidently consists in the ravenous pursuit of wealth
And power and in the exploitation and prostitution
Of women, except the wholly self-sacrificing ones
Who make you crazy with guilt, and since I am going
To be the world, I might as well take an ax to the head
Of this woman who symbolises both usury and the guilt
The virtue and suffering of women induces in men,
And be done with it). I frankly admit the syntax
Of that sentence, like the intestines slithering from the hands
Of the startled boys clutching their belly wounds
At the Somme, has escaped my grip. I step over it
Gingerly. Where were we? Not far from the honey market,
Which is not far from the hay market. It is important
To remember that the teeming cities of the nineteenth century
Were site central for horsewhipping. Humans had domesticated
The race of horses some ten centuries before, harnessed them,
Trained them, whipped them mercilessly for recalcitrance
In vienna, Prague, Naples, London, and Chicago, according
To the novels of the period which may have been noticing this

For the first time or registering an actual statistical increase
In either human brutality or the insurrectionary impulse
In horses, which were fed hay, so there was, of course,
In every European city a hay market like the one in which
Raskolnikov kissed the earth from a longing for salvation.
Grushenka, though Dostoyevsky made her, probably did not
Have much use for novels of ideas. Her younger son,
A master carpenter, eventually took a degree in engineering
From Bucknell University. He married an Irish girl
From Vermont who was descended from the gardener
Of Emily Dickinson, but that's another story. Their son
In Iwo Jima died. Gangrene. But he left behind, curled
In the body of the daughter of a Russian Jewish cigar maker
From Minsk, the fetal curl of a being who became the lead dancer
In the Cleveland Ballet, radiant Tanya, who turned in
A bad knee sometime in early 1971, just after her brother ate it
In Cao Dai Dien, for motherhood, which brings us
To our waiter, Dmitri, who, you will have noticed, is not in Baghdad.
He doesn't even want to be an actor. He has been offered
Roles in several major motion pictures and refused them
Because he is, in fact, under contract to John Ashbery
Who is a sane and humane man and has no intention
Of releasing him from the poem. You can get killed out there.
He is allowed to go home for his mother's birthday and she
Has described to him on the phone – a cell phone, he's
Walking down Christopher Street with such easy bearing
He could be St Christopher bearing innocence across a river –
Having come across a lock, the delicate curl of a honey-
Colored lock of his great-grandmother's Crimean-
Honey-bee-pollen-, Russian-spring-wildflower-sachet-
Scented hair in the attic, where it released for her
In the July heat and raftery midsummer dark the memory
Of an odor like life itself carried to her on the wind.
Here is your sea bass with a light lemon and caper sauce.
Here is your dish of raspberries and chocolate; notice
Their subtle transfiguration of the colors of excrement and blood;
And here are the flecks of crystallised lavender that stipple it.

ROBERT HASS

The Long War

Less passionate the long war throws
its burning thorn about all men,
caught in one grief, we share one wound,
and cry one dialect of pain.

We have forgot who fired the house
whose easy mischief spilled first blood,
under one raging roof we lie
the fault no longer understood

But as our twisted arms embrace
the desert where our cities stood
death's family likeness in each face
must show, at last, our brotherhood.

LAURIE LEE

Letter to My Wife

Beneath, the nether worlds, deep, still, and mute.
Silence howls in my ears, and I cry out.
No answer could come back, it is so far
from that sad Serbia swooned into war.
And you're so distant. But my heart redeems
your voice all day, entangled in my dreams.
So I am still, while close about me sough
the great cold ferns, that slowly stir and bow.

When I'll see you, I don't know. You whose calm
is as the weight and sureness of a psalm,
whose beauty's like the shadow and the light,
whom I could find if I were blind and mute,
hide in the landscape now, and from within
leap to my eye, as if cast by my brain.
You were real once; now you have fallen in
to that deep well of teenage dreams again.

Jealous interrogations: tell me; speak.
Do you still love me? will you on that peak
of my past youth become my future wife?
– But now I fall awake to real life
and know that's what you are: wife, friend of years,
– just far away. Beyond three wild frontiers.
And Fall comes. Will it also leave with me?
Kisses are sharper in the memory.

Daylight and miracles seemed different things.
Above, the echelons of bombers' wings:
skies once amazing blue with your eyes' glow
are darkened now. Tight with desire to blow,
the bombs must fall. I live in spite of these,
a prisoner. All of my fantasies
I measure out. And I will find you still;
for you I've walked the full length of the soul,

the highways of countries! – on coals of fire,
if needs must, in the falling of the pyre,
if all I have is magic, I'll come back;
I'll stick as fast as bark upon an oak!
And now that calm, whose habit is a power
and weapon to the savage, in the hour
of fate and danger, falls as cool and true
as does a wave: the sober two times two.

[*Lager Heideman, August–September 1944*]

MIKLÓS RADNÓTI
translated from the Hungarian by Zsuzsanna Ozsváth & Frederick Turner

NOTE: Miklós Radnóti wrote this poem while on a forced march of 3200
Hungarian Jews from a labour camp in Yugoslavia. Most of those died on
the road. Radnóti was shot by Hungarian fascists in November 1944.
When his body was exhumed from a mass grave in 1946, a small notebook
of poems telling the story of his last six months was found in his coat.

Aspen Tree

Aspen tree, your leaves glance white into the dark.
My mother's hair never turned white.

Dandelion, so green is the Ukraine.
My fair-haired mother did not come home.

Rain cloud, do you linger at the well?
My soft-voiced mother weeps for all.

Rounded star, you coil the golden loop.
My mother's heart was hurt by lead.

Oaken door, who hove you off your hinge?
My gentle mother cannot return.

PAUL CELAN
translated from the German by John Felstiner

The Green Beret

He was twelve years old,
and I do not know his name.
The mercenaries took him and his father,
whose name I do not know,
one morning upon the High Plateau.
Green Beret looked down on the frail boy
with the eyes of a hurt animal and thought,
a good fright will make him talk.
He commanded, and the father was taken away
behind the forest's green wall.
'Right kid tell us where they are,
Tell us where or your father – dead.'
With eyes now bright and filled with horror
the slight boy said nothing.

'You've got one minute kid,' said Green Beret,
'tell us where or we kill father'
and thrust his wrist-watch against a face all eyes,
the second-hand turning, jerking on its way.
'OK boy ten seconds to tell us where they are.'
In the last instant the silver hand shattered the
sky and the forest of trees.
'Kill the old guy' roared Green Beret
and shots hammered out
behind the forest's green wall
and sky and trees and soldiers stood,
in silence, and the boy cried out.
Green Beret stood
in silence, as the boy crouched down
and shook with tears,
as children do when their father dies.
'Christ,' said one mercenary to Green Beret,
'he didn't know a damn thing
we killed the old guy for nothing.'
So they all went away,
Green Beret and his mercenaries.

And the boy knew everything.
He knew everything about them, the caves,
the trails, the hidden places and the names,
and in the moment that he cried out,
in that same instant,
protected by frail tears
far stronger than any wall of steel,
they passed everywhere
like tigers
across the High Plateau.

HO THIEN
translated from the Vietnamese

Night Ambush

We are still, lips swollen with mosquito bites.
A treeline opens out onto paddies
quartered by dikes, a moon in each,
and in the center, the hedged island of a village
floats in its own time, ribboned with smoke.
Someone is cooking fish.
Whispers move across water.
Children and old people. Anyone between
is a target. It is so quiet
you can hear a safety clicked off
all the way on the other side.
Things live in my hair. I do not bathe.
I have thrown away my underwear.
I have forgotten the why of everything.
I sense an indifference larger than anything
I know. All that will remain of us
is rusting metal disappearing in vines.
Above the fog that clots the hill ahead
a red tracer arcs and dims.
A black snake slides off the paddy dike
into the water and makes the moon shiver.

DOUG ANDERSON

How to Kill

Under the parabola of a ball,
a child turning into a man,
I looked into the air too long.
The ball fell in my hand, it sang
in the closed fist: *Open Open
Behold a gift designed to kill.*

Now in my dial of glass appears
the soldier who is going to die.
He smiles, and moves about in ways

his mother knows, habits of his.
The wires touch his face: I cry
NOW. Death, like a familiar, hears

and look, has made a man of dust
of a man of flesh. This sorcery
I do. Being damned, I am amused
to see the centre of love diffused
and the waves of love travel into vacancy.
How easy it is to make a ghost.

The weightless mosquito touches
her tiny shadow on the stone,
and with how like, how infinite
a lightness, man and shadow meet.
They fuse. A shadow is a man
when the mosquito death approaches.

KEITH DOUGLAS

Here, Bullet

If a body is what you want,
then here is bone and gristle and flesh.
Here is the clavicle-snapped wish,
the aorta's opened valves, the leap
thought makes at the synaptic gap.
Here is the adrenaline rush you crave,
that inexorable flight, that insane puncture
into heat and blood. And I dare you to finish
what you've started. Because here, Bullet,
here is where I complete the word you bring
hissing through the air, here is where I moan
the barrel's cold esophagus, triggering
my tongue's explosives for the rifling I have
inside of me, each twist of the round
spun deeper, because here, Bullet,
here is where the world ends, every time.

BRIAN TURNER

The War Works Hard

How magnificent the war is!
How eager
and efficient!
Early in the morning,
it wakes up the sirens
and dispatches ambulances
to various places,
swings corpses through the air,
rolls stretchers to the wounded,
summons rain
from the eyes of mothers,
digs into the earth
dislodging many things
from under the ruins...
Some are lifeless and glistening,
others are pale and still throbbing...
It produces the most questions
in the minds of children,
entertains the gods
by shooting fireworks and missiles
into the sky,
sows mines in the fields
and reaps punctures and blisters,
urges families to emigrate,
stands beside the clergymen
as they curse the devil
(poor devil, he remains
with one hand in the searing fire)...
The war continues working, day and night.
It inspires tyrants
to deliver long speeches,
awards medals to generals
and themes to poets.
It contributes to the industry
of artificial limbs,
provides food for flies,
adds pages to the history books,
achieves equality
between killer and killed,

teaches lovers to write letters,
accustoms young women to waiting,
fills the newspapers
with articles and pictures,
builds new houses
for the orphans,
invigorates the coffin makers,
gives grave diggers
a pat on the back
and paints a smile on the leader's face.
The war works with unparalleled diligence!
Yet no one gives it
a word of praise.

DUNYA MIKHAIL
translated from the Arabic by Elizabeth Winslow

The Place Where We Are Right

From the place where we are right
flowers will never grow
in the spring.

The place where we are right
is hard and trampled
like a yard.

But doubts and loves
dig up the world
like a mole, a plow.
And a whisper will be heard in the place
where the ruined
house once stood.

YEHUDA AMICHAI
translated from the Hebrew by Stephen Mitchell

nothing else

no, i was not at the square when a grenade hit
yes, someone dear to me was hit there
no, i did not sleep in a cellar
yes, i phone every night those who were sleeping there
no, i was not a man and they did not take me to the camp
yes, i met someone coming out of the wires with a bullet in his chest
no, i did not see anyone dying
yes, i saw the corpses floating along the river
no, i did not starve
yes, i sold a wedding ring and bought bread and milk
no, nobody forced me out of my home
yes, someone changed the locks and lay in my bed
no, i did not buy a tiny pistol i spotted in the shop
yes, i liked it, it would fit in my wallet
no, i did not choose the river bank i happened to be at
yes, i know, i could learn to swim
no, i was not scared
yes, i did cry watching the planes passing by
no, they did not hear me, i was far below
yes, i knew they would drop a bomb in your backyard
no, in fact i did not know, i worried they might do that
yes, i remember everything
no, it was not cold, it was a beautiful summer
i walked my baby in a stroller and sang to her
the whole day
what did i sing?
about a cloud and a bird,
a wish and a star,
la la la,
yes, nothing else

TATJANA LUKIC

The Pomegranates of Kandahar

The bald heft of ordnance
A landmine
shrapnel cool in its shell

Red balls
pinioned in pyramids
rough deal tables stacked to the sky

A mirrored shawl
splits
and dozens tumble down –

careering through the marketplace
joyful fruit
caught by the shouts of barefoot children

Assembled, they are jewels –
jewels
of garnet, jewels of ruby

A promise deep as the deep red of poppies
of rouged lips (concealed)
Proud hearts

built of rubble
Come, let us light candles in the dust
and prise them apart –

thrust your knife through the globe
then twist
till the soft flesh cleaves open

to these small shards of sweetness
Tease each jellied cell
from its white fur of membrane

till a city explodes in your mouth
Harvest of goodness,
harvest of blood

SARAH MAGUIRE

A Night Unlike Others

His finger almost touches the bell,
the door, unbelievably slowly,
opens.

He enters.

He goes to his bedroom.
Here they are:
his picture next to his little bed,
his schoolbag, in the dark,
awake.
He sees himself sleeping
between two dreams, two flags.

He knocks on the doors of all the rooms
– he almost knocks. But he does not.
They all wake up:
'He's back!
By God, he's back!' they shout,
but their clamour makes no sound.

They stretch their arms to hug Mohammed
but do not reach his shoulders.

He wants to ask them all
how they are doing
under the night shelling;
he cannot find his voice.

They too say things
but find no voice.

He draws nearer, they draw nearer,
he passes through them, they pass through him,
they remain shadows
and never meet.

They wanted to ask him if he'd had his supper,
if he was warm enough over there, in the earth,
if the doctors could take the bullet and the fear
out of his heart.

Was he still scared?
Had he solved the two arithmetic problems
in order not to disappoint his teacher
the following day?

Had he...?

He, too, simply wanted to say:
I've come to see you
to make sure you're all right.
He said:
Dad will, as usual, forget to take his hypertension pill.
I came to remind him as I usually do.
He said:
my pillow is here, not there.

They said.
He said.
Without a voice.

The doorbell never rang,
the visitor was not in his little bed,
they have not seen him.

The following morning neighbours whispered:
it was all a delusion.
His schoolbag was here
marked by the bullet holes,
and his stained notebooks.

Those who came to give their condolences
had never left his mother.

Moreover, how could a dead child
come back, like this, to his family,
walking,
calmly
under the shelling
of such a very long
night?

MOURID BARGHOUTI
translated from the Arabic by Radwa Ashour

16 Iraqi Policemen

The explosion left a hole in the roadbed
large enough to fit a mid-sized car.
It shattered concrete, twisted metal,
busted storefront windows in sheets
and lifted a BMW chassis up onto a rooftop.

The shocking blood of the men
forms an obscene art: a moustache, alone
on a sidewalk, a blistered hand's gold ring
still shining, while a medic, Doc Lopez,
pauses to catch his breath, to blow it out
hard, so he might cup the left side of a girl's face
in one hand, gently, before bandaging
the half gone missing.

Allah must wander in the crowd
as I do, dazed by the pure concussion
of the blast, among sirens, voices
of the injured, the boots of running soldiers,
not knowing whom to touch first,
for the dead policemen cannot be found,
here a moment before, then vanished.

BRIAN TURNER

Silence

Silence said:
truth needs no eloquence.
After the death of the horseman,
the homeward-bound horse
says everything
without saying anything.

MOURID BARGHOUTI
translated from the Arabic by Radwa Ashour

War

I, too, have declared war:
You'll need to divert part of the force
deployed to wipe out the Arabs –
to drive them out of their homes
and expropriate the land –
and set it against me.
You've got tanks and planes,
and soldiers by the batallion;
you've got the rams' horn in your hands
with which to rouse the masses;
you've got men to interrogate and torture;
you've got cells for detention.
I have only this heart
with which I give shelter
to an Arab child.
Aim your weapon at it;
even if you blow it apart
it will always,
always mock you.

AHARON SHABTAI
translated from the Hebrew by Peter Cole

A Poem of Bliss

We are placed on a wedding cake
like the two dolls, bride and groom.
When the knife strikes
we'll try to stay on the same slice.

RONNY SOMECK
translated from the Hebrew by Yair Mazor

Abd el-Hadi Fights a Superpower

In his life
he neither wrote nor read.
In his life he
didn't cut down a single tree,
didn't slit the throat
of a single calf.
In his life he did not speak
of the *New York Times*
behind its back,
didn't raise
his voice to a soul
except in his saying:
'Come in, please,
by God, you can't refuse.'

*

Nevertheless –
his case is hopeless,
his situation
desperate.
His God-given rights are a grain of salt
tossed into the sea.
Ladies and gentlemen of the jury:
about his enemies
my client knows not a thing.

And I can assure you,
were he to encounter
the entire crew
of the aircraft carrier *Enterprise*,
he'd serve them eggs
sunny-side up,
and labneh
fresh from the bag.

TAHA MUHAMMAD ALI
translated from the Arabic by Peter Cole, Yahya Hijazi & Gabriel Levin

Truce

It begins with one or two soldiers
And one or two following
With hampers over their shoulders.
They might be off wildfowling

As they would another Christmas Day,
So gingerly they pick their steps.
No one seems sure of what to do.
All stop when one stops.

A fire gets lit. Some spread
Their greatcoats on the frozen ground.
Polish vodka, fruit and bread
Are broken out and passed round.

The air of an old German song,
The rules of Patience, are the secrets
They'll share before long.
They draw on their last cigarettes

As Friday-night lovers, when it's over,
Might get up from their mattresses
To congratulate each other
And exchange names and addresses.

PAUL MULDOON

A U-Boat Morning, 1914

will come as we perform the mundane toil,
say, tossing the breakfast scraps astern,
or washing down the maindeck among the oblongs
of sail-shadow. The morning sun
will mint its coins across a lazy sea,
the weather tacks and sheets will rise and fall
in languid intersectings of the sea-rim.

And there, so sudden, ordinary, too close
to dodge, or do anything about but wait for
with quiet interest, will be the thing of hearsay,
cigar profile, stub tower, little gun, so credible,
for all that it will be the first such vessel
we will have seen outside some journal's
crude picture.

Through his loudhailer,
the officer will be polite, but firm,
reading the English translation from a card.
Fifteen minutes. We'll stow such extra food,
water, charts, as time will allow,
also oilskins, a mouth organ, a piece
of unfinished scrimshaw perhaps, nothing bulky,
then lower the boats, and stand off from the barque
at the distance we will have been directed to.
Oddest for our sense of what is proper
will be the sight of the helm unmanned out there
in open sea.

And this will be the manner
a moment in time will surface to say, *Of course*
your lives are free. Of course they are compelled,
as we watch, quiescent, attentive, the lifeboats
gentle as hammock sway in the swell beneath us,
the little gun puffing its little smoke,
and thin smoke oozing from somewhere on board.
Gradually our home will lean into
its odd stricken angle, and spill wheatgrain
from the holes in her side, slipping under,
natural as a sleeper turning under blankets.
When it is done, the captain will salute us
just once, the submarine chug away, routine
as a mailboat.

And without undue hardship
we will survive, but no one there will serve
in sailing ships again. This is how
an ancient confidence will vanish
casually like a fashion in jokes. Instead
we'll live into a time strange to us,

we'll live aware of how the unborn have
their faces turned away from all we took
for granted, as stubborn or quizzical, we will
submit to someone else's scheme of what
is pressing, waste on the floor of life's renewal.
And if this quiet impending morning leaves
one thought in mind, it might be wheatgrain
fanning from a ship across the ocean's dark
like brassy beads, like fabulous golden blood.

ALAN GOULD

The Field-Mouse

Summer, and the long grass is a snare drum.
The air hums with jets.
Down at the end of the meadow,
far from the radio's terrible news,
we cut the hay. All afternoon
its wave breaks before the tractor blade.
Over the hedge our neighbour travels his field
in a cloud of lime, drifting our land
with a chance gift of sweetness.

The child comes running through the killed flowers,
his hands a nest of quivering mouse,
its black eyes two sparks burning.
We know it will die and ought to finish it off.
It curls in agony big as itself
and the star goes out in its eye.
Summer in Europe, the field's hurt,
and the children kneel in long grass,
staring at what we have crushed.

Before day's done the field lies bleeding,
the dusk garden inhabited by the saved, voles,
frogs, a nest of mice. The wrong that woke
from a rumour of pain won't heal,
and we can't face the newspapers.

All night I dream the children dance in grass
their bones brittle as mouse-ribs, the air
stammering with gunfire, my neighbour turned
stranger, wounding my land with stones.

GILLIAN CLARKE

The Goldfinches of Baghdad

These finches are kept in gold cages
or boxes covered in wire mesh;
they are used by falcon trainers as lures,
and rich patriarchs choose these living ornaments
to sing to them on their deathbeds. Their song is pure
and melodious. A goldfinch with a slashed throat
was the subject of a masterpiece painted in the
sixteenth century on the back of a highly
polished mother-of-pearl shell – it burns
tonight in Baghdad, along with the living,
caged birds. Flesh and feathers, hands
and wings. Sirens wail, but the tongues
of poets and the beaks of goldfinches burn.
Those who cannot speak burn along with the
articulate – creatures oblivious of prayer burn
along with those who lament to their god.
Falcons on the silver chains, the children
of the falson trainer, smother in the smoke
of burning feathers and human flesh.
We sing or die, singing death
as our songs feed the flames.

ROBERT ADAMSON

Garden Fragrance

Last night a bomb exploded on the veranda
But sounds of birds sweeten the earth this morning.
I hear the fragrant trees, look in the garden,
Find two silent clusters of ripe guavas.

LAM THI MY DA
translated from the Vietnamese by Martha Collins & Thuy Dinh

Though There Are Torturers

Though there are torturers in the world
There are also musicians.

Though, at this moment,
Men are screaming in prisons
There are jazzmen raising storms
Of sensuous celebration
And orchestras releasing
Glories of the Spirit.

Though the image of God
Is everywhere defiled
A man in West Clare
Is playing the concertina,
The Sistine Choir is levitating
Under the dome of St Peter's
And a drunk man on the road
Is singing for no reason.

MICHAEL COADY

The Ice-Cream Man

Rum and raisin, vanilla, butterscotch, walnut, peach:
You would rhyme off the flavours. That was before
They murdered the ice-cream man on the Lisburn Road
And you bought carnations to lay outside his shop.
I named for you all the wild flowers of the Burren
I had seen in one day: thyme, valerian, loosestrife,
Meadowsweet, twayblade, crowfoot, ling, angelica,
Herb robert, marjoram, cow parsley, sundew, vetch,
Mountain avens, wood sage, ragged robin, stitchwort,
Yarrow, lady's bedstraw, bindweed, bog pimpernel.

MICHAEL LONGLEY

To Whom It May Concern

This poem about ice cream
has nothing to do with government,
with riot, with any political scheme.

It is a poem about ice cream. You see?
About how you might stroll into a shop
and ask: *One Strawberry Split. One Mivvi.*

What did I tell you? No one will die.
No licking tongues will melt like candle wax.
This is a poem about ice cream. Do not cry.

ANDREW MOTION

Wreaths

The Civil Servant

He was preparing an Ulster fry for breakfast
When someone walked into the kitchen and shot him:
A bullet entered his mouth and pierced his skull,
The books he had read, the music he could play.

He lay in his dressing gown and pyjamas
While they dusted the dresser for fingerprints
And then shuffled backwards across the garden
With notebooks, cameras and measuring tapes.

They rolled him up like a red carpet and left
Only a bullet hole in the cutlery drawer:
Later his widow took a hammer and chisel
And removed the black keys from his piano.

The Greengrocer

He ran a good shop, and he died
Serving even the death-dealers
Who found him busy as usual
Behind the counter, organised
With holly wreaths for Christmas,
Fir trees on the pavement outside.

Astrologers or three wise men
Who may shortly be setting out
For a small house up the Shankill
Or the Falls, should pause on their way
To buy gifts at Jim Gibson's shop,
Dates and chestnuts and tangerines.

The Linen Workers

Christ's teeth ascended with him into heaven:
Through a cavity in one of his molars
The wind whistles: he is fastened for ever
By his exposed canines to a wintry sky.

I am blinded by the blaze of that smile
And by the memory of my father's false teeth
Brimming in their tumbler: they wore bubbles
And, outside of his body, a deadly grin.

When they massacred the ten linen workers
There fell on the road beside them spectacles,
Wallets, small change, and a set of dentures:
Blood, food particles, the bread, the wine.

Before I can bury my father once again
I must polish the spectacles, balance them
Upon his nose, fill his pockets with money
And into his dead mouth slip the set of teeth.

MICHAEL LONGLEY

September Twelfth, 2001

Two caught on film who hurtle
from the eighty-second floor,
choosing between a fireball
and to jump holding hands,

aren't us. I wake beside you,
stretch, scratch, taste the air,
the incredible joy of coffee
and the morning light.

Alive, we open eyelids
on our pitiful share of time,
we bubbles rising and bursting
in a boiling pot.

X.J. KENNEDY

I Saw You Walking

I saw you walking in Newark Penn Station
in your shoes of white ash. At the corner
of my nervous glance your dazed passage
first forced me away, tracing the crescent
berth you'd give a drunk, a lurcher, nuzzling
all comers with ill will and his stench, but
not this one, not today: one shirt arm's sheared
clean from the shoulder, the whole bare limb
wet with muscle and shining dimly pink,
the other full-sheathed in cotton, Brooks Bros
type, the cuff yet buttoned at the wrist, a
parody of careful dress, preparedness –
so you had not rolled up your sleeves yet this
morning when your suit jacket (here are
the pants, dark gray, with subtle stripe, as worn
by men like you on ordinary days)
and briefcase (you've none, reverse commuter
come from the pit with nothing to carry
but your life) were torn from you, as your life
was not. Your face itself seemed to be walking,
leading your body north, though the age
of the face, blank and ashen, passing forth
and away from me, was unclear, the sandy
crown of hair powdered white like your feet, but
underneath not yet gray – forty-seven?
forty-eight? the age of someone's father –
and I trembled for your luck, for your broad
dusted back, half shirted, walking away;
I should have dropped to my knees to thank God
you were alive, O my God, in whom I don't believe.

DEBORAH GARRISON

Kidding Myself in Kuta, Bali: A Pantoum

They've hired too many actors for the scene
The piles of bodies really are a laugh
The wounds are so extreme that they're obscene
With limbs ripped off and bodies cut in half

The piles of bodies really are a laugh
The blood however excellently done
With limbs ripped off and bodies cut in half
While all around the crimson rivers run

The blood however excellently done
Confused? Concussed? A little drunk perhaps
While all around the crimson rivers run
I am the one in shock who laughs and claps

Confused? Concussed? A little drunk perhaps
At last it dawns, there is no camera crew
I am the one in shock who laughs and claps
Hawaiian shirt with blood now streaming through

At last it dawns, there is no camera crew
A laugh chokes in my throat, I'm sobbing now
Hawaiian shirt with blood now streaming through
A man in white sticks something on my brow

A laugh chokes in my throat, I'm sobbing now
The frantic search for living victims starts
A man in white sticks something on my brow
He smiles and whispers sorry and departs

The frantic search for living victims starts
A second man comes close, and shakes his head
He smiles and whispers sorry and departs
I can't accept I'm very nearly dead

A second man comes close, and shakes his head
I do not want to face my life's conclusion
I can't accept I'm very nearly dead
It's just a film: my final self delusion

I do not want to face my life's conclusion
They've hired too many actors for the scene
It's just a film: my final self delusion
The wounds are so extreme that they're obscene

ALAN SMITH

While the Record Plays

They heated hatchet blades over gas fires in roadside workshops
and hammered them into cleavers.

They brought wooden blocks on trucks and carried them across
these new provinces grimly, quickly, and steadily: almost
according to ritual.

Because at any time – at noon or midnight – they would arrive at
one of these impure settlements,

where women did not cook nor make beds as theirs did, where men
did not greet one another as they did, where children and
the whole damned company did not pronounce words as
they did, and where the girls kept apart from them.

They would select from these insolent and intolerable people twelve
men, preferably young ones, to take to the marketplace,

and there – because of *blah-blah-blah* and moreover *quack-quack-
quack* and likewise *quack-blah-quack* – would beat and
behead them,

of historical necessity – because of *twaddle-twiddle* and *twiddle-diddle*,
and expertly, for their occupations would be different one
from the other,

agronomist and butcher, bookbinder and engineer, waiter and
doctor, several seminarists, cadets from military academies,
a considerable number of students,

those familiar with Carnot, Beethoven and even Einstein, displaying
their finest talents,

because, after all, nevertheless, *blah-blah-blah* and *twiddle-dee-dee*,

while through loudspeakers records played – music and an
occasional gruff order, and they, the zealous ones, wiped
their foreheads and turned aside every now and then to
urinate since excitement affects the kidneys;

then having washed the blocks and hauled down the large tricolour
which on such occasions always waved above their heads,

they too would march on into the broad future,

past the heads, carefully placed in a circle,

then out of the settlement where now also

and forever and ever,

reason, comfort, and hope would be no –

wrr-wrr-wrr – that is to say – *we-wp*, *wa-rp*, the sound (by now
the only one

without music or words) that the needle makes as the record
grinds on.

GYULA ILLYÉS
translated from the Hungarian by William Jay Smith

Fear

Fear passes from man to man
Unknowing,
As one leaf passes its shudder
To another.

All at once the whole tree is trembling
And there is no sign of the wind.

CHARLES SIMIC

In trying times

They asked that man for his time
so that he could link it to History.
They asked him for his hands,
because for trying times
nothing is better than a good pair of hands.
They asked him for his eyes
that once had tears
so that he should see the bright side
(the bright side of life, especially)
because to see horror one startled eye is enough.
They asked him for his lips,
parched and split, to affirm,
to belch up, with each affirmation, a dream
(the great dream);
they asked him for his legs
hard and knotted
(his wandering legs),
because in trying times
is there anything better than a pair of legs
for building or digging ditches?
They asked him for the grove that fed him as a child,
with its obedient tree.
They asked him for his breast, heart, his shoulders.
They told him
that that was absolutely necessary.
They explained to him later
that all this gift would be useless
unless he turned his tongue over to them,
because in trying times
nothing is so useful in checking hatred or lies.
And finally they begged him,
please, to go take a walk.
Because in trying times
that is, without a doubt, the decisive test.

HEBERTO PADILLA
translated from the Spanish by Alastair Reid & Andrew Hurley

On Living

I

Life's no joke,
you must live it in earnest
    like a squirrel, for example,
expecting nothing outside your life or beyond,
    you must concentrate wholly on living.

You must take living seriously,
so much so that,
your back to the wall, your arms bound behind;
or in a laboratory
    in your white coat and big goggles
    you can die for mankind,
    even for people whose faces you've never seen,
    even though nobody forces you,
    even though you know the best thing, the most real,
        is to live.

You'll take living so seriously,
that even at seventy you'll plant olive trees
not just to leave to your children;
    but because, although you fear death
        you don't believe in it,
        so great is the power of life.

1947

II

Say we're ill enough for a major operation,
I mean that perhaps we won't ever get up
    from the white table.
If we have to feel sorry for leaving a little early,
we can still laugh at Nasreddin Hodja jokes,
and look from the window to see if it rains,
or hang around restless
    for the latest news.

Say we're fighting for something worthwhile,
    at the front, for example;
at the first assault the first day,

we might fall face down and die.
We'll feel a strange anger,
    and not knowing
    the end of that war which could last for years
        will still drive us mad.

Say we're in prison,
our age almost fifty,
eighteen years till they open the iron door;
but we must still live with the world outside,
with its people and animals, its quarrels, its wind,
    the world beyond the wall.

But wherever, however we are,
    we must live as though
    we will never die.

1948

III

This world will grow cold,
a star among stars,
    one of the smallest,
this great world of ours
    a gilded mote on blue velvet.

This world will grow cold one day,
not even as a heap of ice,
or a lifeless cloud,
it will roll like an empty walnut round and round
    in pitch darkness for ever.

For now you must feel this pain,
and endure the sadness,
but so love this world
    that you can say,
    'I have lived'.

February 1948
[Letter to Kemal Tahir from prison]

NAZIM HIKMET
translated from the Turkish by Ruth Christie

Soup

One night our block leader set a competition:
two bowls of soup to the best teller of a tale.
That whole evening the hut filled with words –
tales from the old countries
of wolves and children
potions and love-sick herders
stupid woodsmen and crafty villagers.
Apple-blossom snowed from blue skies,
orphans discovered themselves royal.
Tales of greed and heroes and cunning survival,
soldiers of the empires, the Church, the Reich.

And when they turned to me
I could not speak,
sunk in the horror of that place,
my throat a corridor of bones, my eyes
and nostrils clogged with self pity.
'Speak,' they said, 'everyone has a story to tell.'
And so I closed my eyes and said:
I have no hunger for your bowls of soup, you see
I have just risen from the Shabbat meal –
my father has filled our glasses with wine,
bread has been broken, the maid has served fish.
Grandfather has sung, tears in his eyes, the old songs.
My mother holds her glass by the stem, lifts
it to her mouth, the red glow reflecting on her throat.
I go to her side and she kisses me for bed.
My grandfather's kiss is rough and soft like an apricot.
The sheets on my bed are crisp and flat
like the leaves of a book...

I carried my prizes back to my bunk: one bowl
I hid, the other I stirred
and smelt a long time, so long
that it filled the cauldron of my head,
drowning a family of memories.

TONY CURTIS

I will live and survive

I will live and survive and be asked:
How they slammed my head against a trestle,
How I had to freeze at nights,
How my hair started to turn grey...
But I'll smile. And will crack some joke
And brush away the encroaching shadow.
And I will render homage to the dry September
That became my second birth.
And I'll be asked: 'Doesn't it hurt you to remember?'
Not being deceived by my outward flippancy.
But the former names will detonate in my memory –
Magnificent as old cannon.
And I will tell of the best people in all the earth,
The most tender, but also the most invincible,
How they said farewell, how they went to be tortured,
How they waited for letters from their loved ones.
And I'll be asked: what helped us to live
When there were neither letters nor any news – only walls,
And the cold of the cell, and the blather of official lies,
And the sickening promises made in exchange for betrayal.
And I will tell of the first beauty
I saw in captivity.
A frost-covered window! No spyholes, nor walls,
Nor cell-bars, nor the long endured pain –
Only a blue radiance on a tiny pane of glass,
A cast pattern – none more beautiful could be dreamt!
The more clearly you looked, the more powerfully blossomed
Those brigand forests, campfires and birds!
And how many times there was bitter cold weather
And how many windows sparkled after that one –
But never was it repeated,
That upheaval of rainbow ice!
And anyway, what good would it be to me now,
And what would be the pretext for that festival?
Such a gift can only be received once,
And perhaps is only needed once.

[Labour camp hospital, *30 November 1983*]

IRINA RATUSHINSKAYA
translated from the Russian by David McDuff

355

Skipping Without Ropes

I will, I will skip without your rope
Since you say I should not, I cannot
Borrow your son's skipping rope to
Exercise my limbs, I will skip without

Your rope as you say even the lace
I want will hang my neck until I die
I will create my own rope, my own
Hope and skip without your rope as

You insist I do not require to stretch
My limbs fixed by these fevers of your
Reeking sweat and your prison walls;
I will, will skip with my forged hope;

Watch, watch me skip without your
Rope; watch me skip with my hope –
A-one, a-two, a-three, a-four, a-five
I will, a-seven, I do, will skip, a-ten,

Eleven, I will skip without, will skip
Within and skip I do without your
Rope but with my hope; and I will,
Will always skip you dull, will skip

Your silly rules, skip your filthy walls,
Your weevil pigeon peas, skip your
Scorpions, skip your Excellency Life
Glory. I do, you don't, I can, you can't,

I will, you won't, I see, you don't, I
Sweat, you don't, I will, will wipe my
Gluey brow then wipe you at a stroke
I will, will wipe your horrid, stinking,

Vulgar prison rules, will wipe you all
Then hop about, hop about my cell, my
Home, the mountains, my globe as your
Sparrow hops about your prison yard

Without your hope, without your rope,
I swear, I will skip without your rope, I
Declare, I will have you take me to your
Showers to bathe me where I can resist

This singing child you want to shape me,
I'll fight your rope, your rules, your hope
As your sparrow does under your super-
vision! Guards! Take us for a shower!

JACK MAPANJE

Sorry I Forgot To Clean Up After Myself

Sorry, Sirs and Madams, I forgot to clean up after myself
after the unfortunate incidents of the previous century.

How embarrassing; my apologies. I wouldn't advise you
to stroll around here without safety goggles, and I must insist
that you enter at your own risk. You may, however, leave
your umbrella at the door. Just keep your ticket.

We expected, of course, to have this all cleared away by the time
you arrived. The goal was to present you
with blue and green screens, whitewashed counters.

Unforeseen expenses.
Red tape.
So hard to find good help these days.

But, alas, excuses. Perhaps you will appreciate
the difficulties I've faced in providing you a clean slate.
If you step into a hole, Sirs and Madams, accept the loss
of a shoe or two. Stay the course.

Progress is the mother of invention. Here: take my hand.
Yes, that's right. You can return it on the way back.

PRISCILA UPPAL

It's This Way

I stand in the advancing light,
my hands hungry, the world beautiful.

My eyes can't get enough of the trees –
they're so hopeful, so green.

A sunny road runs through the mulberries,
I'm at the window of the prison infirmary.

I can't smell the medicines –
carnations must be blooming nearby.

It's this way:
being captured is beside the point,
the point is not to surrender.

NÂZIM HIKMET
translated from the Turkish by Randy Blasing & Mutlu Konuk

My Blue Piano

At home I have a blue piano.
But I can't play a note.

It's been in the shadow of the cellar door
Ever since the world went rotten.

Four starry hands play harmonies.
The Woman in the Moon sang in her boat.

Now only rats dance to the clanks.
The keyboard is in bits.

I weep for what is blue. Is dead.
Sweet angels, I have eaten

Such bitter bread. Push open
The door of heaven. For me, for now –

Although I am still alive –
Although it is not allowed.

ELSE LASKER-SCHÜLER
translated from the German by Eavan Boland

Soldiering On

We need another monument. Everywhere
Has Tommy Atkins with his head bowed down
For all his pals, the alphabetical dead,
And that is sweet and right and every year
We freshen the whited cenotaph with red

But no one seems to have thought of standing her
In all the parishes in bronze or stone
With bags, with heavy bags, with bags of spuds
And flour and tins of peas and clinging kids
Lending the bags their bit of extra weight –

Flat-chested little woman in a hat,
Thin as a rake, tough as old boots, with feet
That ache, ache, ache. I've read
He staggered into battle carrying sixty pounds
Of things for killing with. She looked after the pence,

She made ends meet, she had her ports of call
For things that keep body and soul together
Like sugar, tea, a loaf, spare ribs and lard,
And things the big ship brings that light the ends
Of years, like oranges. On maps of France

I've trailed him down the chalky roads to where
They end and her on the oldest A to Z
Down streets, thin as a wraith, year in, year out
Bidding the youngest put her best foot forward,
Lugging the rations past the war memorial.

DAVID CONSTANTINE

'For Those Dead, Our Dead...'

When you get the nomination, the award, the promotion,
think about the ones who died.
When you are at the reception, on the delegation, on the commission,
think about the ones who died.
When you have won the vote, and the crowd congratulates you,
think about the ones who died.
When you're cheered as you go up to the speaker's platform with
    the leaders,
think about the ones who died.
When you're picked up at the airport in the big city,
think about the ones who died.
When it's your turn to talk into the microphone, when the TV
    cameras focus on you,
think about the ones who died.
When you become the one who gives out the certificates, orders,
    permission,
think about the ones who died.
When the little old lady comes to you with her problem, her little
    piece of land,
think about the ones who died.
       See them without shirts, being dragged,
    gushing blood, wearing hoods, blown to pieces,
submerged in tubs, getting electric shocks,
           their eyes gouged out,
    their throats cut, riddled with bullets,
dumped along the side of the road,
      in holes they dug themselves,
      in mass graves,
or just lying on the ground, enriching the soil of wild plants:
You represent them.
The ones who died
delegated you.

ERNESTO CARDENAL
translated from the Spanish by Jonathan Cohen

Sleeping on the Bus

How we drift in the twilight of bus stations,
how we shrink in overcoats as we sit,
how we wait for the loudspeaker
to tell us when the bus is leaving,
how we bang on soda machines
for lost silver, how bewildered we are
at the vision of our own faces
in white-lit bathroom mirrors.

How we forget the bus stations of Alabama,
Birmingham to Montgomery,
how the Freedom Riders were abandoned
to the beckoning mob, how afterwards
their faces were tender and lopsided as spoiled fruit,
fingers searching the mouth for lost teeth,
and how the riders, descendants
of Africa and Europe both, kept riding
even as the mob with pleading hands wept fiercely
for the ancient laws of segregation.

How we forget Biloxi, Mississippi, a decade before,
where no witnesses spoke to cameras,
how a brown man in Army uniform
was pulled from the bus by police
when he sneered at the custom of the back seat,
how the magistrate proclaimed a week in jail
and went back to bed with a shot of whiskey,
how the brownskinned soldier could not sleep
as he listened for the prowling of his jailers,
the muttering and cardplaying of the hangmen
they might become.
His name is not in the index;
he did not tell his family for years.
How he told me, and still I forget.

How we doze upright on buses,
how the night overtakes us
in the babble of headphones,
how the singing and clapping
of another generation

fade like distant radio
as we ride, forehead
heavy on the window,
how we sleep, how we sleep.

MARTÍN ESPADA

News About No One

Those who are
　　　　never in the news,
whom no one remembers –
what wind erased their traces
as if they never walked the earth;
my father, all the others, where
　　　　O where...?

What happened to the
　　　　neighbourhood carpenter
maker of solid beds, and dressers
　　　　　　　　for brides?
How he worshipped the wood!

Where is the silent shoemaker
who hugged his anvil, and bit the bitter nails
between his teeth? Did a "smart" bomb
demolish his hole-in-the-wall
crammed to the ceiling
with battered shoes?

Where the coppersmith,
　　　　　　where the golden tray?

The ear of wheat around the saint's image?
The horseshoe above the door?
What happened to Umm Youssef, the midwife?
How many babies were dragged
　　out of the warm darkness of the womb

into the starkness of this world
   by her dextrous hands
sending them on their way
   with a slap on their bare bottoms
through the crooked valleys of
         their destinies, soldiers who fight
         in dubious battles
         and unjust wars?...

After they got tired
slaving in the mills of poverty
to fill the granaries of the tyrant
did they feel ashamed of the way
                  this world is made?

After the sieges, after the wars
beyond hunger, beyond
         enemies, out of the reach
of the executioner's hand –
         did they go to sleep
   at last?
To sleep, and hug the dust.

SARGON BOULUS
translated from the Arabic by the author

You Will Forget

If you stay in comfort too long
you will not know
the weight of a water pot
on the bald head of the village woman

You will forget
the weight of three bundles of thatch grass
on the sinewy neck of the woman
whose baby cries on her back
for a blade of grass in its eyes

Sure, if you stay in comfort too long
you will not know the pain
of childbirth without a nurse in white

You will forget
the thirst, the cracked dusty lips
of the woman in the valley
on her way to the headman who isn't there

You will forget
the pouring pain of a thorn prick
with a load on the head.
if you stay in comfort too long

You will forget
the wailing in the valley
of women losing a husband in the mines.

You will forget
the rough handshake of coarse palms
full of teary sorrow at the funeral.

If you stay in comfort too long
you will not hear
the shrieky voice of old warriors sing
the songs of fresh storied battlefields.

You will forget
the unfeeling bare feet
gripping the warm soil turned by the plough

You will forget
the voice of the season talking to the oxen.

CHENJERAI HOVE

7

Living in hope

All that is worth remembering in life, is the poetry of it.
Fear is poetry, hope is poetry, love is poetry, hatred is poetry;
contempt, jealousy, remorse, admiration, wonder, pity, despair,
or madness, are all poetry. Poetry is that fine particle within us,
that expands, rarefies, refines, raises our whole being:
without it 'man's life is poor as beast's'.

WILLIAM HAZLITT

VISITING HIS GRANDFATHER'S HOME village of Kilmore in Co. Armagh during
the Second World War, Belfast poet John Hewitt found himself connecting
with his roots. In the excerpts from 'Townland of Peace' (366), part of his
long poem *Freehold* (1986), Hewitt recognises his 'corner of the universe'. Across
the border in Co. Monaghan, Patrick Kavanagh finds universal meaning in his
own local patch in 'Epic' (368) and 'Shancoduff' (369), while the Irish-language
poet Liam Ó Muirthile comes to know that his 'constituency is the nation of
the small townlands' (369).

The human need for home, security and the common language of child-
hood coupled with national, tribal and family loyalties is explored by poets from
many cultures in this section, although sometimes the original home or home-
land may be left behind in forging a new identity. *Staying Alive* also includes
a series of poems relating to exile in section 8 ('My people', SA 327-38), and
this section of *Being Human* has a wider selection of poems on the modern
condition of displacement and the age-old problems of poverty, social inequality
and protecting individual freedom from communal or political intolerance.

Dunya Mikhail (330, 392) worked as a journalist in Baghdad before fleeing
Iraq in 1996 after repeated threats and harassment. Nick Makoha (391) had to
leave Uganda because his family name was shared by someone unrelated on a
government hitlist. Partaw Naderi (394) was imprisoned by the Soviet-backed
regime in Aghanistan during the 1970s and has only recently returned to Kabul
after many years of exile. Nadia Anjuman (393) was a young Persian poet and
journalist from Afghanistan who risked execution under Taliban rule by study-
ing books other than the Qu'ran in one of Herat's renowned "sewing circles"
where women were educated in secret. In 2005 she was killed by a husband
whose family felt shamed by her publication of a book of poems about love,
beauty and the oppression of Afghan women.

from **Freehold**

III *Townland of Peace*

Once in a showery summer, sick of war,
I strode the roads that slanted to Kilmore,
that church-topped mound where half the tombstones wear
my people's name; some notion drew me there,
illogical, but not to be ignored,
some need of roots saluted, some sought word
that might give strength and sense to my slack rein,
by this directed, not to lose again
the line and compass so my head and heart
no longer plunge and tug to drag apart.

Thus walking dry or sheltered under trees,
I stepped clean out of Europe into peace,
for every man I met was relevant
to the harsh clamour of my eager want,
gathering fruit, or leading horse uphill,
sawing his timber, measuring his well.
The crooked apple trees beside the gate
that almost touched the roadside with the weight
of their clenched fruit, the dappled calves that browsed
free in the netted sunlight and unhoused
the white hens slouching round the tar-bright sheds,
the neat-leafed damsons with the smoky beads,
the farm unseen but loud with bucket and dog
and voices moving in a leafy fog,
gave neither hint nor prophecy of change,
save the slow seasons in their circled range;
part of a world of natural diligence
that has forgotten its old turbulence,
save when the spade rasps on a rusted sword
or a child in a schoolbook finds a savage word.

Old John, my father's father, ran these roads
a hundred years ago with other lads
up the steep brae to school, or over the stile
to the far house for milk, or dragging the long mile
to see his mother buried. Every stride

with gable, gatepost, hedge on either side,
companioned so brought nearer my desire
to stretch my legs beside a poet's fire
in the next parish. As the road went by
with meadow and orchard, under a close sky,
and stook-lined field, and thatched and slated house,
and apples heavy on the crouching boughs,
I moved beside him. Change was strange and far
where a daft world gone shabby choked with war
among the crumpled streets or in the plains
spiked with black fire-crisped rafters and buckled lines,
from Warsaw to the Yangtze, where the slow-
phrased people learn such thought that scourge and blow
may school them into strength to find the skill
for new societies of earth and steel,
but here's the age they've lost.
                          The boys I met
munching their windfalls, drifting homeward late,
are like that boy a hundred years ago,
the same bare kibes, the heirloom rags they show;
but they must take another road in time.
Across the sea his fortune summoned him
to the brave heyday of the roaring mills
where progress beckoned with a million wheels.
[...]

Now and for ever through the change-rocked years,
I know my corner in the universe;
my corner, this small region limited
in space by sea, in the time by my own dead,
who are its compost, by each roving sense
henceforward mobilised in its defence,
against the sickness that has struck mankind,
mass-measured, mass-infected, mass-resigned.

Against the anthill and the beehive state
I hold the right of man to stay out late,
to sulk and laugh, to criticise or pray,
when he is moved, at any hour of day,
to vote by show of hands or sit at home,
or stroll on Sunday with a vasculum,
to sing or act or play or paint or write
in any mode that offers him delight.

I hold my claim against the mammoth powers
to crooked roads and accidental flowers,
to corn with poppies fabulously red,
to trout in rivers, and to wheat in bread,
to food unpoisoned, unpolluted air,
and easy pensioned age without a care
other than time's mortality must bring
to any shepherd, commissar, or king.

But these small rights require a smaller stage
than the vast forum of the nations' rage,
for they imply a well-compacted space
where every voice declares its native place,
townland, townquarter, county at the most,
the local word not ignorantly lost
in the smooth jargon, bland and half alive,
which wears no clinging burr upon its sleeve
to tell the ground it grew from, and to prove
there is for sure a plot of earth we love.

JOHN HEWITT

Epic

I have lived in important places, times
When great events were decided: who owned
That half a rood of rock, a no-man's land
Surrounded by our pitchfork-armed claims.
I heard the Duffys shouting 'Damn your soul'
And old McCabe stripped to the waist, seen
Step the plot defying blue cast-steel –
'Here is the march along these iron stones'.
That was the year of the Munich bother. Which
Was most important? I inclined
To lose my faith in Ballyrush and Gortin
Till Homer's ghost came whispering to my mind
He said: I made the *Iliad* from such
A local row. Gods make their own importance.

PATRICK KAVANAGH

Shancoduff

My black hills have never seen the sun rising,
Eternally they look north towards Armagh.
Lot's wife would not be salt if she had been
Incurious as my black hills that are happy
When dawn whitens Glassdrummond chapel.

My hills hoard the bright shillings of March
While the sun searches in every pocket.
They are my Alps and I have climbed the Matterhorn
With a sheaf of hay for three perishing calves
In the field under the Big Forth of Rocksavage.

The sleety winds fondle the rushy beards of Shancoduff
While the cattle-drovers sheltering in the Featherna Bush
Look up and say: 'Who owns them hungry hills
That the water-hen and snipe must have forsaken?
A poet? Then by heavens he must be poor.'
I hear and is my heart not badly shaken?

PATRICK KAVANAGH

The Parlour

You had to get a key to open it. In the cool
Interior your blood was racing, looking for
The secrets of mantelpiece or drawer.

Once the door was quietly locked, I was shut in,
Back among the photographs of forebears,
Devoutly attending this most private altar.

That was where the priest robed for the Stations:
The hiding-place of accordion and saxophone,
Of cattle certificates and papal marriage blessings.

We spent one whole year hiding out on the farm,
Fleeing the polio that was rampant in the City,
Wasting the legs of children in the streets.

Now in that country parlour I am seeking
Something else: that tie we have with the past –
To bring back to the light its blinded citizens.

They all said I looked like my mother's father,
And here's his wedding: cold as the marble shelf
In his bone-collared, high-necked shirt, and my bent nose.

And here's Paddy 'The Russian' Murphy from Sliabh Owen
Who hadn't the remotest interest in farming,
Whose ear they held a gun to in the time of the Tans.

Not that he ever did any act of daring.
He was delicate, and more interested in poetry
Of the *Nation*'s kind from the nineteenth century.

The Kilmichael ambush happened at the far end of the parish;
I used to fancy it was my grandfather who provided
The Volunteers' bucket of tea the night before it.

It wasn't actually; he was too far away.
But people on the run often slept in the settle,
And once the house was cleared for a military court.

My small moments of history; my household gods; my myth,
Revisiting the parlour for my benefit, so now I know
My constituency is the nation of the small townlands.

LIAM Ó MUIRTHILE
translated from the Irish by Bernard O'Donoghue

My real dwelling

My real dwelling
Has no pillars
And no roof either
So rain cannot soak it
And wind cannot blow it down!

IKKYU
translated from the Japanese by John Stevens

Denouement

I have great admiration for ships
and for certain people's handwriting which I attempt to imitate.
Of my entire family, I'm the only one who has seen the ocean,
I describe it over and over; they say 'hmm'
and continue circling the chicken coop with wire.
I tell about the spume, and the wearisome size of the waters;
they don't remember there's such a place as Kenya,
they'd never guess I'm thinking of Tanzania.
Eagerly they show me the lot: this is where the kitchen will be,
that's where we'll put in a garden.
So what do I do with the coast?
It was a pretty afternoon the day I planted myself in the window,
             between uncles,
and saw the man with his fly open,
the trellis angry with roses.
Hours and hours we talked unconsciously in Portuguese
as if it were the only language in the world.
Faith or no, I ask where are my people who are gone;
because I'm human, I zealously cover the pan of leftover sauce.
How could we know how to live a better life than this,
when even weeping it feels so good to be together?
Suffering belongs to no language.
I suffered and I suffer both in Minas Gerais and at the edge of
             the ocean.
I stand in awe of being alive. Oh, moon over the backlands,
oh, forests I don't need to see to get lost in,
oh, great cities and states of Brazil that I love as if I had invented them.
Being Brazilian places me in a way I find moving
and this, which without sinning I can call fate,
gives my desire a rest.
Taken all at once, it's far too intelligible; I can't take it.
Night! Make yourself useful and cover me with sleep.
Me and the thought of death just can't get used to each other.
I'll tremble with fear till the end.
And meanwhile everything is so small.
Compared to my heart's desire
the sea is a drop.

ADÉLIA PRADO
translated from the Portuguese by Ellen Doré Watson

The Broken Home

Crossing the street,
I saw the parents and the child
At their window, gleaming like fruit
With evening's mild gold leaf.

In a room on the floor below,
Sunless, cooler – a brimming
Saucer of wax, marbly and dim –
I have lit what's left of my life.

I have thrown out yesterday's milk
And opened a book of maxims.
The flame quickens. The word stirs.

Tell me, tongue of fire,
That you and I are as real
At least as the people upstairs.

My father, who had flown in World War I,
Might have continued to invest his life
In cloud banks well above Wall Street and wife.
But the race was run below, and the point was to win.

Too late now, I make out in his blue gaze
(Through the smoked glass of being thirty-six)
The soul eclipsed by twin black pupils, sex
And business; time was money in those days.

Each thirteenth year he married. When he died
There were already several chilled wives
In sable orbit – rings, cars, permanent waves.
We'd felt him warming up for a green bride.

He could afford it. He was 'in his prime'
At three score ten. But money was not time.

When my parents were younger this was a popular act:
A veiled woman would leap from an electric, wine-dark car

To the steps of no matter what – the Senate or the Ritz Bar –
And bodily, at newsreel speed, attack

No matter whom – Al Smith or José María Sert
Or Clemenceau – veins standing out on her throat
As she yelled *War mongerer! Pig! Give us the vote!*,
And would have to be hauled away in her hobble skirt.

What had the man done? Oh, made history.
Her business (he had implied) was giving birth,
Tending the house, mending the socks.

Always that same old story –
Father Time and Mother Earth,
A marriage on the rocks.

One afternoon, red, satyr-thighed
Michael, the Irish setter, head
Passionately lowered, led
The child I was to a shut door. Inside,

Blinds beat sun from the bed.
The green-gold room throbbed like a bruise.
Under a sheet, clad in taboos
Lay whom we sought, her hair undone, outspread,

And of a blackness found, if ever now, in old
Engravings where the acid bit.
I must have needed to touch it
Or the whiteness – was she dead?
Her eyes flew open, startled strange and cold.
The dog slumped to the floor. She reached for me. I fled.

Tonight they have stepped out onto the gravel.
The party is over. It's the fall
Of 1931. They love each other still.
She: Charlie, I can't stand the pace.
He: Come on, honey – why, you'll bury us all!

A lead soldier guards my windowsill:
Khaki rifle, uniform, and face.
Something in me grows heavy, silvery, pliable.

How intensely people used to feel!
Like metal poured at the close of a proletarian novel,
Refined and glowing from the crucible,
I see those two hearts, I'm afraid,
Still. Cool here in the graveyard of good and evil,
They are even so to be honored and obeyed.

...Obeyed, at least, inversely. Thus
I rarely buy a newspaper, or vote.
To do so, I have learned, is to invite
The tread of a stone guest within my house.

Shooting this rusted bolt, though, against him,
I trust I am no less time's child than some
Who on the heath impersonate Poor Tom
Or on the barricades risk life and limb.

Nor do I try to keep a garden, only
An avocado in a glass of water –
Roots pallid, gemmed with air. And later,

When the small gilt leaves have grown
Fleshy and green, I let them die, yes, yes,
And start another. I am earth's no less.

A child, a red dog roam the corridors,
Still, of the broken home. No sound. The brilliant
Rag runners halt before wide-open doors.
My old room! Its wallpaper – cream, medallioned
With pink and brown – brings back the first nightmares,
Long summer colds, and Emma, sepia-faced,
Perspiring over broth carried upstairs
Aswim with golden fats I could not taste.

The real house became a boarding school.
Under the ballroom ceiling's allegory
Someone at last may actually be allowed
To learn something; or, from my window, cool
With the unstiflement of the entire story,
Watch a red setter stretch and sink in cloud.

JAMES MERRILL

Back Home

I came back
to where trash
blooms like flowers –
this is the world I longed for.

I came back
to where hatred
clumps like dry dung –
this is the world I longed for.

Where I spit and swear
at the gray sky,
where the scavengers
and gangs
hustle,
yell all night.

I came back
to where girls giggle,
selling their slovenly bodies
green as turnips,
where no one knows how
to fly a flag high on the pole –
this is the world I longed for.

KO UN
translated from the Korean by Clare You & Richard Silberg

Hometown

Home is a faraway place.
The womb where you rested,
the village where you were born,
the neighbourhood where you jumped and played,
those aren't home.

If you go back before you were a man,
that's where your home is.
No, not even there, go back further.

Just try yelling without yearning
in the simple voice of an animal.
What the beast returns to,
the pure land, that's home.

Men won't do anymore.
Animals, mistreated over thousands of years,
transcending greed and foolishness,
are standing up bare in golden sunset.

So nowhere on earth, that's home.

KO UN
translated from the Korean by Clare You & Richard Silberg

Degrees of Gray in Philipsburg

You might come here Sunday on a whim.
Say your life broke down. The last good kiss
you had was years ago. You walk these streets
laid out by the insane, past hotels
that didn't last, bars that did, the tortured try
of local drivers to accelerate their lives.
Only churches are kept up. The jail
turned 70 this year. The only prisoner
is always in, not knowing what he's done.

The principal supporting business now
is rage. Hatred of the various grays
the mountain sends, hatred of the mill,
The Silver Bill repeal, the best liked girls
who leave each year for Butte. One good
restaurant and bars can't wipe the boredom out.
The 1907 boom, eight going silver mines,
a dance floor built on springs –
all memory resolves itself in gaze,
in panoramic green you know the cattle eat

or two stacks high above the town,
two dead kilns, the huge mill in collapse
for fifty years that won't fall finally down.

Isn't this your life? That ancient kiss
still burning out your eyes? Isn't this defeat
so accurate, the church bell simply seems
a pure announcement: ring and no one comes?
Don't empty houses ring? Are magnesium
and scorn sufficient to support a town,
not just Philipsburg, but towns
of towering blondes, good jazz and booze
the world will never let you have
until the town you came from dies inside?

Say no to yourself. The old man, twenty
when the jail was built, still laughs
although his lips collapse. Someday soon,
he says, I'll go to sleep and not wake up.
You tell him no. You're talking to yourself.
The car that brought you here still runs.
The money you buy lunch with,
no matter where it's mined, is silver
and the girl who serves your food
is slender and her red hair lights the wall.

RICHARD HUGO

Conurbation

The day you left they pulled your picture from its frame and tore
the posters from your walls: immaculate, monastic,
boasting no trace that you were ever there, didn't that blank
plaster prove the house had never loved you? Scrub the floor.

Boil the sheets. One day you'll feel the city's dirt
bed down beneath your fingernails; you'll tilt the blinds,
look out over council flats and office blocks,
see lamps appear in living rooms like riding lights

and lose your fear of kitchens in which eggs and bacon
squabble in the pan, where a TV waits on standby in each room,
where children still fall silent at the slam of a door,
where, when a cigarette clears a throat, it passes for conversation.

You'll wonder how you stood it for so long: a house
that never learned how to exhale. You'll close the window, turn
back to the bed as one by one the panes fill up with snow,
and that's where you'll be hiding when you get called home.

PAUL BATCHELOR

Leaf-Huts and Snow-Houses

There's not much to
these verses, only
a few words piled up
at random.
I think
nonetheless
it's fine
to make them, then
for a little while
I have something like a house.
I remember leaf-huts
we built
when we were small:
to creep in and sit
listening to the rain,
feel alone in the wilderness,
drops on your nose
and your hair –
Or snow-houses at Christmas,
to creep in and
close the hole with a sack,
light a candle and stay there
on cold evenings.

OLAV H. HAUGE
translated from the Norwegian by Robin Fulton

Street

Ah these are the poor,
These are the poor –

Bergen street.

Humiliation
Hardship...

Nor are they very good to each other;
It is not that. I want

An end of poverty
As much as anyone

For the sake of intelligence,
'The conquest of existence' –

It has been said, and is true –

And this is real pain,
Moreover. It is terrible to see the children,

The righteous little girls;
So good, they expect to be so good...

GEORGE OPPEN

American Classic

It's a classic American scene –
a car stopped off the road
and a man trying to repair it.

The woman who stays in the car
in the classic American scene
stares back at the freeway traffic.

They look surprised, and ashamed
to be so helpless...
let down in the middle of the road!

To think that their car would do this!
They look like mountain people
whose son has gone against the law.

But every night they set out food
and the robber goes skulking back to the trees.
That's how it is with the car...

it's theirs, they're stuck with it.
Now they know what it's like to sit
and see the world go whizzing by.

In the fume of carbon monoxide and dust
they are not such good Americans
as they thought they were.

The feeling of being left out
through no fault of your own is common.
That's why I say, an American classic.

LOUIS SIMPSON

from Poem VI

Cruising back from 7-11
esta mañana
in my '56 Chevy truckita,
beat up and rankled
farm truck,
clanking between rows
of shiny new cars –

> 'Hey fella! Trees need pruning
> and the grass needs trimming!'
A man yelled down to me
from his 3rd-story balcony.

'Sorry, I'm not the gardener,'
I yelled up to him.

Funny how in the Valley
an old truck symbolises prestige
and in the Heights, poverty.

Worth is determined in the Valley
by age and durability,
and in the Heights, by newness
and impression.

In the Valley,
the atmosphere is soft and worn,
things are shared and passed down.
In the Heights,
the air is blistered with glaze
of new cars and new homes.

How many days of my life
I have spent fixing up
rusty broken things,
charging up old batteries,
wiring pieces of odds and ends together!
Ah, those lovely bricks
and sticks I found in the fields
and took home with me
to make flower boxes!

The old cars I've worked on
endlessly giving them tune-ups,
changing tires, tracing
electrical shorts,
cursing when I've been stranded
between Laguna pueblo and Burque.
It's the process of making-do,
of the life I've lived between
breakdowns and break-ups, that has made life
worth living.

I could not bear a life
with everything perfect.

JIMMY SANTIAGO BACA

Them and You

They wait for the bus.
You spray them with puddles.

They queue for curry and chips.
You phone an order for delivery.

They place themselves under the protection
of the Marian Grotto at the front of their estate.

You put your trust in gilts, managed funds,
income continuation plans.

They look weathered.
You look tanned.

They knock back pints.
You cultivate a taste for vintage wines.

They get drunk.
You get pleasantly inebriated.

Their wives have straw hair.
Yours is blonde.

They are missing one football card
to complete the full set.

You keep an eye out for a matching
Louis XV-style walnut hall table.

They are hoping for a start with a builder.
You play your part in the family firm.

They use loose change, welfare coupons.
You tap your credit card impatiently on the counter.

They lean over the breeze-block wall to gossip.
You put down motions for the Residents' AGM.

They have a hot tip for Newmarket.
You have the inside track on a rights issue.

They go over the top.
You reach it.

They preach better pay.
You practise it.

DENNIS O'DRISCOLL

Cathedral Builders

They climbed on sketchy ladders towards God,
With winch and pulley hoisted hewn rock into heaven,
Inhabited sky with hammers, defied gravity,
Deified stone, took up God's house to meet Him,

And came down to their suppers and small beer;
Every night slept, lay with their smelly wives,
Quarrelled and cuffed the children, lied,
Spat, sang, were happy or unhappy,

And every day took to the ladders again;
Impeded the rights of way of another summer's
Swallows; grew greyer, shakier, became less inclined
To fix a neighbour's roof of a fine evening,

Saw naves sprout arches, clerestories soar,
Cursed the loud fancy glaziers for their luck,
Somehow escaped the plague, got rheumatism,
Decided it was time to give it up,

To leave the spire to others; and stood in the crowd
Well back from the vestments at the consecration,
Envied the fat bishop his warm boots,
Cocked up a squint eye and said, 'I bloody did that.'

JOHN ORMOND

Grit

A doxology

I praise the country women
of my mother's generation
who bred, brought up and boasted
six Australians each –
the nearest doctor fifty miles
on a road cut off by flood;
the women who by wordless men
were courted away from typewriters
and taught themselves to drive –
I praise their style
in the gravel corners.
I praise the snakes they broke in two
and the switch of wire they kept in a cupboard.
I praise what they keep and what they lose –
the long road in to the abattoirs,
the stare which cures
a stockman of shooting swans.
I praise the prints, the wide straw brims
they wore out to the clothes line;
I praise each oily crow that watched them.
I praise the tilting weather –
the dry creeks and the steady floods
and the few good weeks between.
I praise each column in the ledger
they kept up late by mosquito and lamp-light;
the temerity of the banker
reining them in at last – or trying;
the machinations for chequered paddocks
swung on the children's names;
the companies just one step ahead;
the tax clerk, in his way, also.
I praise each one of their six children
discovering in turn
the river in its tempers
the rapids and the river trees;
the children who grew up to horse sweat
and those who made it to the city.
I praise the stringy maxims
that served instead of prayers;

also the day that each child found
a slogan not enough,
surprising themselves in a camera flash
and bringing no extra paddocks.
I praise the boast of country women:
they could have been a wife
to any of a dozen men
and damn well made it work.
I praise what I have seen
to be much more than this.
I praise their politics of leather;
the ideologies in a line of cattle;
the minds that would not
stoop to whisky.
I praise their scorn
for the city of options, the scholars
in their turning chairs and air-conditioned theories.
I praise also that moment
when they headed off in tears –
the car in a toolshed failing to start,
a bootfull of fencing wire.
I praise the forty years
when they did not. I praise
each day and evening of their lives –
that hard abundance year by year
mapped in a single word.

GEOFF PAGE

Intervention Pay Day

I love my wife   she right skin for me   pretty one my wife
young one   found her at the next community over   across
the hills   little bit long way   not far

and from there she give me good kids   funny kids mine   we
always laughing all together   and that wife   she real
good mother   make our wali real nice   flowers and grass
patch and chickens   I like staying home with my kids

and from there I build cubby house   yard for the horse   see
I make them things from leftovers   from the dump   all the
leftovers from fixing the houses   and all the left overs I build
cubby house and chicken house

and in the house we teach the kids   don't make mess   go
to school   learn good so you can work round here later   good
job   good life   and the government will leave you alone

and from there tjamu and nana tell them the story   when the
government was worse   rations   government make all the rules
but don't know culture   can't sit in the sand   oh tjamu and nana
they got the best story   we always laughing us mob

and from there night time when we all asleep   all together on
the grass patch   dog and cat and kids   my wife and me
them kids they ask really good questions   about the olden days
about today   them real ninti them kids   they gunna be right

and from there come intervention   John Howard   he make
new rules   he never even come to see us   how good we was
doing already   Mal Brough   he come with the army   we
got real frightened true   thought he was gonna take the kids
away   just like tjamu and nana bin tell us

I run my kids in the sand hills   took my rifle up there and sat
but they was all just lying   changing their words all the time
wanting meeting today   and meeting tomorrow   we was getting
sick of looking at them   so everyone put their eyes down
and some even shut their ears

and from there I didn't care too much   just kept working
fixing the housing   being happy working hard   kids go to
school   wife working hard too   didn't care too much   we
was right   we always laughing us mob   all together

but then my wife she come home crying   says the money in
quarantine but I didn't know why they do that   we was happy
not drinking and fighting   why they do that we ask the council
to stop the drinking and protect the children   hey you know me ya
bloody mongrel I don't drink   and I look after my kids   I
bloody fight ya you say that again   *hey settle down we not saying
that   Mal Brough saying that   don't you watch the television*

386

he making the rules for all the mobs   every place Northern Territory
he real cheeky whitefella   but he's the boss   we gotta do it

and from there I tell my wife she gets paid half   half in hand
half in the store   her money in the store now   half and half
me too   all us building mob   but I can't buy tobacco   or
work boots   you only get the meat and bread   just like the
mission days   just like tjamu and nana tell us

and from there I went to the store to get meat for our supper
but the store run out only tin food left   so I asked for some
bullets   I'll go shoot my own meat but sorry they said   you
gotta buy food   that night I slept hungry   and I slept by
myself   thinking about it

and from there the government told us our job was finish   the
government been give us the sack   we couldn't believe it   we
been working CDEP for years   slow way park the truck at the
shed   just waiting for something   for someone with tobacco

the other men's reckon fuck this   drive to town for the grog
but I stayed with my kids   started watching the television
trying to laugh   not to worry   just to be like yesterday

and from there the politician man says *I give you real job* tells me
to work again   but different   only half time sixteen hours but
I couldn't understand   it was the same job as before   but more
little   less pay   and my kids can't understand   when they
come home from school   why I cant buy the lolly for them like
I used to before   I didn't want to tell them   I get less money
for us now

and from there they say my wife earns too much money   I gonna
miss out again   I'm getting sick of it   don't worry she says
I'll look after you   but I know that's not right way   I'm get-
ting shame   my brother   he shame too   he goes to town
drinking   leaves his wife behind   leaves his kids

and from there I drive round to see tjamu   he says his money
in the store too   poor bloke   he can't even walk that far
and I don't smile   I look at that old man   he lost his smile too
but nana she cook the damper and tail   she trying to smile
she always like that

and from there when I get home   my wife gone to town with the
sister in law   she gone look for my brother   he might be stupid
on the grog   he not used to it   she gotta find him   might
catch him with another woman   make him bleed   drag him
home

and from there my wife   she come back   real quiet   tells
me she went to casino them others took her   taught her the
machines   she lost all the money   she lost her laughing

and from there all the kids bin watching us   quiet way   not
laughing around   so we all go swimming down the creek   all
the families there together   we happy again them boys   we
take them shooting   chasing the malu in the car   we real
careful with the gun   not gonna hurt my kids no way

and from there my wife   she sorry   she back working hard
save the money   kids gonna get new clothes   I gonna get my
tobacco and them bullets   but she gone change again   getting
her pay   forgetting her family   forget yesterday   only
thinking for town   with the sister in law

and my wife   she got real smart now   drive for miles all
dressed up   going to the casino with them other kungkas   for
the Wednesday night draw

I ready told you I love my kids   I only got five   two pass
away already   and I not complaining bout looking after my
kids   no way   but when my wife gets home   if she spent
all the money   not gonna share with me and the kids

I might hit her   first time

ALI COBBY ECKERMANN

wali: house; *tjamu:* grandfather; *ninti:* clever; *malu:* kangaroo; *kungkas:*
women; *CDEP:* Community Development Employment Projects (Australian
work programme for indigenous people); *grog:* alcohol.

Cable-ship

We fished up the Atlantic cable between Barbados and Tortuga,
held up our lanterns
and patched over the gash on its back,
fifteen degrees north and sixty-one west.
When we put our ears to the gnawed part
we heard the murmuring in the cable.
One of us said: 'It's the millionaires in Montreal and St John's
discussing the price of Cuban sugar
and the lowering of our wages.'

HARRY MARTINSON
translated from the Swedish by Robin Fulton

Imagine the Angels of Bread

This is the year that squatters evict landlords,
gazing like admirals from the rail
of the roofdeck
or levitating hands in praise
of steam in the shower;
this is the year
that shawled refugees deport judges
who stare at the floor
and their swollen feet
as files are stamped
with their destination;
this is the year that police revolvers,
stove-hot, blister the fingers
of raging cops,
and nightsticks splinter
in their palms;
this is the year
that darkskinned men
lynched a century ago
return to sip coffee quietly

with the apologising descendants
of their executioners.

This is the year that those
who swim the border's undertow
and shiver in boxcars
are greeted with trumpets and drums
at the first railroad crossing
on the other side;
this is the year that the hands
pulling tomatoes from the vine
uproot the deed to the earth that sprouts the vine,
the hands canning tomatoes
are named in the will
that owns the bedlam of the cannery;
this is the year that the eyes
stinging from the poison that purifies toilets
awaken at last to the sight
of a rooster-loud hillside,
pilgrimage of immigrant birth;
this is the year that cockroaches
become extinct, that no doctor
finds a roach embedded
in the ear of an infant;
this is the year that the food stamps
of adolescent mothers
are auctioned like gold doubloons,
and no coin is given to buy machetes
for the next bouquet of severed heads
in coffee plantation country.

If the abolition of slave-manacles
began as a vision of hands without manacles,
then this is the year;
if the shutdown of extermination camps
began as imagination of a land
without barbed wire or the crematorium,
then this is the year;
if every rebellion begins with the idea
that conquerors on horseback
are not many-legged gods, that they too drown
if plunged in the river,
then this is the year.

So may every humiliated mouth,
teeth like desecrated headstones,
fill with the angels of bread.

MARTÍN ESPADA

Beatitude

When a rebel leader promises you the world seen in commercials,
he will hold a shotgun to the radio announcer's mouth,
and use a quilt of bristling static to muffle the tears.

When the bodies disappear, discarded like the husk of mangoes.
He will weep with you in those hours of reckoning and judgement
into the hollow night when the crowds disperse.

When by paraffin light his whiskey breath tells you
your mother's wailings in your father's bed, are a song
for our nation and sits with you on the veranda to witness the sunrise,

say nothing. Slaughter your herd. Feed the soldiers
who looted your mills and factories. Let them dance
in your garden while an old man watches.

Then, when they sleep and your blood turns to kerosene,
find your mother gathering water at the well to stave off
the burning. Shave her head with a razor from the kiosk.

When the fury has gathered, take her hand and run
past the fields an odour of blood and bones. Past the checkpoint,
past the swamp to towards the smoky disc flaring in the horizon.

Run till your knuckles become as white as handkerchiefs,
run into the night's fluorescent silence, run till your lungs
become a furnace of flames. Run past the border.

Run till you no longer see yourself in other men's eyes.
Run past sleep, past darkness visible.
Stop when you find a country where they do not know your name.

NICK MAKOHA

I Was in a Hurry

Yesterday I lost a country.
I was in a hurry,
and didn't notice when it fell from me
like a broken branch from a forgetful tree.
Please, if anyone passes by
and stumbles across it,
perhaps in a suitcase
open to the sky,
or engraved on a rock
like a gaping wound,
or wrapped
in the blankets of emigrants,
or canceled
like a losing lottery ticket,
or helplessly forgotten
in Purgatory,
or rushing forward without a goal
like the questions of children,
or rising with the smoke of war,
or rolling in a helmet on the sand,
or stolen in Ali Baba's jar,
or disguised in the uniform of a policeman
who stirred up the prisoners
and fled,
or squatting in the mind of a woman
who tries to smile,
or scattered
like the dreams
of new immigrants in America.
If anyone stumbles across it,
return it to me please.
Please return it, sir.
Please return it, madam.
It is my country...
I was in a hurry
when I lost it yesterday.

DUNYA MIKHAIL
translated from the Arabic by Elizabeth Winslow

The Silenced

I have no desire for talking, my tongue is tied up.
Now that I am abhorred by my time, do I sing or not?
What could I say about honey, when my mouth is as bitter as poison.
Alas! The group of tyrants has muffled my mouth.
This corner of imprisonment, grief, failure and regrets –
I was born for nothing that my mouth should stay sealed.
I know O! my heart, It is springtime and the time for joy.
What could I, a bound bird, do without flight.
Although I have been silent for long, I have not forgotten to sing,
Because my songs whispered in the solitude of my heart.
Oh, I will love the day when I break out of this cage,
Escape this solitary exile and sing wildly.
I am not that weak willow twisted by every breeze.
I am an Afghan girl and known to the whole world.

NADIA ANJUMAN
translated from the Dari by Abdul Salam Shayek

Mother Tongue

Which language do you dream in,
swear in, cry in, asked the questionnaire.
How many languages do you swim in,
drown in, breathe in, mime in?

Do you know how many tongues have adopted
your voice? And when at night you stare
at dark walls and one pair of lips
comes closer, whispering in perfect German

Ich bin deine Mutter –

Or the night shadows enlarge into a Fritz Lang
open scream and *Muttersprache* appears
on the silent movie screen, then:
what do you reply? In which language,

and how clearly, do you say: my mother tongue
is somewhere in the recesses of my mind.
I am not an orphan. I have a mother.
She put me to bed one night

and went away. The film we made
together has long been silent. But I still
hear her voice through the keyhole of my heart.

NORA NADJARIAN

My Voice

I come from a distant land
with a foreign knapsack on my back
with a silenced song on my lips

As I travelled down the river of my life
I saw my voice
(like Jonah)
swallowed by a whale

And my very life lived in my voice

The Mirror

I have spent a lifetime in the mirrors of exile
busy absorbing my reflection
Listen –
I come from the unending conflicts of wisdom
I have grasped the meaning of nothingness

[*Kabul, 1989*]

PARTAW NADERI
two poems translated from the Dari by Sarah Maguire & Yama Yari

It looks so simple from a distance...

The way lives touch,
touch and spring apart,
the pulse synaptic,
local, but its stretch
electric – as when cities
lose themselves in velvet
under winking planes,
binding black hostilities
with gold chains.

ANNE STEVENSON

Local

Two of the countries that share a border with this one
are at war with each other.

My radio, which I've placed
in the shadow of the oleander bush,
tells me which targets are now being bombed
and what weapons are in use.

Not till tomorrow will the pictures come:
those of the ruins.
And those of the dead.

Many of them were alive as recently as yesterday
and many are only half as old as I am.

While I try to tune in to a radio station
with classical music
I think how hard it is to get used
to the local cigarettes.

HENRIK NORBRANDT
translated from the Danish by Robin Fulton

A Second Nature

After a couple of days, the eye gets used
to the squirrel, a gray one, not red as it should be,
to the cars, each of them five feet too long,
to the clear air, against which glistens the wet paint
of billboards, puffy clouds, and fire-escape ladders.

After a couple of weeks, the hand gets used
to the different shape of the digits one and seven,
not to mention skipping diacritical marks in your signature.

After a couple of months, even the tongue knows
how to curl in your mouth the only way that produces a correct *the*.
Another couple of months and, while tying your shoelace in the street,
you realise that you're actually doing it just to tie your shoelace,
and not in order to routinely check
if you're not followed.

After a couple of years, you have a dream:
you're standing at the kitchen sink in the forest cottage near Sieraków,
where you once spent vacation, a high-school graduate unhappily·
       in love;
your left hand holds a kettle, your right one reaches for the faucet
       knob.
The dream, as if having hit a wall, suddenly stops dead,
focusing with painful intensity on a detail that's uncertain:
was that knob made of porcelain, or brass?
Still dreaming, you know with a dazzling clarity that everything
       depends on this.
As you wake up, you know with equal clarity you'll never be able
       to make sure.

STANISŁAV BARAŃCZAK
translated from the Polish by Stanislav Barańczak & Clare Cavanagh

Foreign

Imagine living in a strange, dark city for twenty years.
There are some dismal dwellings on the east side
and one of them is yours. On the landing, you hear
your foreign accent echo down the stairs. You think
in a language of your own and talk in theirs.

Then you are writing home. The voice in your head
recites the letter in a local dialect; behind that
is the sound of your mother singing to you,
all that time ago, and now you do not know
why your eyes are watering and what's the word for this.

You use the public transport. Work. Sleep. Imagine one night
you saw a name for yourself sprayed in red
against a brick wall. A hate name. Red like blood.
It is snowing on the streets, under the neon lights,
as if this place were coming to bits before your eyes.

And in the delicatessen, from time to time, the coins
in your palm will not translate. Inarticulate,
because this is not home, you point at fruit. Imagine
that one of you says *Me not know what these people mean.*
It like they only go to bed and dream. Imagine that.

CAROL ANN DUFFY

Must Escape

At last the word for scream bursts into my notebook.
Damn this sick society
where shadows boast about their own size.
No one understands the absence of the sun.
No one knows that this brightness
is just pretending to be dawn.
No one understands the absence of meaning
in the guises of the chameleon.

These hollow ghosts
with their gorgeous clothes
and dazzling pendants on long chains,
and breadth perfumed with the scent of Europe –
from the pulpit of time, with fancy words
they talk deceit as if it were truth.
I am offended by them, offended
by the pretentiousness of the very small.
I am offended by myself, too:
I just don't understand enough
about the weakness of form and the courage of meaning.
Why do I always fall into step,
and say 'Yay!' to a demon showing off
a ring as big as Solomon's.
Why do I make conversation with nothing
and stitch my words into the hems of the mediocre
like margin prayers or footnotes.
Must escape
must run away to simplicity,
must elevate the best,
must become another example of the sun.
O darling, what can I say, for even you,
choose a dim light-bulb over daylight,
even you with your perceptive glance,
no longer see the absence of the sun.

FARZANEH KHOJANDI
translated from the Tajik by Jo Shapcott & Narguess Farzad

Hijab Scene #7

No, I'm not bald under the scarf
No, I'm not from that country
where women can't drive cars
No, I would not like to defect
I'm already American
But thank you for offering

What else do you need to know
relevant to my buying insurance,
opening a bank account,
reserving a seat on a flight?
Yes, I speak English
Yes, I carry explosives
They're called words
And if you don't get up
Off your assumptions,
They're going to blow you away

MOHJA KAHF

Application for Naturalisation

Country.
Could your mountainous days ever fold around my arrival?
I wait in a room with blank walls that wait.
I go out among the sea, the streets, the sky:
they are too busy to make conversation.

Country:
must I become dust for your moonlight to drink?
You don't open my window.
I lean against the glass,
I hear you talking to the gulls all night.

I am luminous, not transparent,
a spell waiting to be uttered.
Country, become my shadow,
I will become your body.

KAREN PRESS

Front door

Wherever I have lived,
walking out of the front door
every morning
means crossing over
to a foreign country.

One language inside the house,
another out.
The food and clothes
and customs change.
The fingers on my hand turn
into forks.

I call it adaptation
when my tongue switches
from one grammar to another,
but the truth is I'm addicted now,
high on the rush
of daily displacement,
speeding to a different time zone,
heading into altered weather,
landing as another person.

Don't think I haven't noticed
you're on the same trip too.

IMTIAZ DHARKER

Englan Voice

I prepare – an prepare well – fe Englan.
Me decide, and done leave behine
all the voice of ol slave-estate bushman.

None of that distric bad-talk in Englan,
that bush talk of ol slave-estate man.

Hear me speak in Englan, an see
you dohn think I a Englan native.

Me nah go say
'Bwoy, how you du?'
me a-go say 'How are you old man?'

Me nah go say
'Wha yu nyam las night?'
me a-go say 'What did you have for supper?'

Patois talk is bushman talk –
people who talk patois them dam lazy.

Because mi bush voice so settle in me
an might let me down in-a Englan
me a-practise.

Me a-practise talk like teacher
till mi Englan voice come out-a me
like water from hillside rock.

Even if you fellows here
dohn hear mi Englan voice
I have it – an hear it in mi head!

JAMES BERRY

from The arrival of Brighteye

My mommy gone over de ocean
My mommy gone over de sea
she gawn dere to work for some money
an den she gawn sen back for me

one year
two year
tree year gawn

four year
five year
soon six year come

granny seh it don't matter
but supposin I forget her
Blinky Blinky, one two tree
Blinky Blinky, remember me

Mommy sen dis dress fah ma seventh birthday. Ah born de day before chrismas, an she sen de shoes and de hat to match.

Ah wear it dat very chrismas Sunday, an wen ah come out into de square, on de way to church wid Granny, all de ole man dem laughing and chanting

Brighteye Brighteye
red white an blue
Brighteye Brighteye
yuh pretty fi true

an Granny seh don't walk so boasy, mind ah buk up mi toe an fall down an tear up de dress pon rockstone because she going to fold it up an wrap it up back in de crepe paper wid two camphor ball an put it back in de suitcase, dis very evening, as soon as ah tek it aff, put it back in de suitcase dat ah going to carry to Englan.

Crass de sea, girl, yuh going crass de sea, an a likkle water fall from Granny eye which mek er cross an she shake mi han aff er dress where ah was holding on to make sure dat ah don't fall down for de shoes hard to walk in on rockstone, an she wipe er eye wid er kerchief.

An ah looking up in Granny face, ah know Granny face good. She say is me an mi madda an grampa put all de lines in it, an ah wondering which lines is mine, an ah tinking how Granny face look wen sun shine an de flowers bloom, an wen rain full up de water barrel, an wen drought an de bean tree dead, an wen Grampa bus a rude joke, ah know Granny face but now she wipe er eye an lock up er face tight, an ah feel someting tight lack up in my troat, fah ah can't remember mi madda face, ah can't remember mi madda face at all.

An all de time after dat, Granny finger in de silver thimble, flashing, sewing awn de red, white an blue lace she buy at market, sewing it awn to de church hat to mek pretty bonnet to go wid de dress. She say ah mus put awn de whole outfit when ah reach, so mi madda can see how ah pretty, an how she tek good care of mi, an she pack de cod liver oil pill dem in mi bag an say memba to tek one every day on de boat so mi skin would still shine when ah reach, an when we leaving de village in de mawning all de ole man dem singing

> Brighteye, Brighteye,
> going crass de sea
> Brighteye, Brighteye
> madda sen fi she
> Brighteye, Brighteye
> yuh gwine remember we?

an de children, playing ring game an clapping

> Row, row, row your boat
> gently down the stream
> merrily, merrily, merrily, merrrily
> life is but a dream

an de bus to town, an Granny crying, an de boat, an de woman dat Granny put mi in de charge of, an day an night, day an night, an it getting cole, all de way, in a dream, to Englan.

JEAN 'BINTA' BREEZE

Wherever I Hang

I leave me people, me land, me home
For reasons, I not too sure
I forsake de sun
And de hummingbird splendour
Had big rats in de floorboard
So I pick up me new-world-self
And come, to this place call England
At first I feeling like I in dream –
De misty greyness
I touching de walls to see if they real
They solid to de seam
And de people pouring from de underground system
Like beans
And when I look up to de sky
I see Lord Nelson high – too high to lie

And is so I sending home photos of myself
Among de pigeons and de snow
And is so I warding off de cold
And is so, little by little
I begin to change my calypso ways
Never visiting nobody
Before giving them clear warning
And waiting me turn in queue
Now, after all this time
I get accustom to de English life
But I still miss back-home side
To tell you de truth
I don't know really where I belaang

    Yes, divided to de ocean
    Divided to de bone

Wherever I hang me knickers – that's my home

GRACE NICHOLS

Look We Have Coming to Dover!

So various, so beautiful, so new...
MATTHEW ARNOLD, 'Dover Beach'

Stowed in the sea to invade
the alfresco lash of a diesel-breeze
ratcheting speed into the tide, brunt with
gobfuls of surf phlegmed by cushy come-and-go
tourists prow'd on the cruisers, lording the ministered waves.

Seagull and shoal life
vexing their blarnies upon our huddled
camouflage past the vast crumble of scummed
cliffs, scramming on mulch as thunder unbladders
yobbish rain and wind on our escape hutched in a Bedford van.

Seasons or years we reap
inland, unclocked by the national eye
or stabs in the back, teemed for breathing
sweeps of grass through the whistling asthma of parks,
burdened, ennobled – poling sparks across pylon and pylon.

Swarms of us, grafting in
the black within shot of the moon's
spotlight, banking on the miracle of sun:
span its rainbow, passport us to life. Only then
can it be human to hoick ourselves, bare-faced for the clear.

Imagine my love and I,
our sundry others, Blair'd in the cash
of our beeswax'd cars, our crash clothes, free,
we raise our charged glasses over unparasol'd tables
East, babbling our lingoes, flecked by the chalk of Britannia!

DALJIT NAGRA

Half-caste

Excuse me
standing on one leg
I'm half-caste

Explain yuself
wha yu mean
when yu say half-caste
yu mean when picasso
mix red an green
is a half-caste canvas/
explain yuself
wha yu mean
when yu say half-caste
yu mean when light an shadow
mix in de sky
is a half-caste weather/
well in dat case
england weather
nearly always half-caste
in fact some o dem cloud
half-caste till dem overcast
so spiteful dem dont want de sun pass
ah rass/
explain yuself
wha yu mean
when yu say half-caste
yu mean when tchaikovsky
sit down at dah piano
an mix a black key
wid a white key
is a half-caste symphony/

Explain yuself
wha yu mean
Ah listening to yu wid de keen
half of mih ear
Ah lookin at yu wid de keen
half of mih eye
an when I'm introduced to you

I'm sure you'll understand
why I offer yu half-a-hand
an when I sleep at night

I close half-a-eye
consequently when I dream
I dream half-a-dream
an when moon begin to glow
I half-caste human being
cast half-a-shadow
but yu must come back tomorrow

wid de whole of yu eye
an de whole of yu ear
an de whole of yu mind

an I will tell yu
de other half
of my story

JOHN AGARD

Half-and-Half

The thin line running from my navel downwards
meant, I thought, that I was half-and-half,

like the coffee my mother drank in restaurants.
That was sophisticated –

but to be half-and-half oneself? And one part
stemmed from a country that wasn't whole –

West and East Pakistan, on different sides
of the pendulous India, because powerful people

had carved up the world like the Sunday joint.
Pakistan belonged to the politicians, the priests.

And to my geography teacher who leapt across
ditches on field trips, and enlightened me

briskly as to where I was born.
Discomfited, I put the pin on the map.

MONIZA ALVI

Bilingual Blues

Soy un ajiaco de contradicciones.
I have mixed feelings about everything.
Name your tema, I'll hedge;
name your cerca, I'll straddle it
like a cubano.

I have mixed feelings about everything.
Soy un ajiaco de contradicciones.
Vexed, hexed, complexed,
hyphenated, oxygenated, illegally alienated,
psycho soy, cantando voy:
You say tomato,
I say tu madre;
You say potato,
I say Pototo.
Let's call the hole
un hueco, the thing
a cosa, and if the cosa goes into the hueco,
consider yourself en casa,
consider yourself part of the family.

Soy un ajiaco de contradicciones,
un puré de impurezas:
a little square from Rubik's Cuba
que nadie nunca acoplará.
(Cha-cha-chá.)

GUSTAVO PÉREZ FIRMAT

The Truth Is

In my left pocket a Chickasaw hand
rests on the bone of the pelvis.
In my right pocket
a white hand. Don't worry. It's mine
and not some thief's.
It belongs to a woman who sleeps in a twin bed
even though she falls in love too easily,
and walks along with hands
in her own empty pockets
even though she has put them in others
for love not money

About the hands, I'd like to say
I am a tree, grafted branches
bearing two kinds of fruit,
apricots maybe and pit cherries.
It's not that way. The truth is
we are crowded together
and knock against each other at night.
We want amnesty.

Linda, girl, I keep telling you
this is nonsense
about who loved who
and who killed who.

Here I am, taped together
like some old civilian conservation corps
passed by from the great depression
and my pockets are empty.
It's just as well since they are masks
for the soul, and since coins and keys
both have the sharp teeth of property.

Girl, I say,
it is dangerous to be a woman of two countries.
You've got your hands in the dark
of two empty pockets. Even though
you walk and whistle like you aren't afraid

you know which pocket the enemy lives in
and you remember how to fight
so you better keep on walking.
And you remember who killed who.
For this you want amnesty
and there's that knocking on the door
in the middle of the night.

Relax, there are other things to think about.
Shoes, for instance.
Now those are the true masks of the soul.
The left shoe
and the right one with its white foot.

LINDA HOGAN

Painting a Room
(for Irina Kendall)

Here on a March day in '89
I blanch the ceiling and walls with bluish lime.
Drop cloths and old newspapers hide
the hardwood floors. All my furniture has been sold,
or given away to bohemian friends.
There is nothing to eat but bread and wine.

An immigration visa in my pocket, I paint
the small apartment where I've lived for ten years.
Taking a break around 4 P.M.,
I sit on the last chair in the empty kitchen,
smoke a cigarette and wipe my tears
with the sleeve of my old pullover.
I am free from regrets but not from pain.

Ten years of fears, unrequited loves, odd jobs,
of night phone calls. Now they've disconnected the line.
I drop the ashes in the sink, pour turpentine
into a jar, stirring with a spatula. My heart throbs
in my right palm when I pick up the brush again.

For ten years the window's turquoise square
has held my eyes in its simple frame.
Now, face to face with the darkening sky,
what more can I say to the glass but thanks
for being transparent, seamless, wide
and stretching perspective across the size
of the visible.

Then I wash the brushes and turn off the light.
This is my last night before moving abroad.
I lie down on the floor, a rolled-up coat
under my head. This is the last night.
Freedom smells of a freshly painted room,
of wooden floors swept with a willow broom,
and of stale raisin bread.

KATIA KAPOVICH

The Mercy

The ship that took my mother to Ellis Island
Eighty-three years ago was named 'The Mercy'.
She remembers trying to eat a banana
without first peeling it and seeing her first orange
in the hands of a young Scot, a seaman
who gave her a bite and wiped her mouth for her
with a red bandana and taught her the word,
'orange', saying it patiently over and over.
A long autumn voyage, the days darkening
with the black waters calming as night came on,
then nothing as far as her eyes could see and space
without limit rushing off to the corners
of creation. She prayed in Russian and Yiddish
to find her family in New York, prayers
unheard or misunderstood or perhaps ignored
by all the powers that swept the waves of darkness
before she woke, that kept 'The Mercy' afloat
while smallpox raged among the passengers
and crew until the dead were buried at sea
with strange prayers in a tongue she could not fathom.

'The Mercy', I read on the yellowing pages of a book
I located in a windowless room of the library
on 42nd Street, sat thirty-one days
offshore in quarantine before the passengers
disembarked. There a story ends. Other ships
arrived, 'Tancred' out of Glasgow, 'The Neptune'
registered as Danish, 'Umberto IV',
the list goes on for pages, November gives
way to winter, the sea pounds this alien shore.
Italian miners from Piemonte dig
under towns in western Pennsylvania
only to rediscover the same nightmare
they left at home. A nine-year-old girl travels
all night by train with one suitcase and an orange.
She learns that mercy is something you can eat
again and again while the juice spills over
your chin, you can wipe it away with the back
of your hands and you can never get enough.

PHILIP LEVINE

Miracle

Not the one who takes up his bed and walks
But the ones who have known him all along
And carry him in –

Their shoulders numb, the ache and stoop deeplocked
In their backs, the stretcher handles
Slippery with sweat. And no let up

Until he's strapped on tight, made tiltable
and raised to the tiled roof, then lowered for healing.
Be mindful of them as they stand and wait

For the burn of the paid-out ropes to cool,
Their slight lightheadedness and incredulity
To pass, those who had known him all along.

SEAMUS HEANEY

Optimistic Little Poem

Now and then it happens
that somebody shouts for help
and somebody else jumps in at once
and absolutely gratis.

Here in the thick of the grossest capitalism
round the corner comes the shining fire brigade
and extinguishes, or suddenly
there's silver in the beggar's hat.

Mornings the streets are full
of people hurrying here and there without
daggers in their hands, quite equably
after milk or radishes.

As though in a time of deepest peace.

A splendid sight.

HANS MAGNUS ENZENSBERGER
translated from the German by David Constantine

The Spaces of Hope

I have experienced the spaces of hope,
The spaces of a moderate mercy. Experienced
The places which suddenly set
Into a random form: a lilac garden,
A street in Florence, a morning room,
A sea smeared with silver before the storm,
Or a starless night lit only
By a book on the table. The spaces of hope
Are in time, not linked into
A system of miracles, nor into a unity;
They merely exist. As in Kanfanar,
At the station; wind in a wild vine
A quarter-century ago: one space of hope.

413

Another, set somewhere in the future,
Is already destroying the void around it,
Unclear but real. Probable.

In the spaces of hope light grows,
Free of charge, and voices are clearer,
Death has a beautiful shadow, the lilac blooms later,
But for that it looks like its first-ever flower.

IVAN V. LALIC
translated from the Serbian by Francis R. Jones

Hope

It hovers in dark corners
before the lights are turned on,
it shakes sleep from its eyes
and drops from mushroom gills,
it explodes in the starry heads
of dandelions turned sages,
it sticks to the wings of green angels
that sail from the tops of maples.
It sprouts in each occluded eye
of the many-eyed potato,
it lives in each earthworm segment
surviving cruelty,
it is the motion that runs the tail of a dog,
it is the mouth that inflates the lungs
of the child that has just been born.
It is the singular gift
we cannot destroy in ourselves,
the argument that refutes death,
the genius that invents the future,
all we know of God.
It is the serum which makes us swear
not to betray one another;
it is in this poem, trying to speak.

LISEL MUELLER

Hope

I want to be unconstrained –
therefore I care not a fig for noble styles.
I roll up my sleeves.
The poem's dough is rising...
Oh what a pity
that I cannot bake cathedrals...
Highness of forms –
goal of persistent longing.
Child of the present –
does your spirit not have a proper shell?
Before I die
I shall bake a cathedral.

EDITH SÖDERGRAN
translated from the Swedish by David McDuff

Living Space

There are just not enough
straight lines. That
is the problem.
Nothing is flat
or parallel. Beams
balance crookedly on supports
thrust off the vertical.
Nails clutch at open seams.
The whole structure leans dangerously
towards the miraculous.

Into this rough frame,
someone has squeezed
a living space

and even dared to place
these eggs in a wire basket,

fragile curves of white
hung out over the dark edge
of a slanted universe,
gathering the light
into themselves,
as if they were
the bright, thin walls of faith.

IMTIAZ DHARKER

Little of Distinction

Little of distinction, guide-books had said –
a marshy common and a windy hill:
a renovated church, a few old graves
with curly stones and cherubs with blind eyes:
yews with split trunks straining at rusty bands;
and past the church, a house or two, a farm,
not picturesque, not even very old.
And yet, the day I went there, life that breaks
so many promises, gave me a present
it had not promised – I found this place
had beauty after all. How could I have seen
how a verandah's fantastic curlicues
would throw a patterned shadow on the grass?
or thought how delicate ash-leaves would stir
against a sky of that young blue? or known
trees and grey walls would have such truthful beauty,
like an exact statement? And least of all
could I have foreseen the miles on hazy miles
of Radnorshire and Breconshire below,
uncertain in the heat – the mystery
that complements precision. So much sweeter
was this day than the expectation of it.

RUTH BIDGOOD

Emerging

A man says yes without knowing
how to decide even what the question is,
and is caught up, and then is carried along
and never again escapes from his own cocoon;
and that's how we are, forever falling
into the deep well of other beings;
and one thread wraps itself around our necks,
another entwines a foot, and then it is impossible,
impossible to move except in the well –
nobody can rescue us from other people.

It seems as if we don't know how to speak;
it seems as if there are words which escape,
which are missing, which have gone away and left us
to ourselves, tangled up in snares and threads.

And all at once, that's it; we no longer know
what it's all about, but we are deep inside it,
and now we will never see with the same eyes
as once we did when we were children playing.
Now these eyes are closed to us,
now our hands emerge from different arms.

And therefore, when you sleep, you are alone in your dreaming,
and running freely through the corridors
of one dream only, which belongs to you.
Oh never let them come to steal our dreams,
never let them entwine us in our bed.
Let us hold on to the shadows
to see if, from our own obscurity,
we emerge and grope along the walls,
lie in wait for the light, to capture it,
till, once and for all time,
it becomes our own, the sun of every day.

PABLO NERUDA
translated from the Spanish by Alastair Reid

Yes

I love the word
And hear its long struggle with no
Even in the bird's throat
And the budging crocus.
Some winter's night
I see it flood the faces
Of my friends, ripen their laughter
And plant early flowers in
Their conversation.

You will understand when I say
It is for me a morning word
Though it is older than the sea
And hisses in a way
That may have given
An example
To the serpent itself.
It is this ageless incipience
Whose influence is found
In the first and last pages of books,
In the grim skin of the affirmative battler
And in the voices of women
That constitutes the morning quality
Of yes.

        We have all
Thought what it must be like
Never to grow old,
The dreams of our elders have mythic endurance
Though their hearts are stilled
But the only agelessness
Is yes.
I am always beginning to appreciate
The agony from which it is born.
Clues from here and there
Suggest such agony is hard to bear
But is the shaping God
Of the word that we
Sometimes hear, and struggle to be.

BRENDAN KENNELLY

Yes

A smile says: Yes.
A heart says: Blood.
When the rain says: Drink
The earth says: Mud.

The kangaroo says: Trampoline.
Giraffes say: Tree.
A bus says: Us
While a car says: Me.

Lemon trees say: Lemons.
A jug says: Lemonade.
The villain says: You're wonderful.
The hero: I'm afraid.

The forest says: Hide and Seek.
The grass says: Green and Grow.
The railway says: Maybe.
The prison says: No.

The millionaire says: Take.
The beggar says: Give.
The soldier cries: Mother!
The baby sings: Live.

The river says: Come with me.
The moon says: Bless.
The stars says: Enjoy the light.
The sun says: Yes.

ADRIAN MITCHELL

Yes, But

Even if it were true,
Even if I were dead and buried in Verona,
I believe I would come out and wash my face
In the chill spring.

I believe I would appear
Between noon and four, when nearly
Everybody else is asleep or making love,
And all the Germans turned down, the motorcycles
Muffled, chained, still.

Then the plump lizards along the Adige by San Giorgio
Come out and gaze,
Unpestered by temptation, across the water.
I would sit among them and join them in leaving
The golden mosquitoes alone.
Why should we sit by the Adige and destroy
Anything, even our enemies, even the prey
God caused to glitter for us
Defenseless in the sun?
We are not exhausted. We are not angry, or lonely,
Or sick at heart.
We are in love lightly, lightly. We know we are shining,
Though we cannot see one another.
The wind doesn't scatter us,
Because our very lungs have fallen and drifted
Away like leaves down the Adige
Long ago.

We breathe light.

JAMES WRIGHT

Dreams

Hold fast to dreams
For if dreams die
Life is a broken-winged bird
That cannot fly.

Hold fast to dreams
For when dreams go
Life is a barren field
Frozen with snow.

LANGSTON HUGHES

8

Body and soul

We don't read and write poetry because it's cute. We read and
write poetry because we are members of the human race. And the
human race is filled with passion. And medicine, law, business,
engineering, these are noble pursuits and necessary to sustain life.
But poetry, beauty, romance, love, these are what we stay alive for.

DEAD POETS SOCIETY

THIS SECTION BEGINS with a series of poems on 'the human beast' (422-42) in
which animals – and how we view and treat them – speak to our humanity.
As Henri Cole observes in 'Ape House, Berlin Zoo' (422), 'part of me lives in
you, / or is it the reverse, as it was with my father / before all of him went
into a pint of ash'. These poems can be read alongside those in section 6 of
Staying Alive ('Man and beast', SA 217-48), and with others in my Bloodaxe
anthology *Earth Shattering: ecopoems* (2007) whose particular focus is ecological
balance and environmental destruction. Because that important area of con-
temporary poetry is covered so comprehensively in *Earth Shattering*, I haven't
given it much space in *Being Human*. Ecopoetry goes beyond traditional nature
poetry to take on distinctly contemporary issues, recognising the interdepen-
dence of all life on earth, the wildness and otherness of nature, and the irre-
sponsibility of our attempts to tame and plunder nature.

The first poems in the next part of this section (443-49) concern the human
body: what it is and what it means beyond the physical – before becoming that
'pint of ash'. Subsequent poems explore the relationship between body and
soul, self and identity as well as perception and spiritual awareness. This sel-
ection complements section 1 of *Staying Alive* ('Body and soul', SA 29-52). For
a broader gathering of poems covering this area, I would recommend another
Bloodaxe anthology, *Soul Food: nourishing poems for starved minds* (2008), which
I edited with Pamela Robertson-Pearce. This includes poets from many trad-
itions, periods and places, ranging from Rumi, Kabir, Chuang-tzu and Tung-
shan to Herbert, Blake, Rilke, Hopkins, Dickinson and Mary Oliver.

Little known in his lifetime, Kenji Miyazawa (462) is now recognised as
Japan's greatest modern poet as well as being a much loved children's author.
Influenced by Buddhism and by his strong personal identification with nature,
many of his poems and tales are set in a remote prefecture where he travelled
from village to village, teaching the science of rice cultivation. He died from
TB at the age of 37.

Ape House, Berlin Zoo

Are the lost like this,
living not like a plant, an inch to drink each week,
but like the grass snake under it,
gorging itself before a famine?
Gazing at me longer than any human has in a long time,
you are my closest relative in thousands of miles.
When your soul looks out through your eyes,
looking at me looking at you, what does it see?
Like you, I was born in the East;
my arms are too long and my spine bowed;
I eat leaves, fruits and roots; I curl up when I sleep; I live alone.
As your mother once cradled you, mine cradled me,
pushing her nipple between my gums.
Here, where time crawls forward, too slow for human eyes,
neither of us rushes into the future,
since the future means living with a self
that has fed on the squalor that is here.
I cannot tell which of us absorbs the other more;
I am free but you are not,
if freedom means traveling long distances to avoid boredom.
When a child shakes his dirty fist in your face,
making a cry like a buck at rutting time,
you are not impressed. Indolence has made you philosophical.
From where I stand, you are beautiful and ugly at once,
    like a weed or a human.
We are children meeting for the first time,
each standing in the other's light.
Instruments of darkness have not yet told us truths;
love has not yet made us jealous or cruel,
though it has made us look like one another.
It is understood that part of me lives in you,
or is it the reverse, as it was with my father,
before all of him went into a pint of ash?
Sitting in a miasma of excrement and straw,
combing aside hair matted on your ass,
picking an insect from your breast, chewing a plant bulb,
why are you not appalled by my perfect teeth
and scrupulous dress? How did you lose what God gave you?
Bowing to his unappealable judgment, do you feel a lack?

Nakedness, isolation, bare inanity: these are the soil
and entanglement of actual living.
There are no more elegant redemptive plots.
Roaming about the ape house, I cannot tell which of us,
with naked, painful eyes, is shielded behind Plexiglas.
How can it be that we were not once a family
and now we've come apart? How can it be that it was Adam
who brought death into the world?
Roaming about the ape house, I am sweat and contemplation
    and breath.
I am active and passive, darkness and light, chaste and corrupt.
I am martyr to nothing. I am rejected by nothing.
All the bloated clottings of a life – family disputes,
    lost inheritances,
vulgar lies, festering love, ungovernable passion, hope wrecked –
bleed out of the mind. Pondering you,
as you chew on a raw onion and ponder me,
I am myself as a boy, showering with my father, learning not
    to be afraid,
spitting mouthfuls of water into the face of the loved one,
the only thing to suffer for.

HENRI COLE

With No Experience in Such Matters

To hold a damaged sparrow
under water until you feel it die
is to know a small something
about the mind; how, for example,
it blames the cat for the original crime,
how it wants praise for its better side.

And yet it's as human
as pulling the plug on your Dad
whose world has turned
to faeces and fog, human as...
Well, let's admit, it's a mild thing
as human things go.

But I felt the one good wing
flutter in my palm –
the smallest protest, if that's what it was,
I ever felt or heard.
Reminded me of how my eyelid has twitched,
the need to account for it.
Hard to believe no one notices.

STEPHEN DUNN

Elegy for a Dead Labrador

Here there may be, in the midst of summer,
a few days when suddenly it's fall.
Thrushes sing on a sharper note.
The rocks stand determined out in the water.
They know something. They have always known it.
We know it too, and we don't like it.
On the way home, in the boat, on just such evenings,
you would stand stock-still in the bow, collected,
scouting the scents coming across the water.
You read the evening, the faint streak of smoke
from a garden, a pancake frying
half a mile away, a badger
standing somewhere in the same twilight
sniffing the same way. Our friendship
was of course a compromise; we lived
together in two different worlds: mine,
mostly letters, a text passing through life;
yours, mostly smells. You had knowledge
I would have given much to have possessed:
the ability to let a feeling – eagerness, hate, or love –
run like a wave through your body
from nose to tip of tail, the inability
to ever accept the moon as a fact.
At the full moon you always complained loudly against it.
You were a better Gnostic than I am. And consequently
you lived continually in paradise.

You had a habit of catching butterflies on the leap
and munching them, which some people thought disgusting.
I always liked it. Why
couldn't I learn from you? And doors.
In front of doors you lay down and slept,
sure that sooner or later one would come
who'd open up the door. You were right,
I was wrong. Now I ask myself, now this
long mute friendship is forever finished,
if possibly there was anything I could do
which impressed you. Your firm conviction
that I called up the thunderstorms
doesn't count. That was a mistake. I think
my certain faith that the ball existed,
even when hidden behind the couch,
somehow gave you an inkling of my world.
In my world most things were hidden
behind something else. I called you 'dog',
I really wonder whether you perceived me
as a larger, noisier 'dog'
or as something different, forever unknown,
which is what it is, existing in that attribute
it exists in, a whistle
through the nocturnal park one has got used to
returning to without actually knowing
what it is one is returning to. About you,
and who you were, I knew no more.
One might say, from this more objective
standpoint, we were two organisms. Two
of those places where the universe makes a knot,
in itself, short-lived, complex structures
of proteins that have to complicate themselves
more and more in order to survive, until everything
breaks and turns simple once again, the knot
dissolved, the riddle gone. You were a question
asked of another question, nothing more,
and neither had the answer to the other.

LARS GUSTAFSSON
translated from the Swedish by Yvonne L. Sandstroem

Looking at the Invisible

About looking, he thought, do animals look?
Animals look at the visible, we the invisible.
We look at hopeless loves, at the dead, night and day,
at poverty, fears and angers,
we see reasons, results, tomorrows.
But a craftsman must have smeared a little yellow, a little green on his
    hands,
a cart appears before us, laden with hay, decorated all round,
we see our craftsman, his cottage, his yard, his geranium at the window.

OKTAY RIFAT
translated from the Turkish by Ruth Christie

From Underneath

> *A giant sea turtle saved the life of a 52 year-old woman
> lost at sea for two days after a shipwreck in the Southern
> Philippines. She rode on the turtle's back.*
> SYRACUSE POST-STANDARD

When her arms were no longer
strong enough to tread water
it came up beneath her, hard
and immense, and she thought
this is how death comes,
something large between your legs
and then the plunge.
She dived off instinctively,
but it got beneath her again
and when she realised what it was
she soiled herself, held on.

God would have sent something winged,
she thought. *This* came from beneath,
a piece of hell that killed a turtle
on the way and took its shape.
How many hours passed?

She didn't know, but it was night
and the waves were higher.
The thing swam easily in the dark.

She swooned into sleep.
When she woke in the morning,
the sea calm, her strange raft
still moving. She noticed the elaborate
pattern of its shell, map-like,
the leathery neck and head
as if she'd come up behind
an old longshoreman
in a hard-backed chair.
She wanted and was afraid to touch
the head – one finger
just above the eyes –
the way she would touch her cat
and make it hers.
The more it swam a steady course
the more she spoke to it
the jibberish of the lost.
And when the laughter
located at the bottom
of oneself, unstoppable.

The call went from sailor to sailor
on the fishing boat: A woman
riding an 'oil drum'
off the starboard side.
But the turtle was already swimming
toward the prow
with its hysterical, foreign cargo
and when it came up alongside
it stopped
until she could be hoisted off.
Then it circled three times
and went down.
The woman was beyond all language,
the captain reported:
the crew was afraid of her
for a long, long time.

STEPHEN DUNN

Giuseppe

My uncle Giuseppe told me
that in Sicily in World War Two,
in the courtyard behind the aquarium,
where the bougainvillea grows so well,
the only captive mermaid in the world
was butchered on the dry and dusty ground
by a doctor, a fishmonger, and certain others.

She, it, had never learned to speak
because she was simple, or so they'd said.
But the priest who held one of her hands
while her throat was cut,
said she was only a fish, and fish can't speak.
But she screamed like a woman in terrible fear.

And when they took a ripe golden roe
from her side, the doctor said
this was proof she was just a fish
and anyway an egg is not a child,
but refused when some was offered to him.

Then they put her head and her hands
in a box for burial
and someone tried to take her wedding ring,
but the others stopped him,
and the ring stayed put.

The rest they cooked and fed to the troops.
They said a large fish had been found on the beach.

Starvation forgives men many things,
my uncle, the aquarium keeper, said,
but couldn't look me in the eye,
for which I thank God.

RODERICK FORD

The Gun

Bringing a gun into a house
changes it.

You lay it on the kitchen table,
stretched out like something dead
itself: the grainy polished wood stock
jutting over the edge,
the long metal barrel
casting a grey shadow
on the green-checked cloth.

At first it's just practice:
perforating tins
dangling on orange string
from trees in the garden.
Then a rabbit shot
clean through the head.

Soon the fridge fills with creatures
that have run and flown.
Your hands reek of gun oil
and entrails. You trample
fur and feathers. There's a spring
in your step; your eyes gleam
like when sex was fresh.

A gun brings a house alive.

I join in the cooking: jointing
and slicing, stirring and tasting –
excited as if the King of Death
had arrived to feast, stalking
out of winter woods,
his black mouth
sprouting golden crocuses.

VICKI FEAVER

429

City Animals

Just before the tunnel, the train
lurches through a landscape
snatched from a dream. Flame blurts

from high up on the skeletal refinery,
all pipes and tanks. Then a tail of smoke.

The winter twilight looks like fire, too,

smeared above the bleached grasses
of the marsh, and in the shards of water

where an egret the color of newspaper
holds perfectly still, like a small angel

come to study what's wrong with the world.

In the blond reeds, a cat picks her way
from tire to oil drum,

hunting in the petrochemical stink.

Row of nipples, row of sharp ribs.
No fish in the iridescence.
Maybe a sick pigeon, or a mouse.

Across the Hudson,
Manhattan's black geometry begins to spark

as the smut of evening rises in the streets.

Somewhere in it,
a woman in fur with a plastic bag in her hand
follows a dachshund in a purple sweater,

letting him sniff a small square of dirt
studded with cigarette butts.
And in the park a scarred Dobermann

drags on his choke chain toward another fight,

but his master yanks him back.
It's like the Buddhist vision of the beasts
in their temporary afterlife, each creature

locked in its own cell of misery,
the horse pulling always uphill
with its terrible load, the whip

flicking bits of skin from its back,
the cornered bear woofing with fear,

the fox's mouth red from the leg in the trap.

Animal islands, without comfort between them.
Which shall inherit the earth?

Not the interlocking kittens frozen in the trash.

Not the dog yapping itself to death
on the twentieth floor. And not the egret,
fishing in the feculent marsh

for the condom and the drowned gun.

No, the earth belongs to the spirits
that haunt the air above the sewer grates,

the dark plumes trailing the highway's
diesel moan, the multitudes
pouring from the smokestacks of the citadel

into the gaseous ocean overhead.

Where will the angel rest itself?
What map will guide it home?

CHASE TWICHELL

Skunk Hour

(for Elizabeth Bishop)

Nautilus Island's hermit
heiress still lives through winter in her Spartan cottage;
her sheep still graze above the sea.
Her son's a bishop. Her farmer
is first selectman in our village;
she's in her dotage.

Thirsting for
the hierarchic privacy
of Queen Victoria's century,
she buys up all
the eyesores facing her shore,
and lets them fall.

The season's ill –
we've lost our summer millionaire,
who seemed to leap from an L.L. Bean
catalogue. His nine-knot yawl
was auctioned off to lobstermen.
A red fox stain covers Blue Hill.

And now our fairy
decorator brightens his shop for fall;
his fishnet's filled with orange cork,
orange, his cobbler's bench and awl;
there is no money in his work,
he'd rather marry.

One dark night,
my Tudor Ford climbed the hill's skull;
I watched for love-cars. Lights turned down,
they lay together, hull to hull,
where the graveyard shelves on the town....
My mind's not right.

A car radio bleats,
'Love, O careless Love....' I hear
my ill-spirit sob in each blood cell,
as if my hand were at its throat....

I myself am hell;
nobody's here –

only skunks, that search
in the moonlight for a bite to eat.
They march on their soles up Main Street:
white stripes, moonstruck eyes' red fire
under the chalk-dry and spar spire
of the Trinitarian Church.

I stand on top
of our back steps and breathe the rich air –
a mother skunk with her column of kittens swills the garbage pail
She jabs her wedge-head in a cup
of sour cream, drops her ostrich tail,
and will not scare.

ROBERT LOWELL

The Armadillo
(for Robert Lowell)

This is the time of year
when almost every night
the frail, illegal fire balloons appear.
Climbing the mountain height,

rising toward a saint
still honored in these parts,
the paper chambers flush and fill with light
that comes and goes, like hearts.

Once up against the sky it's hard
to tell them from the stars –
planets, that is – the tinted ones:
Venus going down, or Mars,

or the pale green one. With a wind,
they flare and falter, wobble and toss;
but if it's still they steer between
the kite sticks of the Southern Cross,

433

receding, dwindling, solemnly
and steadily forsaking us,
or, in the downdraft from a peak,
suddenly turning dangerous.

Last night another big one fell.
It splattered like an egg of fire
against the cliff behind the house.
The flame ran down. We saw the pair

of owls who nest there flying up
and up, their whirling black-and-white
stained bright pink underneath, until
they shrieked up out of sight.

The ancient owls' nest must have burned.
Hastily, all alone,
a glistening armadillo left the scene,
rose-flecked, head down, tail down,

and then a baby rabbit jumped out,
short-eared, to our surprise.
So soft! – a handful of intangible ash
with fixed, ignited eyes.

Too pretty, dreamlike mimicry!
O falling fire and piercing cry
and panic, and a weak mailed fist
clenched ignorant against the sky!

ELIZABETH BISHOP

Song

Listen: there was a goat's head hanging by ropes in a tree.
All night it hung there and sang. And those who heard it
Felt a hurt in their hearts and thought they were hearing
The song of a night bird. They sat up in their beds, and then
They lay back down again. In the night wind, the goat's head

Swayed back and forth, and from far off it shone faintly
The way the moonlight shone on the train track miles away
Beside which the goat's headless body lay. Some boys
Had hacked its head off. It was harder work than they had imagined.
The goat cried like a man and struggled hard. But they
Finished the job. They hung the bleeding head by the school
And then ran off into the darkness that seems to hide everything.
The head hung in the tree. The body lay by the tracks.
The head called to the body. The body to the head.
They missed each other. The missing grew larger between them,
Until it pulled the heart right out of the body, until
The drawn heart flew toward the head, flew as a bird flies
Back to its cage and the familiar perch from which it trills.
Then the heart sang in the head, softly at first and then louder,
Sang long and low until the morning light came up over
The school and over the tree, and then the singing stopped....
The goat had belonged to a small girl. She named
The goat Broken Thorn Sweet Blackberry, named it after
The night's bush of stars, because the goat's silky hair
Was dark as well water, because it had eyes like wild fruit.
The girl lived near a high railroad track. At night
She heard the trains passing, the sweet sound of the train's horn
Pouring softly over her bed, and each morning she woke
To give the bleating goat his pail of warm milk. She sang
Him songs about girls with ropes and cooks in boats.
She brushed him with a stiff brush. She dreamed daily
That he grew bigger, and he did. She thought her dreaming
Made it so. But one night the girl didn't hear the train's horn,
And the next morning she woke to an empty yard. The goat
Was gone. Everything looked strange. It was as if a storm
Had passed through while she slept, wind and stones, rain
Stripping the branches of fruit. She knew that someone
Had stolen the goat and that he had come to harm. She called
To him. All morning and into the afternoon, she called
And called. She walked and walked. In her chest a bad feeling
Like the feeling of the stones gouging the soft undersides
Of her bare feet. Then somebody found the goat's body
By the high tracks, the flies already filling their soft bottles
At the goat's torn neck. Then somebody found the head
Hanging in a tree by the school. They hurried to take
These things away so that the girl would not see them.
They hurried to raise money to buy the girl another goat.

They hurried to find the boys who had done this, to hear
Them say it was a joke, a joke, it was nothing but a joke....
But listen: here is the point. The boys thought to have
Their fun and be done with it. It was harder work than they
Had imagined, this silly sacrifice, but they finished the job,
Whistling as they washed their large hands in the dark.
What they didn't know was that the goat's head was already
Singing behind them in the tree. What they didn't know
Was that the goat's head would go on singing, just for them,
Long after the ropes were down, and that they would learn to listen,
Pail after pail, stroke after patient stroke. They would
Wake in the night thinking they heard the wind in the trees
Or a night bird, but their hearts beating harder. There
Would be a whistle, a hum, a high murmur, and, at last, a song,
The low song a lost boy sings remembering his mother's call.
Not a cruel song, no, no, not cruel at all. This song
Is sweet. It is sweet. The heart dies of this sweetness.

BRIGIT PEGEEN KELLY

The Mower

The mower stalled, twice; kneeling, I found
A hedgehog jammed up against the blades,
Killed. It had been in the long grass.

I had seen it before, and even fed it, once.
Now I had mauled its unobtrusive world
Unmendably. Burial was no help:

Next morning I got up and it did not.
The first day after a death, the new absence
Is always the same; we should be careful

Of each other, we should be kind
While there is still time.

PHILIP LARKIN

The Caterpillars

On the headland to the lighthouse,
a brown detour of caterpillars
crimped end-to-end across the road.

Poke away the pilot and the line
would break up, rioting,
fingering for the scent.
Put him back, they'd straighten.
You could imagine them humming
their queue numbers.

I've only seen such blind following
in the patient, dull dole queues,
or old photos of the Doukhobors
the world's first march of naked people.

I watched over the line for hours
warding off birds whose wings, getting close,
were like the beating of spoons
in deep bowls. I put a finger to the ground
and soft prickles pushed over,
a warm chain of hair.

This strange sect, wrapped in the sun
like their one benefit blanket
marched in brotherhood and exile.

Later, a group of boys
(their junta-minds set on torture),
picked off the leader.
Each creature contorted,
shut into its tight burr.
I could only stand like a quiet picket
and watch the rough panic.

I remember them, those caterpillars,
pacifists following their vegetable passion –
lying down in the road and dying
when they could no longer touch each other.

JUDITH BEVERIDGE

Another Feeling

Once you saw a drove of young pigs
crossing the highway. One of them
pulling his body by the front feet,
the hind legs dragging flat.
Without thinking,
you called the Humane Society.
They came with a net and went for him.
They were matter of fact, uniformed;
there were two of them,
their truck ominous, with a cage.
He was hiding in the weeds. It was then
you saw his eyes. He understood.
He was trembling.
After they took him, you began to suffer regret.
Years later, you remember his misfit body
scrambling to reach the others.
Even at this moment, your heart
is going too fast; your hands sweat.

RUTH STONE

The Oldest Living Thing in L.A.

At Wilshire & Santa Monica I saw an opossum
Trying to cross the street. It was late, the street
Was brightly lit, the opossum would take
A few steps forward, then back away from the breath
Of moving traffic. People coming out of the bars
Would approach, as if to help it somehow.
It would lift its black lips & show them
The reddened gums, the long rows of incisors,
Teeth that went all the way back beyond
The flames of Troy & Carthage, beyond sheep
Grazing rock-strewn hills, fragments of ruins
In the grass at San Vitale. It would back away

Delicately & smoothly, stepping carefully
As it always had. It could mangle someone's hand
In twenty seconds. Mangle it for good. It could
Sever it completely from the wrist in forty.
There was nothing to be done for it. Someone
Or other probably called the LAPD, who then
Called animal control, who woke a driver, who
Then dressed in mailed gloves, the kind of thing
Small knights once wore into battle, who gathered
Together his pole with a noose on the end,
A light steel net to snare it with, someone who hoped
The thing would have vanished by the time he got there.

LARRY LEVIS

Tarantulas on the Lifebuoy

For some semitropical reason
when the rains fall
relentlessly they fall

into swimming pools, these otherwise
bright and scary
arachnids. They can swim
a little, but not for long

and they can't climb the ladder out.
They usually drown – but
if you want their favor,
if you believe there is justice,
a reward for not loving

the death of ugly
and even dangerous (the eel, hog snake,
rats) creatures, if

you believe these things, then
you would leave a lifebuoy
or two in your swimming pool at night.

And in the morning
you would haul ashore
the huddled, hairy survivors

and escort them
back to the bush, and know,
be assured that at least these saved,
as individuals, would not turn up

again someday
in your hat, drawer,
or the tangled underworld

of your socks, and that even –
when your belief in justice
merges with your belief in dreams –
they may tell the others

in a sign language
four times as subtle
and complicated as man's

that you are good,
that you love them,
that you would save them again.

THOMAS LUX

The Eel

The eel, siren
of cold seas, who leaves
the Baltic for our seas,
our estuaries, rivers, rising
deep beneath the downstream flood
from branch to branch, from twig to smaller twig,
ever more inward,
bent on the heart of rock,
infiltrating muddy

rills until one day
light glancing off the chestnuts
fires her flash
in stagnant pools,
in the ravines cascading down
the Apennine escarpments to Romagna;
eel, torch, whiplash,
arrow of Love on earth,
whom only our gullies
or dessicated Pyrenean brooks lead back
to Edens of generation;
green spirit seeking life
where only drought and desolation sting;
spark that says that everything begins
when everything seems charcoal,
buried stump;
brief rainbow, iris,
twin to the one your lashes frame
and you set shining virginal among
the sons of men, sunk in your mire –
can you fail to see her as a sister?

EUGENIO MONTALE
translated from the Italian by Jonathan Galassi

The Cows on Killing Day

All me are standing on feed. The sky is shining.

All me have just been milked. Teats all tingling still
from that dry toothless sucking by the chilly mouths
that gasp loudly in in in, and never breathe out.

All me standing on feed, move the feed inside me.
One me smells of needing the bull, that heavy urgent me,
the back-climber, who leaves me humped, straining, but light
and peaceful again, with crystalline moving inside me.

Standing on wet rock, being milked, assuages the calf-sorrow in me.
Now the me who needs mounts on me, hopping, to signal the bull.

The tractor comes trotting in its grumble; the heifer human
bounces on top of it, and cud comes with the tractor,
big rolls of tight dry feed: lucerne, clovers, buttercup, grass,
that's been bitten but never swallowed, yet is cud.
She walks up over the tractor and down it comes, roll on roll
and all me following, eating it, and dropping the good pats.

The heifer human smells of needing the bull human
and is angry. All me look nervously at her
as she chases the dog me dream of horning dead: our enemy
of the light loose tongue. Me'd jam him in his squeals.

Me, facing every way, spreading out over feed.

One me is still in the yard, the place skinned of feed.
Me, old and sore-boned, little milk in that me now,
licks at the wood. The oldest bull human is coming.

Me in the peed yard. A stick goes out from the human
and cracks, like the whip. Me shivers and falls down
with the terrible, the blood of me, coming out behind an ear.
Me, that other me, down and dreaming in the bare yard.

All me come running. It's like the Hot Part of the sky
that's hard to look at, this that now happens behind wood
in the raw yard. A shining leaf, like off the bitter gum tree
is with the human. It works in the neck of me
and the terrible floods out, swamped and frothy. All me make the Roar,
some leaping stiff-kneed, trying to horn that worst horror.
The wolf-at-the-calves is the bull human. Horn the bull human!

But the dog and the heifer human drive away all me.

Looking back, the glistening leaf is still moving.
All of dry old me is crumpled, like the hills of feed,
and a slick me like a huge calf is coming out of me.

The carrion-stinking dog, who is calf of human and wolf,
is chasing and eating little blood things the humans scatter
and all me run away, over smells, toward the sky.

LES MURRAY

Little Aster

(FROM 'Morgue')

A drowned truck-driver was propped on the slab.
Someone had stuck a lavender aster
between his teeth.
As I cut out the tongue and the palate,
through the chest
under the skin
with a long knife,
I must have touched the flower, for it slid
into the brain lying next.
I packed it into the cavity of the chest
among the excelsior
as it was sewn up.
Drink yourself full in your vase!
Rest softly,
Little aster!

GOTTFRIED BENN
translated from the German by Babette Deutsch

Poem by Gottfried Benn

I had to go out but a poem by Gottfried Benn
stopped me in my tracks – you've no idea
quite how disturbing that poem was

A flower fell apart in the middle of an autopsy
and the doctor who'd cut open the corpse
saw how those petals landed among the inner organs

Even the medic's rubber gloves were covered
with petals and blood it was utterly breathtaking
but only a poem and I had to go out

I'm not sure if I left but the images
of that poem by Benn – frankly not
a very appealing figure – never left they stayed here

But how they stayed here those images the ghosts
of those lacerating images is something I must
come to terms with it won't be easy but I have to do it

DAVID HUERTA
translated from the Spanish by Jamie McKendrick

Body, Remember...

Body, remember not only how much you were loved,
not only the beds you lay on,
but also those desires that glowed openly
in eyes that looked at you,
trembled for you in the voices –
only some chance obstacle frustrated them.
Now that it's all finally in the past,
it seems almost as if you gave yourself
to those desires too – how they glowed,
remember, in eyes that looked at you,
remember, body, how they trembled for you in those voices.

C.P. CAVAFY
translated from the Greek by Edmund Keeley & Philip Sherrard

'A body is given to me...'

A body is given to me – what am I to make
From this thing that is my own and is unique?

Tell me who it is I must thank for giving
The quiet joy of breathing and of living?

I am the gardener, the flower as well,
Never alone in the world's prison cell.

My warmth, my breathing have already lain
Upon eternity's clear pane.

Imprinted on the glass a pattern shows,
But nowadays a pattern no one knows.

Let the dregs of the moment drain away –
The pattern's loveliness must stay.

OSIP MANDELSTAM
translated from the Russian by Robert Tracy

Disappearing Act

No, soul doesn't leave the body.

My body is leaving my soul.
Tired of turning fried chicken and
coffee to muscle and excrement,
tried of secreting tears, wiping them,
tired of opening eyes on another day,
tired especially of that fleshy heart,
pumping, pumping. More,
that brain spinning nightmares.
Body prepares:
disconnect, unplug, erase.

But here, I think, a smallish altercation
arises.
Soul seems to shake its fist.
Wants brain? Claims dreams and nightmares?
Maintains a codicil bequeathes it shares?

There'll be a fight. A deadly struggle.
We know, of course, who'll win....

But who's this, watching?

ELEANOR ROSS TAYLOR

Body

I'll wear it out perhaps
To a suit of wrinkle, a skin
Too large
With the soul shrinking;

The will gone out of it,
Yet all the daily rent to pay;
Flesh that cannot last,
Soul that never got under way:

Too much houseroom now;
Tomorrow none;
But paying either way
For journey done, for journey not begun.

PADRAIC FALLON

A Hindu to His Body

Dear pursuing presence,
dear body: you brought me
curled in womb and memory.

Gave me fingers to clutch
at grace, at malice; and ruffle
someone else's hair; to fold a man's
shadow back on his world;
to hold in the dark of the eye
through a winter and a fear
the poise, the shape of a breast;
a pear's silence, in the calyx
and the noise of a childish fist.

You brought me: do not leave me
behind. When you leave all else,
my garrulous face, my unkissed
alien mind, when you muffle
and put away my pulse

to rise in the sap of trees
let me go with you and feel the weight
of honey-hives in my branching
and the burlap weave of weaver-birds
in my hair.

A.K. RAMANUJAN

Pocket Mirror

In this small grey circle I am
cropped, a moony snippet, an eye
the size of a world,
a doubled pupil. Shelled in
like a snail, I seal all space:
my sight is minuscule. Here

Is the hinge, the gap
between what there is
and what I see – and the glass
is cool and deep
as a well. Within, words bend
and flex in mindless echo.

I stare, I stare –
I am cut from clear air,
brutal and planetary. Call
my name, I won't answer. Twist
my arm, I won't yell.
My cell, my cell –

This black rictus,
it's hell – still I stand,
smudged, in this circle.
Just to see
glass to eye, eye to glass,
what I am.

SARAH HOLLAND-BATT

Mirror

When you look
into a mirror
it is not
yourself you see,
but a kind
of apish error
posed in fearful
symmetry

JOHN UPDIKE

Theory My Natural Brown Ass

I've paid for too many degrees,
posited too many historical positions,
made too many semiotic apologetics,
forwarded far too many feminist responses
to too many textual materialities

to have an ass this big.

In theory, my ass
does not signify.

But this insistence of the body,
this non-linguistic expression
of inertia and caloric lust,
is a corporeal truth that mental exercise
can't deconstruct.

Or is it just an inverted absence?
The presence of the lack
of any Aryan heritage?

I'm the post-colonial girl
who went abroad and squatted and lunged
while the maid, snapping out

wet laundry, watched.
Skinny brown bitch, was what I thought!
The poor men looked at my ass
like it was a pair of Boston Cremes.

But I was raised
on white girls' dreams.
This juicy back might fly in hip hop,
but I meant to fit
into tinier social circles,
and JLo's butt's already taking up
two stools at the representation bar.
Missy E's already gone
bonh bo bonh bonh
all the way to the bank.

My ass doesn't give a shit
that my mind is post third wave.
It is imperialist, a booty-Gap,
expanding into a third space: the place

beyond my seams. Who cares
that sizes are all 'seems' anyway:
you shop, you walk
the slippery significatory slope
on which an 'S', 'M', or 'L' might fall.
The mall

is the spatial organisation
of desire, I know, but
does that make my ass look small?

SONNET L'ABBÉ

The Idea of Mountain

And of that kind of permanence –
we long for it sometimes,
the obstinacy of a single stone
and its mindlessness. To be less alive
to each particular sadness. Monolithic.

Unmoved as the old man who wakes
and knows no pleasure or disgrace
can harm his tired heart any more
because he has lived, in practical terms, for *ever*.
Beyond cold or heat. Beyond all of it
except our *itness*. Five years I lived
by that black mountain range, the heights
of which let nothing grow, not yellow aspen
or even blue spruce, just the barren peaks
shouldering the snow and sun and surviving.
I would lie in the thistle-grass and watch
wasps mating below the sheer persisting rock,
frantic, their torsos the bright colour of pollen,
their heads the purest black –
and I saw, finally, how our last hours play out
against the continuing earth; how we wake
consoled by the morning's petty smallness,
the kettle's steam, fat hissing on the stove,
and the cat nudging our ankles, its hunger and our own
never fully appeased. But I would have it still –
the aspens, the hunger, the wasps,
and this happiness, sidling slow
as a foal towards the phosphorescence of new grass:
naïve, and wedded to a predictable end.

SARAH HOLLAND-BATT

Proof

I would like all things to be free of me,
Never to murder the days with presupposition,
Never have to feel they suffer the imposition
Of having to be this or that. How easy
It is to maim the moment
With expectation, to force it to define
Itself. Beyond all that I am, the sun
Scatters its light as though by accident.

The fox eats its own leg in the trap
To go free. As it limps through the grass
The earth itself appears to bleed.
When the morning light comes up
Who knows what suffering midnight was?
Proof is what I do not need.

BRENDAN KENNELLY

View with a Grain of Sand

We call it a grain of sand,
but it calls itself neither grain nor sand.
It does just fine without a name,
whether general, particular,
permanent, passing,
incorrect, or apt.

Our glance, our touch mean nothing to it.
It doesn't feel itself seen and touched.
And that it fell on the windowsill
is only our experience, not its.
For it, it is no different from falling on anything else
with no assurance that it has finished falling
or that it is falling still.

The window has a wonderful view of a lake,
but the view doesn't view itself.
It exists in this world
colourless, shapeless,
soundless, odourless, and painless.

The lake's floor exists floorlessly,
and its shore exists shorelessly.
Its water feels itself neither wet nor dry
and its waves to themselves are neither singular nor plural.
They splash deaf to their own noise
on pebbles neither large nor small.

And all this beneath a sky by nature skyless
in which the sun sets without setting at all
and hides without hiding behind an unminding cloud.
The wind ruffles it, its only reason being
that it blows.

A second passes.
A second second.
A third.
But they're three seconds only for us.

Time has passed like courier with urgent news.
But that's just our simile.
The character is inverted, his haste is make-believe,
his news inhuman.

WISŁAWA SZYMBORSKA
translated from the Polish by Stanisław Barańczak & Clare Cavanagh

The Bright Field

I have seen the sun break through
to illuminate a small field
for a while, and gone my way
and forgotten it. But that was the pearl
of great price, the one field that had
the treasure in it. I realise now
that I must give all that I have
to possess it. Life is not hurrying

on to a receding future, nor hankering after
an imagined past. It is the turning
aside like Moses to the miracle
of the lit bush, to a brightness
that seemed as transitory as your youth
once, but is the eternity that awaits you.

R.S. THOMAS

Keeping Things Whole

In a field
I am the absence
of field.
This is
always the case.
Wherever I am
I am what is missing.

When I walk
I part the air
and always
the air moves in
to fill the spaces
where my body's been.

We all have reasons
for moving.
I move
to keep things whole.

MARK STRAND

Almost

There is a quiet substance to things –
The way the world fits together in spite of itself;
You feel it when driving encapsuled in the rain,
Slipping into a silent hospital at night,
Or scanning half-familiar faces on the screen
That almost return your strange satellite gaze.

There is a substance also to emptiness,
But it can never truly be exchanged with another;
Like an absence, or the impulse to despair
At the hole in the universe your substance almost fills.

ALEX SKOVRON

Oddments, inklings, omens, moments

Oddments, as when
you see through skin,
when flowers appear
to be eavesdropping,
or music somewhere
declares your mood;
when sleep fulfils
a feel of dying
or fear makes ghosts
of clothes on a chair.

Inklings, as when
some room rhymes
with a lost time,
or a book reads
like a well-known dream;
when a smell recalls
portraits, funerals,
when a wish happens
or a mirror sees
through distances.

Omens, as when
a shadow from nowhere
falls on a wall,
when a bird seems
to mimic your name,
when a cat eyes you
as though it knew
or, heavy with augury,
a crow caws
cras cras from a tree.

Moments, as when
the air's awareness
makes guesses true,
when a hand's touch
speaks past speech
or when, in poise,

two sympathies
lighten each other,
and love occurs
like song, like weather.

ALASTAIR REID

Feet

Feet clench, make themselves small, run away,
creasing their wretchedness and fear in lines
identical to those on our palms and different.
Feet are extensions of God
(which is why they are low down),
hence their distress, their rounded bulk, their lack of balance.
Feet are like startled crayfish.
Such vulnerable things, feet.
When they make love they clench and huddle together
as though they were their own subjects.
So feet are not made, then,
to grip, wasp-like
with every stab,
each branch of the soul that might shape them there.
They are more wings than feet,
tiny and fragile and human.
However much we overlook them.

PEDRO SERRANO
translated from the Spanish by Anna Crowe

The Gateway

Now the heart sings with all its thousand voices
To hear this city of cells, my body, sing.
The tree through the stiff clay at long last forces
Its thin strong roots and taps the secret spring.

And the sweet waters without intermission
Climb to the tips of its green tenement;
The breasts have borne the grace of their possession,
The lips have felt the pressure of content.

Here I come home: in this expected country
They know my name and speak it with delight.
I am the dream and you my gates of entry,
The means by which I waken into light.

A.D. HOPE

The Gift

Time wants to show you a different country. It's the one
that your life conceals, the one waiting outside
when curtains are drawn, the one Grandmother hinted at
in her crochet design, the one almost found
over at the edge of the music, after the sermon.

It's the way life is, and you have it, a few years given.
You get killed now and then, violated
in various ways. (And sometimes it's turn about.)
You get tired of that. Long-suffering, you wait
and pray, and maybe good things come – maybe
the hurt slackens and you hardly feel it any more.
You have a breath without pain. It is called happiness.

It's a balance, the taking and passing along,
the composting of where you've been and how people
and weather treated you. It's a country where
you already are, bringing where you have been.
Time offers this gift in its millions of ways,
turning the world, moving the air, calling,
every morning, 'Here, take it, it's yours.'

WILLIAM STAFFORD

Flesh

Sitting in a doorway,
in October sunlight,
eating
peppers, onions, tomatoes,
stale bread sodden with olive oil –

and the air high and clean,
and the red taste of tomatoes,
and the sharp bite of onions,
and the pepper's scarlet crunch –

the body
coming awake again,
thinking,
maybe there's more to life than sickness,
than the body's craving for oblivion,
than the hunger of the spirit to be gone –

and maybe the body belongs in the world,
maybe it knows a thing or two,
maybe it's even possible
it may once more remember

sweetness,
absence of pain.

KERRY HARDIE

Toward the End

Toward the end you don't really care if you're still yourself
everything that has lived in you has the right to exist
you speak with others' voices
you dream other people's dreams
they can feed you with porridge or tears
no one owes you anything anymore
and you've earned a little of it all
your sins are countless and your love for life spills over

you're a man of the world
but your curiosity isn't yet gone
you take in the twilight on the river till it hurts
you take in the gray engraving of the city in the rain
and the suddenly uncovered sky
cherished by a wreath of clouds
you've never felt such comfort
even though you've never gotten anything said to the end
and all the things you've done are far from perfect
the only art you're learning
is the art of saying goodbye
yet why are you supposed to leave without regret
regret is the only form of payment for what you have received

JULIA HARTWIG
translated from the Polish by Stanislav Barańczak & Clare Cavanagh

The God Abandons Antony

When suddenly, at midnight, you hear
an invisible procession going by
with exquisite music, voices,
don't mourn your luck that's failing now,
work gone wrong, your plans
all proving deceptive – don't mourn them uselessly.
As one long prepared, and graced with courage,
say goodbye to her, the Alexandria that is leaving.
Above all, don't fool yourself, don't say
it was a dream, your ears deceived you:
don't degrade yourself with empty hopes like these.
As one long prepared, and graced with courage,
as is right for you who proved worthy of this kind of city,
go firmly to the window
and listen with deep emotion, but not
with the whining, the pleas of a coward;
listen – your final delectation – to the voices,
to the exquisite music of that strange procession,
and say goodbye to her, to the Alexandria you are losing.

C.P. CAVAFY
translated from the Greek by Edmund Keeley & Philip Sherrard

Tree

It is foolish
to let a young redwood
grow next to a house.

Even in this
one lifetime,
you will have to choose.

That great calm being,
this clutter of soup pots and books –

Already the first branch-tips brush at the window.
Softly, calmly, immensity taps at your life.

JANE HIRSHFIELD

The Garden

It was a closed space. From the moment I saw it
I knew I could depend on it.
To hell with the endless weathers
Passing above, and the high apartments
Shadowing it. Down here
On the stone bench, of an autumn morning,
I felt, for a moment, the heat of sun on my face
As it angled around the corner
Out of sight. My patch of sky
Went blue then, or grey,
And I went inside.
                    But it was always there,
The garden. At its centre
A tree, a plum tree
As I discovered, when the bluish fruit
Appeared through the leaves in September,
Gave it core, and strength, and definition.
Yellow courgettes, and ripening tomatoes

Bound to their splints. And tough carnations
Half in love with the wire that fenced them in.
And the clay, of course, rich and black
After rain, or a dry brown bath
For thrushes and sparrows.
And day after day, the same man
Clearing weeds, or laying a path
According to some unspecified plan.

No need to mention where all this was.
I had travelled enough, by then,
To dispense with where. Sufficient to say
A horse's tail appeared, one day,
Above a gable, or a streak of cirrus –
Time and the future, far away.
Woodsmoke, the waft of cooking,
Brought me back to earth –
I was here, in the garden. An old woman
With green fingers, fed me generic names
Like Flower, or Tree,
As if nothing else mattered
But the garden, and having your own key.

HARRY CLIFTON

Sweeping the Garden

Slowly learning again to love
ourselves working. Paul Éluard

said the body
is that part of the soul
perceptible by the five senses. To love
the body to love its work
to love the hand that praises both to praise
the body and to love the soul
that dreams and wakes us back alive
against the slothful odds: fatigue
depression loneliness
the perishable still recognition –
what needs

be done. *Sweep the garden, any size*
said the roshi. Sweeping sweeping

alone as the garden grows
large or small. Any song
sung working the garden brings
up from sand gravel soil through
straw bamboo wood and less
tangible elements Power
song for the hands Healing
song for the senses what can
and cannot be perceived
of the soul.

OLGA BROUMAS

from **Of Gravity and Light**
(enlightenment)

What we need most, we learn from the menial tasks:
the novice raking sand in Buddhist texts,
or sweeping leaves, his hands chilled to the bone,
while understanding hovers out of reach;
the changeling in a folk tale, chopping logs,
poised at the dizzy edge of transformation;

and everything they do is gravity:
swaying above the darkness of the well
to haul the bucket in; guiding the broom;
finding the body's kinship with the earth
beneath their feet, the lattice of a world
where nothing turns or stands outside the whole;

and when the insight comes, they carry on
with what's at hand: the gravel path; the fire;
knowing the soul is no more difficult
than water, or the fig tree by the well
that stood for decades, barren and inert,
till every branch was answered in the stars.

JOHN BURNSIDE

Nobody

If you can't bring yourself to build
a snowman or even to clench
a snowball or two to fling
at the pine tree trunk, at least
find some reason to take you out

of yourself: scrape a patch of grass clear
for the birds maybe; prod at your shrubs
so they shake off the weight, straighten up;
or just stump about leaving prints
of your boots, your breath steaming out.

Promise. Don't let yourself in
for this moment again: the end
of the afternoon, drawing the curtains
on the glare of the garden, a whole
day of snow nobody's trodden.

MICHAEL LASKEY

Strong in the Rain

Strong in the rain
Strong in the wind
Strong against the summer heat and snow
He is healthy and robust
Free from desire
He never loses his temper
Nor the quiet smile on his lips
He eats four *go* of unpolished rice
Miso and a few vegetables a day
He does not consider himself
In whatever occurs...his understanding
Comes from observation and experience
And he never loses sight of things

He lives in a little thatched-roof hut
In a field in the shadows of a pine tree grove
If there is a sick child in the east
He goes there to nurse the child
If there's a tired mother in the west
He goes to her and carries her sheaves
If someone is near death in the south
He goes and says, 'Don't be afraid'
If there are strife and lawsuits in the north
He demands that the people put an end to their pettiness
He weeps at the time of drought
He plods about at a loss during the cold summer
Everyone calls him Blockhead
No one sings his praises
Or takes him to heart...

That is the kind of person
I want to be

KENJI MIYAZAWA
translated from the Japanese by Roger Pulvers

Prayer

May things stay the way they are
in the simplest place you know.

May the shuttered windows
keep the air as cool as bottled jasmine.
May you never forget to listen
to the crumpled whisper of sheets
that mould themselves to your sleeping form.
May the pillows always be silvered
with cat-down and the muted percussion
of a lover's breath.
May the murmur of the wall clock
continue to decree that your providence
run ten minutes slow.

May nothing be disturbed
in the simplest place you know
for it is here in the foetal hush
that blueprints dissolve
and poems begin,
and faith spreads like the hum of crickets,
faith in a time
when maps shall fade,
nostalgia cease
and the vigil end.

ARUNDATHI SUBRAMANIAM

Prayer

Echo of the clocktower, footstep
in the alleyway, sweep
of the wind sifting the leaves.

Jeweller of the spiderweb, connoisseur
of autumn's opulence, blade of lightning
harvesting the sky.

Keeper of the small gate, choreographer
of entrances and exits, midnight
whisper travelling the wires.

Seducer, healer, deity or thief,
I will see you soon enough –
in the shadow of the rainfall,

in the brief violet darkening a sunset –
but until then I pray watch over him
as a mountain guards its covert ore

and the harsh falcon its flightless young.

DANA GIOIA

9

More to love

This is the true function of the love poem: to remind us of who we are, and who we are capable of being: while our everyday social roles define us as persons, love reminds us that we are also spirits.

JOHN BURNSIDE

HUMAN UNDERSTANDING AND INTIMACY are created not out of order or perfection but through acceptance of difficulty, inadequacy, imperfection, making do, shortage of time. Alan Dugan's marriage in 'Love Song: I and Thou' (486) is a house in which 'Nothing is plumb, level, or square: / the studs are bowed, the joists / are shaky by nature, no piece fits / any other piece without a gap / or pinch'. In Michael Blumenthal's poem 'A Marriage' (487), you are 'holding up a ceiling / with both arms', but then, unexpectedly, 'something wonderful happens' and someone 'holds their arms up / to the ceiling beside you'. These two practical but loving views of a marriage by American poets remind me of U.A. Fanthorpe's very English poem 'Atlas' in *Being Alive* (BA 209) which proclaims 'a kind of love called maintenance, / Which stores the WD40 and knows when to use it', and which upholds the 'permanently ricketty elaborate / structures of living...the sensible side of love'.

In these and other poems, not just in this section but throughout *Being Human*, there's a strong sense that we're all human beings, we're all in this together and we don't have that much time, so let's accept our differences, work around difficulties and try somehow to make it all work. We can still be loving and passionate with each other, and we can relish the sensual delights of our physical world together, as in the poems by Kim Addonizio (466), Jericho Brown (467) and Edwin Morgan (468); we can 'live out our lives' in the togetherness of 'The Present' (Michael Donaghy, 477) and in 'This Hour' (Sharon Olds, 478); and we can appreciate each other knowing that 'There's more to love. / And more ways to love it' (Herman de Coninck, 485).

These poems showing 'There's more to love' add another dimension to the selections in *Staying Alive* (7: 'In and out of love', 249-94), which starts with passion and ends with heartbreak, and *Being Alive*, which has two complementary sections, one covering the nature of love (4: 'Love Life', 179-210), and the other, gender and the nature of relationships (5: 'Men and Women', 211-56). See also my Bloodaxe anthology *Passionfood* (2005) for its selection of classic and contemporary poems celebrating desire and passionate love as well as lasting love and lifelong friendship.

You Don't Know What Love Is

but you know how to raise it in me
like a dead girl winched up from a river. How to
wash off the sludge, the stench of our past.
How to start clean. This love even sits up
and blinks; amazed, she takes a few shaky steps.
Any day now she'll try to eat solid food. She'll want
to get into a fast car, one low to the ground, and drive
to some cinderblock shithole in the desert
where she can drink and get sick and then
dance in nothing but her underwear. You know
where she's headed, you know she'll wake up
with an ache she can't locate and no money
and a terrible thirst. So to hell
with your warm hands sliding inside my shirt
and your tongue down my throat
like an oxygen tube. Cover me
in black plastic. Let the mourners through.

KIM ADDONIZIO

Like That

Love me like a wrong turn on a bad road late at night, with no moon and
        no town anywhere
and a large hungry animal moving heavily through the brush in the ditch.
Love me with a blindfold over your eyes and the sound of rusty water
blurting from the faucet in the kitchen, leaking down through
the floorboards to hot cement. Do it without asking,
without wondering or thinking anything, while the machinery's
shut down and the watchman's slumped asleep before his small TV
showing the empty garage, the deserted hallways, while the thieves slice
        through
the fence with steel clippers. Love me when you can't find
a decent restaurant open anywhere, when you're alone in a glaring diner
with two nuns arguing in the back booth, when your eggs are greasy
and your hash browns underdone. Snick the buttons off the front of my dre

and toss them one by one into the pond where carp lurk just beneath the
     surface,
their cold fins waving. Love me on the hood of a truck no one's driven
in years, sunk to its fenders in weeds and dead sunflowers;
and in the lilies, your mouth on my white throat, while turtles drag
their bellies through slick mud, through the footprints of coots and ducks.

Do it when no one's looking, when the riots begin and the planes open up,
when the bus leaps the curb and the driver hits the brakes and the pedal
     sinks to the floor,
while someone hurls a plate against the wall and picks up another,
love me like a freezing shot of vodka, like pure agave, love me
when you're lonely, when we're both too tired to speak, when you don't believe
in anything, listen, there isn't anything, it doesn't matter; lie down
with me and close your eyes, the road curves here, I'm cranking up the radio
and we're going, we won't turn back as long as you love me,
as long as you keep on doing it exactly like that.

KIM ADDONIZIO

Track 1: Lush Life

The woman with the microphone sings to hurt you,
To see you shake your head. The mic may as well
Be a leather belt. You drive to the center of town
To be whipped by a woman's voice. You can't tell
The difference between a leather belt and a lover's
Tongue. A lover's tongue might call you *bitch*,
A term of endearment where you come from, a kind
Of compliment preceded by the word *sing*
In certain nightclubs. A lush little tongue
You have: you can yell, *Sing bitch*, and, *I love you*,
With a shot of Patrón at the end of each phrase
From the same barstool every Saturday night, but you can't
Remember your father's leather belt without shaking
Your head. That's what satisfies her, the woman
With the microphone. She does not mean to entertain
You, and neither do I. Speak to me in a lover's tongue –
Call me your bitch, and I'll sing the whole night long.

JERICHO BROWN

467

Strawberries

There were never strawberries
like the ones we had
that sultry afternoon
sitting on the step
of the open french window
facing each other
your knees held in mine
the blue plates in our laps
the strawberries glistening
in the hot sunlight
we dipped them in sugar
looking at each other
not hurrying the feast
for one to come
the empty plates
laid on the stone together
with the two forks crossed
and I bent towards you
sweet in that air
in my arms
abandoned like a child
from your eager mouth
the taste of strawberries
in my memory
lean back again
let me love you

let the sun beat
on our forgetfulness
one hour of all
the heat intense
and summer lightning
on the Kilpatrick hills

let the storm wash the plates

EDWIN MORGAN

Low

It's not happiness, but something else; waiting
for the light to change; a bakery.

It's a lake. It emerges from darkness into the next day surrounded
        by pines.
There's a couple.

It's a living room. The upholstery is yellow and the furniture is walnut.
They used to lie down on the carpet

between the sofa and the coffee table, after the guests had left.

The cups and saucers were still.

Their memories of everything that occurred took place
with the other's face as a backdrop and sometimes

the air was grainy like a movie about evening, and sometimes there
        was an ending
in the air that looked like a scene from a different beginning,

in which they are walking.

It took place alongside a scene in which one of them looks up at a
        brown rooftop
early in March. The ground hadn't softened.

One walked in front of the other breathing.
The other saw a small house as they passed and breathed. The
        reflections in the windows

made them hear the sounds on the hill: a crow, a dog, and branches –
and they bent into the hour that started just then, like bending to
        walk under branches.

ARDA COLLINS

The Shipfitter's Wife

I loved him most
when he came home from work,
his fingers still curled from fitting pipe,
his denim shirt ringed with sweat,
and smelling of salt, the drying weeds
of the ocean. I'd go to him where he sat
on the edge of the bed, his forehead
anointed with grease, his cracked hands
jammed between his thighs, and unlace
the steel-toed boots, stroke his ankles,
his calves, the pads and bones of his feet.
Then I'd open his clothes and take
the whole day inside me – the ship's
gray sides, the miles of copper pipe,
the voice of the first man clanging
off the hull's silver ribs. Spark of lead
kissing metal. The clamp, the winch,
the white fire of the torch, the whistle,
and the long drive home.

DORIANNE LAUX

The Net

Quick, woman, in your net
Catch the silver I fling!
O I am deep in your debt,
Draw tight, skin-tight, the string,
And rake the silver in.
No fisher every yet
Drew such a cunning ring.

Ah, shifty as the fin
Of any fish this flesh
That, shaken to the shin,
Now shoals into your mesh,
Bursting to be held in;

Purse-proud and pebble-hard,
Its pence like shingle showered.

Open the haul, and shake
The fill of shillings free,
Let all the satchels break
And leap about the knee
In shoals of ecstasy.
Guineas and gills will flake
At each gull-plunge of me.

Though all the angels, and
Saint Michael at their head,
Nightly contrive to stand
On guard about your bed,
Yet none dare take a hand
But each can only spread
His eagle-eye instead.

But I, being man, can kiss
And bed-spread-eagle too;
All flesh shall come to this,
Being less than angel is,
Yet higher far in bliss
As it entwines with you.

Come, make no sound, my sweet;
Tyrn down the candid lamp
And draw the equal quilt
Over our naked guilt.

W.R. RODGERS

Tamer and Hawk

I thought I was so tough,
But gentled at your hands,
Cannot be quick enough
To fly for you and show
That when I go I go
At your commands.

Even in flight above
I am no longer free:
You seeled me with your love,
I am blind to other birds –
The habit of your words
Has hooded me.

As formerly, I wheel
I hover and I twist,
But only want the feel,
In my possessive thought,
Of catcher and of caught
Upon your wrist.

You but half civilise,
Taming me in this way.
Through having only eyes
For you I fear to lose,
I lose to keep, and choose
Tamer as prey.

THOM GUNN

Tigers

What are we now but voices
who promise each other a life
neither one can deliver
not for lack of wanting
but wanting won't make it so.
We cling to a vine
at the cliff's edge.
There are tigers above
and below. Let us love
one another and let go.

ELIZA GRISWOLD

Romantic Moment

After seeing the documentary we walk down Canyon Road,
onto the plaza of art galleries and high end clothing stores

where the mock orange trees are fragrant in the summer night
And the smooth adobe walls glow fleshlike in the dark.

It is just our second date, and we sit down on a bench,
holding hands, not looking at each other,

and if I were a bull penguin right now I would lean over
and vomit softly into the mouth of my beloved

and if I were a peacock I'd flex my gluteal muscles to
erect and spread the quills of my Cinemax tail.

If she were a female walkingstick bug she might
insert her hypodermic probiscus delicately into my neck

and inject me with a rich hormonal sedative
before attaching her egg sac to my thoracic undercarriage,

and if I were a young chimpanzee I would break off a nearby tree limb
and smash all the windows in the plaza jewelry stores.

And if she was a Brazilian leopardfrog she would wrap her impressive
tongue three times around my right thigh and

pummel me lightly against the surface of our pond
and I would know her feelings were sincere.

Instead we sit awhile in silence, until
she remarks that in the relative context of tortoises and iguanas,

human males seem to be actually rather expressive
And I say that female crocodiles really don't receive

enough credit for their gentleness.
Then she suggests that it is time for us to go

do something personal, hidden, and human.

TONY HOAGLAND

Before You Came

Before you came,
things were as they should be:
the sky was the dead-end of sight,
the road was just a road, wine merely wine.

Now everything is like my heart,
a colour at the edge of blood:
the grey of your absence, the colour of poison, of thorns,
the gold when we meet, the season ablaze,
the yellow of autumn, the red of flowers, of flames,
and the black when you cover the earth
with the coal of dead fires.

And the sky, the road, the glass of wine?
The sky is a shirt wet with tears,
the road a vein about to break,
and the glass of wine a mirror in which
the sky, the road, the world keep changing.

Don't leave now that you're here –
Stay. So the world may become like itself again:
so the sky may be the sky,
the road a road,
and the glass of wine not a mirror, just a glass of wine.

FAIZ AHMED FAIZ
translated from the Urdu by Agha Shahid Ali

True Ways of Knowing

Not an ounce excessive, not an inch too little,
Our easy reciprocations. You let me know
The way a boat would feel, if it could feel,
The intimate support of water.

The news you bring me has been news forever,
So that I understand what a stone would say

474

If only a stone could speak. Is it sad a grassblade
Can't know how it is lovely?

Is it sad that you can't know, except by hearsay
(My gossiping failing words) that you are the way
A water is that can clench its palm and crumple
A boat's confiding timbers?

But that's excessive, and too little. Knowing
The way a circle would describe its roundness,
We touch two selves and feel, complete and gentle,
The intimate support of being.

The way that flight would feel a bird flying
(If it could feel) is the way a space that's in
A stone that's in a water would know itself
If it had our way of knowing.

NORMAN MacCAIG

'i carry your heart with me'

i carry your heart with me(i carry it in
my heart)i am never without it(anywhere
i go you go,my dear;and whatever is done
by only me is your doing,my darling)
                                    i fear
no fate(for you are my fate,my sweet)i want
no world(for beautiful you are my world,my true)
and it's you are whatever a moon has always meant
and whatever a sun will always sing is you

here is the deepest secret nobody knows
(here is the root of the root and the bud of the bud
and the sky of the sky of a tree called life;which grows
higher than the soul can hope or mind can hide)
and this is the wonder that's keeping the stars apart

i carry your heart(i carry it in my heart)

E.E. CUMMINGS

The Song

How shall I hold my soul that it
does not touch yours? How shall I lift
it over you to other things?
If it would only sink below
into the dark like some lost thing
or slumber in some quiet place
which did not echo your soft heart's beat.
But all that ever touched us – you and me –
touched us together
                like a bow
that from two strings could draw one voice.
On what instrument were we strung?
And to what player did we sing
our interrupted song?

DANA GIOIA
version after the German of Rainer Maria Rilke

He Wishes for the Cloths of Heaven

Had I the heavens' embroidered cloths,
Enwrought with golden and silver light,
The blue and the dim and the dark cloths
Of night and light and the half-light,
I would spread the cloths under your feet:
But I, being poor, have only my dreams;
I have spread my dreams under your feet;
Tread softly because you tread on my dreams.

W.B. YEATS

The Dream Keeper

Bring me all of your dreams,
You dreamers,
Bring me all your
Heart melodies
That I may wrap them
In a blue cloud-cloth
Away from the too-rough fingers
Of the world.

LANGSTON HUGHES

The Present

For the present there is just one moon,
though every level pond gives back another.

But the bright disc shining in the black lagoon,
perceived by astrophysicist and lover,

is milliseconds old. And even that light's
seven minutes older than its source.

And the stars we think we see on moonless nights
are long extinguished. And, of course,

this very moment, as you read this line,
is literally gone before you know it.

Forget the here-and-now. We have no time
but this device of wantonness and wit.

Make me this present then: your hand in mine,
and we'll live out our lives in it.

MICHAEL DONAGHY

This Hour

We could never really say what it is like,
this hour of drinking wine together
on a hot summer night, in the living-room
with the windows open, in our underwear,
my pants with pale-gold gibbon monkeys on them
gleaming in the heat. We talk about our son disap-
pearing between the pine boughs,
we could not tell what was chrysalis or
bough and what was him. The wine
is powerful, each mouthful holds
for a moment its amber agate shape,
I think of the sweat I sipped from my father's
forehead the hour before his death. We talk about
those last days – that I was waiting for him to die.
You are lying on the couch, your underpants
a luminous white, your hand resting
relaxed, alongside your penis,
we talk about your father's illness,
your nipple like a pure circle of
something risen to the surface of your chest.
Even if we wanted to,
we could not describe it,
the end of the second glass when I sometimes
weep and you start to get sleepy – I love
to drink and cry with you, and end up
sobbing to a sleeping man, your
long body filling the couch and
draped slightly over the ends, the
untrained soft singing of your snore, it cannot be given.
Yes, we know we will make love, but we're
not getting ready to make love,
nor are we getting over making love,
love is simply our element,
it is the summer night, we are in it.

SHARON OLDS

Supper

You made crusty bread rolls filled with chunks of brie
And minced garlic drizzled with olive oil
And baked them until the brie was bubbly
And we ate them lovingly, our legs coiled
Together under the table. And salmon with dill
And lemon and whole-wheat couscous
Baked with garlic and fresh ginger, and a hill
Of green beans and carrots roasted with honey and tofu.
It was beautiful, the candles, the linen and silver,
The sun shining down on our northern street,
Me with my hand on your leg. You, my lover,
In your jeans and green T-shirt and beautiful bare feet.
   How simple life is. We buy a fish. We are fed.
   We sit close to each other, we talk and then we go to bed.

GARRISON KEILLOR

& Forgive Us Our Trespasses

Of which the first is love. The sad, unrepeatable fact
that the loves we shouldn't foster burrow faster and linger longer
than sanctioned kinds can. Loves that thrive on absence, on lack
of return, or worse, on harm, are unkillable, Father.
They do not die in us. And you know how we've tried.
Loves nursed, inexplicably, on thoughts of sex,
a return to touched places, a backwards glance, a sigh –
they come back like the tide. They are with us at the terminus
when cancer catches us. They have never been away.
Forgive us the people we love – their dragnet influence.
Those disallowed to us, those who frighten us, those who stay
on uninvited in our lives and every night revisit us.
Accept from us the inappropriate
by which our dreams and daily scenes stay separate.

SINÉAD MORRISSEY

from **A Red Cherry on a White-tiled Floor**

2

How foolish:
Whenever my heart
hears a
knocking
it opens its doors

42

This evening
a man will go out
to
look for
prey
to satisfy
the secrets of his desires

This evening
a woman
will go out
to look for
a man who will make her
mistress of his bed

This
evening
predator and prey will meet
and mix
and perhaps
perhaps
they will
exchange
roles

45

He has two women
One sleeps in his bed
the other

sleeps
in the bed of his dreams

He has two women who love him
One ages
beside him
The other offers him her youth
then droops

He has two women
One
in the heart of his house
One in the house of his heart

53

He taught her
to open up
like a
pomegranate blossom
and to listen
to the whispers of her body
and to scream
out
instead
of muffling her sighs
as she
fell
like a trembling
leaf

64

She came
to offer
him
her pores
and her nails
adorned with cherries
which he
ate
ravenously

She left
with the basket
of her heart
emptied
out

MARAM AL-MASSRI
translated from the Arabic by Khaled Mattawa

Sounds of the day

When a clatter came,
it was horses crossing the ford.
When the air creaked, it was
a lapwing seeing us off the premises
of its private marsh. A snuffling puff
ten yards from the boat was the tide blocking and
unblocking a hole in a rock.
When the black drums rolled, it was water
falling sixty feet into itself.

When the door
scraped shut, it was the end
of all the sounds there are.

You left me
beside the quietest fire in the world.

I thought I was hurt in my pride only,
forgetting that,
when you plunge your hand in freezing water,
you feel
a bangle of ice round your wrist
before the whole hand goes numb.

NORMAN MacCAIG

from 100 Love Sonnets

XCIV

If I die, survive me with such a pure force
you make the pallor and the coldness rage;
flash your indelible eyes from south to south,
from sun to sun, till your mouth sings like a guitar.

I don't want your laugh or your footsteps to waver;
I don't want my legacy of happiness to die;
don't call to my breast: I'm not there.
Live in my absence as in a house.

Absence is such a large house
that you'll walk through the walls,
hang pictures in sheer air.

Absence is such a transparent house
that even being dead I will see you there,
and if you suffer, Love, I'll die a second time.

PABLO NERUDA
translated from the Spanish by Stephen Tapscott

Should You Die First

Let me at least collect your smells
as specimens: your armpits, woollen sweater,
fingers yellow from smoke. I'd need
to take an imprint of your foot
and make recordings of your laugh.

These archives I shall carry into exile;
my body a St Helena where ships no longer dock,
a rock in the ocean, an outpost where the wind howls
and polar bears beat down the door.

ANNABELLE DESPARD

Anti-Love Poem

Sometimes you don't want to love the person you love
you turn your face away from that face
whose eyes lips might make you give up anger
forget insult   steal sadness of not wanting
to love   turn away then turn away   at breakfast
in the evening   don't lift your eyes from the paper
to see that face in all its seriousness   a
sweetness of concentration   he holds his book
in his hand   the hard-knuckled winter wood-
scarred fingers   turn away   that's all you can
do   old as you are to save yourself   from love

GRACE PALEY

Love

Dark falls on this mid-western town
where we once lived when myths collided.
Dusk has hidden the bridge in the river
which slides and deepens
to become the water
the hero crossed on his way to hell.

Not far from here is our old apartment.
We had a kitchen and an Amish table.
We had a view. And we discovered there
love had the feather and muscle of wings
and had come to live with us,
a brother of fire and air.

We had two infant children one of whom
was touched by death in this town
and spared: and when the hero
was hailed by his comrades in hell
their mouths opened and their voices failed and
there is no knowing what they would have asked
about a life they had shared and lost.

I am your wife.
It was years ago.
Our child was healed. We love each other still.
Across our day-to-day and ordinary distances
we speak plainly. We hear each other clearly.

And yet I want to return to you
on the bridge of the Iowa river as you were,
with snow on the shoulders of your coat
and a car passing with its headlights on:

I see you as a hero in a text –
the image blazing and the edges gilded –
and I long to cry out the epic question
my dear companion:

Will we ever live so intensely again?
Will love come to us again and be
so formidable at rest it offered us ascension
even to look at him?

But the words are shadows and you cannot hear me.
You walk away and I cannot follow.

EAVAN BOLAND

For Each Other

Then I loved only your eyes.
Now also the crow's feet around them.
Just as an old word, like *compassion*,
has more in it than a new word. Before, there was only haste

to have what one had, over and over.
Then there was only now. Now there's also then.
There's more to love.
And more ways to love it.

Even doing nothing is one of them.
Just sitting here together with a book.
Or not together, in the café around the corner.

Or not seeing each other for a few days
and missing each other. But always each other,
now almost seven years after all.

HERMAN DE CONINCK
translated from the Flemish by Laure-Anne Bosselaar & Kurt Brown

Say I forgot

Say I forgot how to love you, the way
when I was eight I forgot how to swim?
Could you steel yourself as my mother did
when she enrolled me in lessons for the holiday,
sat up in the stalls with a four-year-old
every morning for a month and afternoons
took me swimming herself in a learner pool
let me grip her hands willing me to let go?
I don't know what makes a child doubt
the water is able to keep her afloat,
think that the other side is too remote
but if I froze, could you wait it out
until I'm propelled again towards your smile
and wrapped tight in your towel like the first time?

LORRAINE MARINER

Love Song: I and Thou

Nothing is plumb, level, or square:
    the studs are bowed, the joists
are shaky by nature, no piece fits
    any other piece without a gap
or pinch, and bent nails
    dance all over the surfacing
like maggots. By Christ
    I am no carpenter. I built
the roof for myself, the walls

for myself, the floors
for myself, and got
    hung up in it myself. I
danced with a purple thumb
    at this house-warming, drunk
with my prime whiskey: rage.
    Oh I spat rage's nails
into the frame-up of my work:
    it held. It settled plumb,
level, solid, square and true
    for that great moment. Then
it screamed and went on through,
    skewing as wrong the other way.
God damned it. This is hell,
    but I planned it, I sawed it,
I nailed it, and I
    will live in it until it kills me.
I can nail my left palm
    to the left-hand crosspiece but
I can't do everything myself.
    I need a hand to nail the right,
a help, a love, a you, a wife.

ALAN DUGAN

A Marriage

You are holding up a ceiling
with both arms. It is very heavy,
but you must hold it up, or else
it will fall down on you. Your arms
are tired, terribly tired,
and, as the day goes on, it feels
as if either your arms or the ceiling
will soon collapse.

But then,
unexpectedly,
something wonderful happens:

Someone,
a man or a woman,
walks into the room
and holds their arms up
to the ceiling beside you.

So you finally get
to take down your arms.
You feel the relief of respite,
the blood flowing back
to your fingers and arms.
And when your partner's arms tire,
you hold up your own
to relieve him again.

And it can go on like this
for many years
without the house falling.

MICHAEL BLUMENTHAL

Thank You, My Fate

Great humility fills me,
great purity fills me,
I make love with my dear
as if I made love dying
as if I made love praying,
tears pour
over my arms and his arms.
I don't know whether this is joy
or sadness, I don't understand
what I feel, I'm crying,
I'm crying, it's humility
as if I were dead,
gratitude, I thank you, my fate,
I'm unworthy, how beautiful
my life.

ANNA SWIR
translated by Czeslaw Milosz & Leonard Nathan

ACKNOWLEDGEMENTS

The poems in this anthology are reprinted from the following books, all by permission of the publishers listed unless stated otherwise. Thanks are due to all the copyright holders cited below for their kind permission: **Robert Adamson:** *The Kingfisher's Soul* (Bloodaxe Books, 2009). **Fleur Adcock:** *Poems 1960-2000* (Bloodaxe Books, 2000). **Kim Addonizio:** 'You Don't Know What Love Is' from *What Is This Thing Called Love* (W.W. Norton & Company, 2004); 'Like That' from *Tell Me* (BOA Editions, USA, 2000), www.boaeditions.org. **John Agard:** *Alternative Anthem: Selected Poems* (Bloodaxe Books, 2009). **Elizabeth Alexander:** *American Blue: Selected Poems* (Bloodaxe Books, 2006). **Maram al-Massri:** *A Red Cherry on a White-tiled Floor,* tr. Khaled Mattawa (Bloodaxe Books, 2004). **Agha Shahid Ali:** *The Half-Inch Himalayas* (Wesleyan University Press, 1987). **Keith Althaus:** *Ladder of Hours: Poems 1969-2005* (Ausable Press, 2005), by permission of Copper Canyon Press, www.coppercanyonpress.org. **Moniza Alvi:** *Split World: Poems 1990-2005* (Bloodaxe Books, 2008). **Yehuda Amichai:** 'A Quiet Joy' from *Selected Poems,* ed. Ted Hughes & Daniel Weissbort (Faber & Faber, 2000); 'Inside the Apple', 'The Place Where We Are Right' and 'A Man in His Life' from *The Selected Poetry of Yehuda Amichai,* tr. Chana Bloch & Stephen Mitchell (HarperCollins, 1986; rev. ed. University of California Press, 1996), by permission of the University of California Press. **Doug Anderson:** *The Moon Reflected Fire* (Alice James Books, 1994), by permission of the author. **Nadia Anjuman:** 'The Silenced', tr. Abdul Salam Shayek, from *Naweed Monthly,* issue 5 & 6, by permission of the translator. **Simon Armitage:** *The Universal Home Doctor* (Faber & Faber, 2002). **W.H. Auden:** *Collected Poems,* ed. Edward Mendelson (Faber & Faber, 1991), by permission of the Wylie Agency. **Margaret Avison:** *Always Now: The Collected Poems* in three volumes (Porcupine's Quill, Canada, 2003), by permission of the publisher and the Estate of Margaret Avison.

Jimmy Santiago Baca: *Martin and Meditations on the South Valley* (New Directions Publishing Corporation, 1987). **Mary Jo Bang:** *Elegy* (Graywolf Press, 2007), www.graywolfpress.org. **Stanisław Baranczak:** 'A Second Nature', tr. Stanislaw Baranczak & Clare Cavanagh, from *Polish Poetry of the Last Two Decades of Communist Rule: Spoiling Cannibals Fun,* ed. & tr. Stanislaw Baranczak & Clare Cavanagh (Northwestern University Press, 1991), by permission of the publisher. **Mourid Barghouti:** *Midnight and other poems,* tr. Radwa Ashour (Arc, 2008). **Paul Batchelor:** *The Sinking Road* (Bloodaxe Books, 2008). **Patricia Beer:** *Collected Poems* (Carcanet Press, 1990). **Gottfried Benn:** Little Aster [poem 1 from 'Morgue'], tr. Babette Deutsch, from *Primal Vision: Selected Writings of Gottfried Benn,* ed. E.B. Ashton (New Directions Publishing Corporation, 1971). **James Berry:** *Windrush Songs* (Bloodaxe Books, 2007), from *The Story I Am In: Selected Poems* (Bloodaxe Books, 2011). **Judith Beveridge:** *The Domesticity of Giraffes* (Black Lightning Press, Australia, 1987). **Sujata Bhatt:** *Brunizem* (Carcanet Press, 1988), from *Point No Point: Selected Poems* (Carcanet Press, 1997). **Ruth Bidgood:** *New & Selected Poems* (Seren Books, 2004). **Elizabeth Bishop:** *Complete Poems 1927-1979* (Farrar, Straus and Giroux, 1983), copyright © 1979, 1983 by Alice Helen Methfessel, by permission of Farrar, Straus and Giroux, LLC. **Richard Blessing:** *A Closed Book* (University of Washington Press, Seattle, 1981), by permission of the Estate of Richard Blessing. **Adrian Blevins:** *The Brass Girl Brouhaha* (Ausable Press, 2003), by permission of Copper Canyon Press, www.coppercanyonpress.org. **Michael Blumenthal:** 'What I Believe' from *Days We Would Rather Know* (Pleasure Boat Studio, NY, 2005) and 'A Marriage' from *Against Romance* (Pleasure Boat Studio, NY, 2006), by permission of the author. **Eavan Boland:** *New Collected Poems* (Carcanet Press, 2005). **Jorge Luis Borges:** *Selected Poems,* ed. Alexander Coleman (Penguin Books, 1999). **Sargon Boulus:** *Knife Sharpener: Selected Poems,* tr. author (Banipal Books, 2009). **Coral Bracho:** *Poems,* tr. Katherine Pierpoint & Tom Boll (Poetry Translation Centre, 2010). **Charles Brasch:** *Collected Poems* (Oxford University Press, New Zealand, 1984). **Jean 'Binta' Breeze:** *The arrival of Brighteye and other poems* (Bloodaxe Books, 2000), from *Third World Girl: Selected Poems* (Bloodaxe Books, 2011). **Olga Broumas:** *Rave: Poems 1975-1999* (Copper Canyon Press, 1999), www.coppercanyonpress.org. **Jericho Brown:** *Please* (New Issues Poetry Press, 2008), by permission of the author. **John Burnside:** 'September Evening: Deer at Big Basin' from *The Myth of the Twin* (Jonathan Cape, 1994), '(enlightenment)', part I of 'Of Gravity and Light', from *The Light Trap* (Jonathan Cape, 2002), 'Anniversary' from *The Good Neighbour* (Jonathan Cape, 2005), by permission of the Random House Group Ltd; 'Marginal jottings on the prospect of dying', part V of 'Varieties of Religious Experience', from *Gift Songs* (Jonathan Cape, 2007), by permission of the author and Rogers, Coleridge and White.

David Campbell: *Collected Poems* (Angus & Robertson, Australia, 1989). **Moya Cannon:** 'The Train' from *Poetry Ireland Review,* 86 (May 2006), by permission of the author. **Edip Cansever:** *Dirty August,* tr. Julia Clare Tillinghast & Richard Tillinghast (Talisman House, USA, 2009), by permission of the translators. **Ernesto Cardenal:** *From Nicaragua with Love: Poems 1979-1986,* tr. Jonathan Cohen (City Lights Books, 1987). **Raymond Carver:** *All of Us: Collected Poems* (Harvill Press, 1996), copyright © 1996 Tess Gallagher, by permission of the Wylie Agency. **C.P. Cavafy:** *Collected Poems,* revised edition, tr. Edmund Keeley & Philip Sherrard (Chatto & Windus, 1998). **Paul Celan:** *Selected Poems and Prose*

490

and United Agents. **Gustavo Pérez Firmat:** *Bilingual Blues* (Bilingual Press/Editorial Bilingüe, Tempe, Arizona, 1995). **Jean Follain:** 'Life' from *Into the Deep Street: Seven Modern French Poets 1938-2008*, ed. & tr. Jennie Feldman & Stephen Romer (Anvil Press Poetry, 2009), translation of 'Vie' from *Exister* (1947) © Editions Gallimard, Paris. **Carolyn Forché:** *The Country Between Us* (Jonathan Cape, 1983), by permission of the Virginia Barber Literary Agency, Inc. **Roderick Ford:** *The Green Crown* (Bradshaw Books 2010), by permission of Bradshaw Books, 50, Popes Quay, Cork, Ireland. **Tua Forsström:** *I studied once at a wonderful faculty*, tr. David McDuff & Stina Katchadourian (Bloodaxe Books, 2006). **Janet Frame:** *Storms Will Tell: Selected Poems* (Bloodaxe Books, 2008). **Robert Frost:** *The Poetry of Robert Frost*, ed. Edward Connery Lathem (Jonathan Cape, 1967), by permission of Random House Group Ltd. **Tess Gallagher:** *My Black Horse: New & Selected Poems* (Bloodaxe Books, 1995), by permission of Graywolf Press, www.graywolfpress.org. **Deborah Garrison:** *The Second Child* (Bloodaxe Books, 2008). **Jack Gilbert:** *Transgressions: Selected Poems* (Bloodaxe Books, 2006). **Alan Gillis:** *Somebody, Somewhere* (Gallery Press, 2004), by permission of the Gallery Press, Loughcrew, Oldcastle, Co. Meath, Ireland. **Dana Gioia:** 'Nothing Is Lost' from *Daily Horoscope* (Graywolf Press, 1986); 'The Song' and 'Prayer' from *The Gods of Winter* (Graywolf Press, 1991), by permission of Graywolf Press, www.graywolfpress. org. **Nikki Giovanni:** *The Collected Poetry of Nikki Giovanni 1968-1998* (William Morrow, 2003), by permission of the author. **John Glenday:** *Grain* (Picador, 2009), by permission of Macmillan Publishers Ltd. **Louise Glück:** 'Matins' from *The Wild Iris* (Carcanet Press, 1992); Louise Glück: 'Screened Porch' from *The Seven Ages* (Carcanet Press, 2001); 'Lullaby' from *The Wild Iris* (Carcanet Press, 1992). **Lorna Goodison:** *Goldengrove: New and Selected Poems* (Carcanet Press, 2005). **Jan Gould:** *The Past Completes Me: Selected Poems 1973-2003* (University of Queensland Press, 2005). **Lavinia Greenlaw:** *Minsk* (Faber & Faber, 2003). **Eamon Grennan:** *Out of Breath* (Gallery Press, 2003), by permission of the Gallery Press, Loughcrew, Oldcastle, Co. Meath, Ireland. **Kevin Griffith:** 'Spinning' from *Mid-American Review*, Vol. 26, no. 2 (2006), by permission of the author. **Eliza Griswold:** *Wideawake Field* (Farrar, Straus and Giroux, 2007). **Vona Groarke:** *Juniper Street* (Gallery Press, 2006), by permission of the Gallery Press, Loughcrew, Oldcastle, Co. Meath, Ireland. **Philip Gross:** *Deep Field* (Bloodaxe Books, 2011). **Thom Gunn:** *Collected Poems* (Faber & Faber, 1993). **Lars Gustafsson:** 'Elegy for a Dead Labrador', tr. Yvonne L. Sandstroem, from *The Stillness of the World Before Bach: New Selected Poems* (New Directions Publishing, 1988); 'The Girl', tr. John Irons, from *A Time in Xanadu* (Copper Canyon Press, 2008), www.coppercanyonpress.org.

Jen Hadfield: *Nigh-No-Place* (Bloodaxe Books, 2008). **Patricia Hampl:** *Resort* (Carnegie Mellon University Press, 2001). **Peter Handke:** 'Song of Childhood' and excerpts of dialogue from *Wings of Desire* by permission of Suhrkamp Verlag GmbH and the author. **Kerry Hardie:** 'May' from *A Furious Place* (Gallery Press, 1996); 'Flesh' from *The Silence Came Close* (Gallery Press, 2006); 'Helplessness' and 'Humankind' from *Only This Room* (Gallery Press, 2009); three of these also in *Selected Poems* (Gallery Press/Bloodaxe Books, 2011), by permission of the Gallery Press, Loughcrew, Oldcastle, Co. Meath, Ireland. **Tony Harrison:** *Collected Poems* (Viking Penguin, 1987), by permission of Gordon Dickerson and the author. **Michael Hartnett:** *The Killing of Dreams* (Gallery Press, 1992), by permission of the Gallery Press, Loughcrew, Oldcastle, Co. Meath, Ireland. **Julia Hartwig:** 'Toward the End', tr. Stanislaw Baranczak & Clare Cavanagh, from *Polish Poetry of the Last Two Decades of Communist Rule: Spoiling Cannibals Fun*, ed. & tr. Stanislaw Baranczak & Clare Cavanagh (Northwestern University Press, 1991). **Francis Harvey:** *Collected Poems* (Dedalus Press, Dublin, 2007). www.dedaluspress.com. **Robert Hass:** *The Apple Trees at Olema: New & Selected Poems* (Bloodaxe Books, 2011). **Olav H. Hauge:** *Leaf-Huts and Snow-Houses: Selected Poems*, tr. Robin Fulton (Anvil Press Poetry, 2003). **Terrance Hayes:** *Hip Logic* (Penguin Books, USA, 2008). **Seamus Heaney:** 'A Sofa in the Forties' from *Opened Ground: Poems 1966-1996* (Faber & Faber, 1998); 'Miracle' from *Human Chain* (Faber & Faber, 2010). **Anthony Hecht:** *Collected Earlier Poems* (Alfred A. Knopf, Inc, 1990). **Stuart Henson:** 'The Price' from *Ember Music* (Peterloo Poets, 1994), by permission of the author. **Toeti Heraty:** *Poems*, tr. Carole Satyamurti & Ulrich Katz (Poetry Translation Centre, 2008). **John Hewitt:** *Collected Poems*, ed. Frank Ormsby (Blackstaff Press, 1991). **Rita Ann Higgins:** *Throw in the Vowels: New & Selected Poems* (Bloodaxe Books, 2005). **Nâzim Hikmet:** 'Things I Didn't Know I Loved' and 'It's This Way' from *Poems of Nâzim Hikmet*, tr. Randy Blasing & Mutlu Konuk (Persea Books, Inc, NY, 1994; second edition, 2002); 'On Living', tr. Ruth Christie from *Beyond the Walls: Selected Poems*, tr. Ruth Christie & Richard McKane (Anvil Press Poetry, 2002). **Selima Hill:** *Gloria: Selected Poems* (Bloodaxe Books, 2008). **Jane Hirshfield:** 'The Weighing' and 'Tree' from *Each Happiness Ringed by Lions: Selected Poems* (Bloodaxe Books, 2005); 'Burlap Sack' from *After* (Bloodaxe Books, 2006). **Ho Thien:** 'Green Beret' from *Axed Between the Ears*, ed. David Kitchen (Heinemann Publishers, 1987). **Tony Hoagland:** *Unincorporated Persons in the Late Honda Dynasty* (Graywolf Press, USA; Bloodaxe Books, UK, 2010), by permission of Graywolf Press, www.graywolfpress.org. **Philip Hodgins:** 'Leaving' from *Up on All Fours* (HarperCollins/Angus & Robertson, Australia, 1993); 'Death Who' from *Blood and Bone* (Collins/Angus & Robertson, Australia, 1986). **Linda Hogan:** *Seeing through the Sun* (University of Massachusetts Press, 1995). **Sarah Holland-Batt:** *Aria* (University of Queensland Press, 2008). **A.D. Hope:** *Selected Poems* (Carcanet Press, 1986), by permission of Curtis Brown. **Frances Horovitz:** *Collected Poems*, ed. Roger Garfitt (Bloodaxe Books,

1985). **Chenjerai Hove:** 'You Will Forget', first published by Baobab Books, Harare, Zimbabwe, by permission of the author. **Marie Howe:** *The Kingdom of Ordinary Time* (W.W. Norton & Company, 2008). **David Huerta:** *Poems*, tr. Jamie McKendrick, ed. Tom Boll (Poetry Translation Centre, 2010). **Langston Hughes:** *The Collected Poems of Langston Hughes* (Alfred A. Knopf, Inc, 1994), by permission of David Higham Associates. **Ted Hughes:** *Birthday Letters* (Faber & Faber, 1998), from *Collected Poems* (Faber & Faber, 2003). **Richard Hugo:** *Making Certain It Goes On: The Collected Poems of Richard Hugo* (W.W. Norton & Company, 1984). **Lynda Hull:** *Collected Poems* (Graywolf Press, 2006), copyright © 2006 by the Estate of Lynda Hull, by permission of Graywolf Press, www.graywolfpress.org. **Ikkyu:** 'My real dwelling' from *Wild Ways: Zen Poems of Ikkyu*, tr. John Stevens (White Pine Press, USA, 2003). **Gyula Illyés:** *What You Have Almost Forgotten: Selected Poems*, tr. William Jay Smith (Curbstone Press, 1999), by permission of Northwestern University Press.

    Kathleen Jamie: *Jizzen* (Picador, 1999), by permission of Macmillan Publishers Ltd. **Randall Jarrell:** *The Complete Poems* (Faber & Faber, 1981). **Elizabeth Jennings:** *New Collected Poems* (Carcanet Press, 2002), by permission of David Higham Associates. **Evan Jones:** *Understandings: poems* (Melbourne University Press, 1967), by permission of the author. **Rodney Jones:** *Salvation Blues: One Hundred Poems 1985-2005* (Houghton Mifflin, 2006). **Roberto Juarroz:** *Vertical Poetry*, tr. W.S. Merwin (North Point Press, 1988), copyright © 1988 by W.S. Merwin, by permission of the Wylie Agency, Spanish original from *Cuarta poesia vertical, poema 1* (Buenos Aires: Aditor, 1969), republished by Emecé in *Poesia vertical, 1958-1982* (Buenos Aires: Emecé, 1993), *Poesía vertical I* (Buenos Aires: Emecé, 2005). **Donald Justice:** *Collected Poems* (Anvil Press Poetry, 2006).

    Mohja Kahf: *E-mails from Scheherazad* (University of Florida Press, 2003). **Anna Kamienska:** 'Funny', tr. Stanisław Barańczak & Clare Cavanagh, from *Polish Poetry of the Last Two Decades of Communist Rule: Spoiling Cannibals Fun*, ed. & tr. Stanisław Barańczak & Clare Cavanagh (Northwestern University Press, 1991). **Jaan Kaplinski:** *Selected Poems* (Bloodaxe Books, 2011). **Katia Kapovich:** *Gogol in Rome* (Salt Publishing, 2004). **Doris Kareva:** *Shape of Time*, tr. Tiina Aleman (Arc, 2010). **Julia Kasdorf:** *Sleeping Preacher* (University of Pittsburgh Press, 1992). **Patrick Kavanagh:** *Collected Poems*, ed. Antoinette Quinn (Allen Lane, 2004), by permission of the Trustees of the Estate of the late Katherine B. Kavanagh, and through the Jonathan Williams Literary Agency. **Jackie Kay:** *Darling: New & Selected Poems* (Bloodaxe Books, 2007). **Garrison Keillor:** *77 Love Sonnets* (Bloodaxe Books, 2011), by permission of the author. **Brigit Pegeen Kelly:** *Poems: Song AND The Orchard* (Carcanet Press, 2008). **X.J. Kennedy:** *The Lords of Misrule: Poems 1992-2001*, p.88, © 2002 X.J. Kennedy, by permission of The Johns Hopkins University Press. **Brendan Kennelly:** *Familiar Strangers: New & Selected Poems 1960-2004* (Bloodaxe Books, 2004). **Jane Kenyon:** *Let Evening Come: Selected Poems* (Bloodaxe Books, 2005), copyright © 2005 Estate of Jane Kenyon, from *Collected Poems* by permission of Graywolf Press, Minneapolis, www.graywolfpress.org. **Farzaneh Khojandi:** *Poems*, tr. Jo Shapcott & Narguess Farzad (Poetry Translation Centre, 2008). **Galway Kinnell:** *Selected Poems* (Bloodaxe Books, 2001). **Irena Klepfisz:** *A Few Words in the Mother Tongue: Poems Selected and New 1971-1990* (The Eighth Mountain Press, 1991). **Arun Kolatkar:** *Collected Poems in English*, ed. Arvind Krishna Mehrotra (Bloodaxe Books, 2010). **Yusef Komunyakaa:** *Scandalize My Name: Selected Poems* (Picador, 2002). **Ko Un:** *Three Way Tavern: Selected Poems*, tr. Clare You & Richard Silberg (University of California Press, 2006). **Stanley Kunitz:** *Passing Through: The Later Poems, New and Selected* (W.W. Norton & Company, 1995).

    Sonnet L'Abbé: *Killarnoe* (McClelland & Stewart, Toronto, 2007), by permission of the author. **Ivan V. Lalic:** *The Passionate Measure*, tr. Francis R. Jones (Anvil Press Poetry, 1989). **Philip Larkin:** *Collected Poems*, ed. Anthony Thwaite (Faber & Faber, 1990). **Else Lasker-Schüler:** 'My Blue Piano', from *Eavan Boland (ed. & tr.) After Every War: Twentieth-Century Women Poets*, ed. & tr. Eavan Boland (Princeton University Press, 2004). **Michael Laskey:** *Permission to Breathe* (Smith/Doorstop Books, 2004). **Dorianne Laux:** *Smoke* (BOA Editions, 2000), www.boaeditions.org. **Anthony Lawrence:** *The Darkwood Aquarium* (Penguin Australia, 1993), by permission of the author. **Laurie Lee:** *Selected Poems* (Penguin, 1985), by permission of United Agents. **Denise Levertov:** *The Life Around Us: selected poems on nature* (New Directions Publishing Corporation, 1997). **Philip Levine:** *Selected Poems* (Bloodaxe Books, 2006), by permission of Alfred A. Knopf, Inc. **Larry Levis:** 'The Oldest Living Thing in LA' from *The Selected Levis*, ed. David St John (University of Pittsburgh Press, 2000, 2003), by permission of the publisher; 'The Morning After My Death' from *The Afterlife* (University of Iowa Press, 1977), by permission of the Estate of Larry Levis. **Frances Leviston:** *Public Dream* (Picador, 2007), by permission of Macmillan Publishers Ltd. **Emma Lew:** *Anything the Landlord Touches* (Shearsman, 2002), by permission of the author. **Luljeta Lleshanaku:** *Haywire: New & Selected Poems* (Bloodaxe Books, 2011). **Michael Longley:** *Collected Poems* (Jonathan Cape, 2006), by permission of the Random House Group Ltd. **Robert Lowell:** *Collected Poems* (Faber & Faber, 2003). **Tatjana Lukic:** *la, la, la* (Five Islands Press, NZ, 2009), by permission of the Estate of Tatjana Lukic. **Thomas Lux:** *New and Selected Poems 1975-1995* (Houghton Mifflin, 1997).

    Norman MacCaig: *The Poems of Norman MacCaig*, ed. Ewen McCaig (Polyon/Birlinn, 2009). **Roger McGough:** *Collected Poems* (Viking, 2003), by permission of Peters, Fraser & Dunlop. **Heather McHugh:** *Hinge & Sign: Poems 1968-1993* (Wesleyan University Press. 1994). **Louis MacNeice:** *Collected*

Poems, ed. Peter McDonald (Faber, 2007), by permission of David Higham Associates Ltd. **Didem Madak**: 'Sir, I Want to Write Poems with Flowers', tr. Murat Nemet-Nejat, from *Eda: An Anthology of Contemporary Turkish Poetry*, ed. Murat Nemet-Nejat (Talisman House, NJ, 2004), by permission of the translator. **Sarah Maguire**: *The Pomegranates of Kandahar* (Chatto, 2007), by permission of the Random House Group Ltd. **Derek Mahon**: 'Thunder Shower' from *An Autumn Wind* (Gallery Press, 2010); 'Kinsale' from *Collected Poems* (Gallery Press, 1999); 'Ignorance' from *Words in the Air: a selection of poems by Philippe Jaccottet* (Gallery Press, 1996), by permission of the Gallery Press, Loughcrew, Oldcastle, Co. Meath, Ireland. **Nick Makoha**: 'Beatitude' from *Ten: new poets from Spread the Word*, ed. Bernardine Evaristo & Daljit Nagra (Bloodaxe Books/Spread the Word, 2010), by permission of the author. **Osip Mandelstam**: *Stone*, trs. Robert Tracy (Collins Harvill, 1991). **Bill Manhire**: *Lifted* (Carcanet Press, 2007). **Eeva-Liisa Manner**: *Bright, Dusky, Bright*, tr. Emily Jeremiah (Waterloo Press, 2009), original text from Eeva-Liisa Manner, *Kirkas, hämärä, kirkas: Kootut runot* (Tammi, 2008). **Jack Mapanje**: *The Last of the Sweet Bananas: New & Selected Poems* (Bloodaxe Books, 2004). **Harry Martinson**: *Chickweed Wintergreen: Selected Poems*, tr. Robin Fulton (Bloodaxe Books, 2010). **Joan Margarit**: *Tugs in the Fog: Selected Poems*, tr. Anna Crowe (Bloodaxe Books, 2006). **E.A. Markham**: *Looking Out, Looking in: New and Selected Poems* (Anvil Press Poetry, 2009). **Lorraine Mariner**: *Furniture* (Picador, 2009), by permission of Macmillan Publishers Ltd. **William Matthews**: *Search Party: Collected Poems*, ed. Sebastian Matthews & Stanley Plumly (Houghton Mifflin Harcourt, 2004). **Paula Meehan**: *The Man Who Was Marked by Winter* (Gallery Press, 1991), by permission of the author. **Arvind Krishna Mehrotra**: *The Transfiguring Places* (Ravi Dayal, 1998), by permission of the author. **Samuel Menashe**: *New and Selected Poems* (Bloodaxe Books, 2009). **James Merrill**: *Collected Poems* (Alfred A. Knopf, 2001). **W.S. Merwin**: *The Shadow of Sirius* (Bloodaxe Books, 2009). **Dunya Mikhail**: *The War Works Hard* (Carcanet Press, 2006). **Czeslaw Milosz**: *New & Collected Poems 1931-2001* (Allen Lane The Penguin Press, 2001), copyright © Czeslaw Milosz Royalties Inc., 1988, 1991, 1995, 2001. **Adrian Mitchell**: 'Yes' from *Blue Coffee: Poems 1985-1996* (Bloodaxe Books, 1996); 'Human Beings' from *The Shadow Knows: Poems 2001-2004* (Bloodaxe Books, 2004); 'Death Is Smaller Than I Thought' from *Tell Me Lies: Poems 2005-2008* (Bloodaxe Books, 2009), by permission of United Agents. **Susan Mitchell**: *The Water Inside the Water* (HarperCollins, USA, 2004). **Kenji Miyazawa**: *Strong in the Rain: Selected Poems*, tr. Roger Pulvers (Bloodaxe Books, 2007). **John Montague**: *Collected Poems* (Gallery Press, 1995), by permission of the Gallery Press, Loughcrew, Oldcastle, Co. Meath, Ireland. **Eugenio Montale**: *Collected Poems 1920-1954*, tr. Jonathan Galassi (Farrar, Straus & Giroux, 2000). **Dom Moraes**: *Collected Poems 1954-2004* (Penguin India, 2004), by permission of Saraju Ahuja. **Esther Morgan**: *Grace* (Bloodaxe Books, 2011). **Edwin Morgan**: *Collected Poems* (Carcanet Press, 1996). **Sinéad Morrissey**: *Between Here and There* (Carcanet Press, 2002). **Andrew Motion**: 'To Whom It May Concern' from *Selected Poems 1976-1997* (Faber & Faber, 1998); 'The Cinder Path' from *The Cinder Path* (Faber & Faber, 2009). **Taha Muhammad Ali**: *So What: New & Selected Poems 1971-2005* (Bloodaxe Books, 2007). **Lisel Mueller**: *Alive Together: New & Selected Poems* (Louisiana State University Press, 1996). **Paul Muldoon**: *New Selected Poems 1968-1994* (Faber & Faber, 1994). **Les Murray**: *New Collected Poems* (Carcanet Press, 2003).

Partaw Naderi: *Poems*, tr. Sarah Maguire & Yama Yari (Poetry Translation Centre, 2008). **Nora Nadjarian**: *Cleft in Twain* (Strovolos, Nicosia, Cyprus, 2003), by permission of the author. **Daljit Nagra**: *Look We Have Coming to Dover!* (Faber & Faber, 2007). **Amjad Nasser**: *Selected Poems*, tr. Khaled Mattawa (Banipal Books, 2009). **María Negroni**: *Night Journey*, tr. Anne Twitty (Princeton University Press, 2002). **Pablo Neruda**: 'If I die, survive me with such a pure force', sonnet XCIV, from *100 Love Sonnets / Cien sonetos de amor*, tr. Stephen Tapscott (University of Texas Press, 1986); 'The great table-cloth', 'Emerging' and 'Keeping quiet' from *Extravagaria*, tr. Alastair Reid (Farrar, Straus and Giroux, 2001). **Eiléan Ní Chuilleanáin**: *The Girl Who Married the Reindeer* (Gallery Press, 2001), by permission of the Gallery Press, Loughcrew, Oldcastle, Co. Meath, Ireland. **Grace Nichols**: *I Have Crossed an Ocean: Selected Poems* (Bloodaxe Books, 2010). **Henrik Nordbrandt**: *My Life, My Dream: Selected Poems*, tr. Robin Fulton (Dedalus Books, Dublin, 2002), www.dedaluspress.com. **Leslie Norris**: *The Complete Poems*, ed. Meic Stephens (Seren Books, 2008), by permission of Meic Stephens. **Naomi Shihab Nye**: *Red Suitcase* (BOA Editions, USA, 2004) and *Tender Spot: Selected Poems* (Bloodaxe Books, UK, 2008), by permission of BOA Editions, www.boaeditions.org.

Julie O'Callaghan: *Tell Me This Is Normal: New & Selected Poems* (Bloodaxe Books, 2008). **Bernard O'Donoghue**: *Gunpowder* (Chatto, 1995), by permission of the author. **Dennis O'Driscoll**: *New and Selected Poems* (Anvil Press Poetry, 2004). **Sharon Olds**: 'This Hour', 'I Go Back to May 1937' and 'The Race' from *Selected Poems* (Jonathan Cape, 2005); 'Self-portrait, Rear View' from *One Secret Thing* (Jonathan Cape, 2009), by permission of the Random House Group Ltd. **Liam Ó Muirthile**: 'The Parlour', tr. Bernard O'Donoghue, from *Modern Poetry in Translation*, series 3 no.1 (2004), by permission of *MPT* and the translator. **George Oppen**: *Collected Poems* (New Directions Publishing Corporation, 1975). **John Ormond**: *Selected Poems* (Seren Books, 1987). **Micheal O'Siadhail**: *Tongues* (Bloodaxe Books, 2010). **Alice Oswald**: *Woods etc.* (Faber & Faber, 2005).

Heberto Padilla: *Legacies: Selected Poems*, tr. Alastair Reid & Andrew Hurley (Farrar, Straus and Giroux, 1982). **Geoff Page**: *Selected Poems* (HarperCollins/Angus & Robertson, 1991). **Dan Pagis**: *The*

Selected Poetry of Dan Pagis, tr. Stephen Mitchell (University of California Press, 1996). **Grace Paley:** 'This Life' from *Begin Again: Collected Poems* (Farrar, Straus & Giroux, 2001); 'Anti-Love Poem' from *Fidelity* (Farrar, Straus & Giroux, 2009). **Francesc Parcerisas:** 'Shave', tr. Cyrus Cassells, from *Words Without Borders*, March 2011, by permission of the translator. **Nii Ayikwei Parkes:** *The Makings of You* (Peepal Tree, 2010). **Linda Pastan:** 'To a Daughter Leaving Home' from *The Imperfect Paradise* (W.W. Norton & Company, 1988); 'Things I Didn't Know I Loved' from *Queen of a Rainy Country* (W.W. Norton & Company, 2006). **Kenneth Patchen:** *Selected Poems* (New Directions Publishing Corporation, 1957). **Molly Peacock:** *Original Love* (W.W. Norton & Company, 1995). **Lucia Perillo:** *Luck Is Luck* (Random House, USA, 2005). **Fernando Pessoa:** *A Little Larger Than the Entire Universe: Selected Poems*, tr. Richard Zenith (Penguin Books, 2006). **Pascale Petit:** *The Zoo Father* (Seren Books, 2001). **Sylvia Plath:** *Collected Poems* (Faber & Faber, 1981). **Patricia Pogson:** *Holding* (Flambard Press, 2002). **Katha Pollitt:** *The Mind-Body Problem* (Random House, USA, 2009). **Vasko Popa:** *Collected Poems* (Anvil Press Poetry, 1997). **Adélia Prado:** *The Alphabet in the Park*, tr. Ellen Doré Watson (Wesleyan University Press, 1990). **Karen Press:** *Home* (Carcanet Press, 2000). **Sheenagh Pugh:** *Stonelight* (Seren Books, 1999).

Salvatore **Quasimodo:** *Complete Poems*, tr. Jack Bevan (Anvil Press Poetry, 1983). **Raymond Queneau:** *Poems* (Unicorn Press, 1971), translation by Teo Savory of 'L'espèce humaine' from *L'Instant fatal* (1948) © Editions Gallimard, Paris.

Miklós **Radnóti:** *Foamy Sky: The Major Poems of Miklós Radnóti*, tr. Zsuzsanna Ozsváth & Frederick Turner (Corvina, Budapest, 2002), by permission of the Estate of Miklós Radnóti. **A.K. Ramanujan:** *The Oxford India Ramanujan*, ed. Molly Daniels-Ramanujan (Oxford University Press, 2004). **Irina Ratushinskaya:** *No, I'm Not Afraid*, tr. David McDuff (Bloodaxe Books, 1986), by permission of Andrew Nurnberg Associates. **Alastair Reid:** *Inside Out: Selected Poetry and Translations* (Polygon, 2008), by permission of Birlinn Limited. **Christopher Reid:** *A Scattering* (Areté Books, 2009), by permission of the author and Rogers Coleridge and White. **Oktay Rifat:** *Poems of Oktay Rifat*, tr. Ruth Christie & Richard McKane (Anvil Press Poetry, 2007). **Rainer Maria Rilke:** 'Archaic Torso of Apollo' from *Ahead of All Parting: The Selected Poetry and Prose of Rainer Maria Rilke*, ed. & tr. Stephen Mitchell (The Modern Library, New York, 1995), copyright © 1995 Stephen Mitchell, by permission of Modern Library a division of Random House, Inc.; 'Childhood' from *The Poems of Rilke*, tr. Edward Snow (North Point Press, 2009), by permission of Farrar, Straus and Giroux. **W.R. Rodgers:** *Poems*, ed. Michael Longley (Gallery Press, 1993), by permission of the Gallery Press, Loughcrew, Oldcastle, Co. Meath, Ireland. **Robyn Rowland:** *Silence & its tongues* (Five Islands Press, Melbourne, 2006), by permission of the author. **Rumi:** *The Essential Rumi: Translations* by Coleman Barks (HarperSanFrancisco, USA, 1995; expanded edition, 2004), copyright in both volumes © Coleman Barks, also by kind permission of the Reid Boates Literary Agency.

Lawrence **Sail:** *Waking Dreams: New & Selected Poems* (Bloodaxe Books, 2010). **Carole Satyamurti:** *Stitching the Dark: New & Selected Poems* (Bloodaxe Books, 2005). **Vernon Scannell:** *Collected Poems 1950-1993* (Faber Finds, 2010), by permission of the Estate of Vernon Scannell. **David Scott:** *Selected Poems* (Bloodaxe Books, 1998). **George Seferis:** *Complete Poems*, tr. Edmund Keeley & Philip Sherrard (Anvil Press Poetry, 1995). **Pedro Serrano:** 'Feet'/'Los pies', tr. Anna Crowe, *Mexican Poetry Today, 20/20 Voices: a bilingual anthology*, ed. Brandel France de Bravo (Shearman, 2010), by permission of the author and translator. **Aharon Shabtai:** *J'Accuse*, tr. Peter Cole (New Directions Publishing Corporation, 2003). **Ravi Shankar:** 'Plumbing the Deepening Grove' from *Fulcrum*, by permission of the author. **Jo Shapcott:** *Of Mutability* (Faber & Faber, 2010). **Izumi Shikibu:** *The Ink Dark Moon: Love Poems by Ono no Komachi and Izumu Shikibu, Women of the Ancient Court of Japan*, tr. Jane Hirshfield with Mariko Aratani (Scribner's 1988; Vintage Classics, 1990), copyright © 1990 Jane Hirshfield, by permission of Vintage Books, a division of Random House Inc. **Penelope Shuttle:** *Taxing the Rain* (Oxford University Press, 1992), by permission of the author and David Higham Associates Ltd. **Charles Simic:** *Dismantling the Silence* (Braziller/Jonathan Cape, 1971), by permission of the author. **Louis Simpson:** *The Owner of the House: New Collected Poems 1940-2001* (BOA Editions, 2001) and *Voices in the Distance: Selected Poems* (Bloodaxe Books, 2010), reprinted by permission of BOA Editions, www. boaeditions.org. **Alex Skovron:** *Infinite City* (Five Islands Press, Melbourne, 1999), by permission of the author. **Alan Smith:** *The Poet of Oz* (Robyn Smith/Lulu, 2008), by permission of the author. **Catherine Smith:** *Lip* (Smith/Doorstop Books, 2007), by permission of the author. **Iain Crichton Smith:** *New Collected Poems* (Carcanet Press, 2011), by permission of the author. **Ken Smith:** *Shed: Poems 1980-2001* (Bloodaxe Books, 2002). **Tracy K. Smith:** *Duende* (Graywolf Press, 2007), www.graywolfpress.org. **Edith Södergran:** *Complete Poems*, tr. David McDuff (Bloodaxe Books, 1984), by permission of the translator. **Ronny Someck:** 'A Poem of Bliss' tr. Yair Mazor from *The Space Between Our Footsteps: Poems & Paintings from the Middle East*, ed. Naomi Shihab Nye (Simon & Schuster, 1998), by permission of the translator Yair Mazor. **Marin Sorescu:** *The Bridge* (Bloodaxe Books, 2004). **William Stafford:** 'The Way It Is' from *The Way It Is: New & Selected Poems* (Graywolf Press, 1998), www.graywolfpress.org'; 'The Gift' from *Even in Quiet Places* (Confluence Press, Lewiston, Idaho, 1996), by permission of the publisher. **Mary Stanley:** *Starveling Year and other poems* (Auckland University Press, New Zealand, 1994), by permission of Alexandra Smithyman and the publisher. **Anne Stevenson**: 'It looks so simple from a distance' from *Poems 1955-2005* (Bloodaxe Books, 2005); 'On Harlech Beach', first published in *The New Yorker*, 2011, by permission of the author and *The New Yorker*. **Greta Stoddart**: *Salvation Jane* (Anvil Press Poetry, 2008). **Ruth Stone**: 'Another Feeling' from *In the Dark* (Copper Canyon Press, 2004); other poems from *What Love Comes To: New & Selected Poems* (Bloodaxe Books, 2009). **Mark Strand**: 'Keeping Things Whole' from *Selected Poems* (Carcanet Press, 1995); 'Old Man Leaves Party' from *Blizzard of One* (Alfred A. Knopf, 1998). **Arundhathi Subramaniam**: *Where I Live: New & Selected Poems* (Bloodaxe Books, 2009). **Matthew Sweeney**: *Black Moon* (Jonathan Cape, 2007), by permission of the Random House Group Ltd. **Anna Swir**: *Talking to My Body*, tr. Czeslaw Miłosz & Leonard Nathan (Copper Canyon Press, USA, 1996), English translation, copyright © 1996 Czeslaw Miłosz & Leonard Nathan, by the permission of Copper Canyon Press, www.coppercanyonpress.org. **Anna T. Szabo**: 'She Leaves Me', tr. Clive Wilmer & George Gömöri, from *New Order: Hungarian Poets of the Post 1989 Generation*, ed. George Szirtes (Arc, 2010). **George Szirtes**: *New & Collected Poems* (Bloodaxe Books, 2008). **Wisława Szymborska**: 'Could Have' and 'View with a Grain of Sand': *Poems New & Collected*, tr. Stanisław Barańczak & Clare Cavanagh (Faber & Faber, 1999); Wisława Szymborska: 'A Note' from *Here*, tr. Stanisław Barańczak & Clare Cavanagh (Houghton Mifflin Harcourt, 2011).

Eleanor Ross Taylor: *Captive Voices: New and Selected Poems* (Louisiana State University Press, 2009). **Toon Tellegen**: *About Love and About Nothing Else*, tr. Judith Wilkinson (Shoestring Press, 2008). **Susana Thénon**: 'Nuptial Song', tr. María Negroni & Anne Twitty, by permission of María Negroni. **Henri Thomas**: 'Audides' from *Into the Deep Street: Seven Modern French Poets 1938-2008*, ed. & tr. Jennie Feldman & Stephen Romer (Anvil Press Poetry, 2009), translation of 'Audides' from *Travaux d'aveugle* (1941) © Editions Gallimard, Paris. **R.S. Thomas**: 'The Bright Field' from *Collected Poems 1945-1990*, by permission of J.M. Dent & Sons, a division of the Orion Publishing Group Ltd, and Gwydion Thomas; 'Comparisons' and 'No Time' from *Collected Later Poems 1988-2000* (Bloodaxe Books, 2004). **Rosemary Tonks**: *Iliad of Broken Sentences* (Bodley Head, 1967). **Tomas Tranströmer**: *New Collected Poems*, tr. Robin Fulton (Bloodaxe Books, 1997/2011); Natasha Trethewey: *Domestic Work* (Graywolf Press, 2000), www.graywolfpress.org. **Brian Turner**: *Here, Bullet* (Bloodaxe Books, 2007). **Chase Twichell**: *Horses Where the Answers Should Have Been: New & Selected Poems* (Bloodaxe Books, 2010). **John Updike**: *Collected Poems 1953-1993* (Alfred A. Knopf, 1995). **Priscila Uppal**: *Successful Tragedies: Poems 1998-2010* (Bloodaxe Books, 2010).

Derek Walcott: *Collected Poems* (Faber & Faber, 1976), by permission of the author and publisher. **Susan Wicks**: *Night Toad: New & Selected Poems* (Bloodaxe Books, 2003). **C.K. Williams**: *Wait* (Bloodaxe Books, 2010). **Miller Williams**: *Living on the Surface: New and Selected Poems* (Louisiana State University Press, 1990). **C.D. Wright**: *Like Something Flying Backwards: New & Selected Poems* (Bloodaxe Books, 2007). **Franz Wright**: *Ill Lit: Selected & New Poems* (Oberlin College Press, 1998), copyright © Franz Wright 1998, by permission of Oberlin College Press, www.oberlin.edu/ocpress. **James Wright**: *Above the River: Complete Poems* (Bloodaxe Books, 1992), by permission of Wesleyan University Press. **Robert Wrigley**: *Earthly Meditations: New and Selected Poems* (Penguin, 2006), by permission of the author. **Mark Wunderlich**: *Voluntary Servitude* (Graywolf Press, 2004), www.graywolfpress.org. **Lynne Wycherley**: 'Apple Tree in Blossom', from *Into the Further Reaches*, ed. Jay Ramsay (PS Avalon, 2007), by permission of the author.

Kevin Young: 'Crowning' from *The New Yorker*, 23 February 2009, by permission of the author. **Adam Zagajewski**: *Selected Poems* (Faber & Faber, 2004).

Every effort has been made to trace copyright holders of the poems published in this book. The editor and publisher apologise if any material has been included without permission or without the appropriate acknowledgement, and would be glad to be told of anyone who has not been consulted.

The editorial commentaries include quotations from the following sources: 21a: Maya Angelou, *The Independent*, 23 March 1992; 21b: Donald Hall, cited in *The Southern Review*, Spring 1994; 21c: William Matthews, 'A Poetry Reading at West Point', *Search Party: Collected Poems*, ed. Sebastian Matthews & Stanley Plumly (Houghton Mifflin Harcourt, 2004); T.R. Hummer, *PBS Bulletin* (Winter 2005); David Constantine, *Magma* (Summer 2004). 39a: W.H. Auden, *The Dyer's Hand and other essays* (Faber & Faber, 1963); 39b: Mark Doty, 'On "Archaic Torso of Apollo"', Academy of American Poets' Online Poetry Classroom Summer Institute (2007). 95a: William Blake, 'The Sick Rose' (1794), *Songs of Innocence and of Experience*; 95b: Pablo Neruda, 'Sobre una poesía sin pureza' (1938), translated as 'Toward an Impure Poetry' by Ben Belitt in *Five Decades: Poems 1925-1970* (Grove Press, 1974). 161: Billy Collins, interviewed by Judith Palmer at Ledbury Poetry Festival, July 2010. 245: 'Mary Jo Bang Examines Grief's Poetic Form, the Elegy', *PBS Newshour*, 10 April 2008. 307: John F. Kennedy, 'Poetry and Power', *Atlantic Monthly*, February 1964. 356: William Hazlitt, *Lectures on the English Poets*, 1818. 421: *Dead Poets Society* (1989), directed by Peter Weir, original screenplay by Tom Schulman: John Keating played by Robin Williams. 465: John Burnside, 'Strong Words'; *Strong Words: modern poets on modern poetry*, ed. W.N. Herbert & Matthew Hollis (Bloodaxe Books, 2000). I am indebted to Dennis O'Driscoll for three quotations from *The Bloodaxe Book of Poetry Quotations* (Bloodaxe Books, 2006).

INDEX OF WRITERS

INDEX OF TITLES & FIRST LINES

508